The 30-Minute Cook

Acclaim for Nigel Slater:

'The flavors in *The 30-Minute Cook* are drawn from all over the globe – fried fish in the Moroccan style, grilled chicken in a Greek marinade, 10-minute pigeon – but there is nothing here beyond the reach of even the most hapless cook ... utterly mouthwatering'
– John McKenna in the *Irish Times*

'Nigel Slater offers us a decade's worth of fresh, original cookery ideas with spoonfuls of wit' – Leslie Forbes in the *Observer*

'I love this man: his wit and greed make him irresistible'
– Nigella Lawson in *The Times*

'Neither Slater's writing nor his cooking is labored. There is liveliness, freshness and intelligence in all that he does'
– Philippa Davenport in the *Financial Times*

'Nigel Slater has cornered the market in writing simplified fast recipes that are as delicious to eat as they are simple to make ...
[*The 30-Minute Cook*] is highly recommended' – *SHE* magazine

Nigel Slater is Food Columnist of the *Observer*. Prior to that he was Food Editor of *Marie Claire* from its launch in 1988 until 1993. His simple, down-to-earth style of cooking has gained him something of a following. In 1989 he won a Glenfiddich Award and in 1995 he won both the coveted Glenfiddich Trophy and the Cookery Writer of the Year Award. Nigel Slater's first book, *Real Fast Food*, has been a bestseller ever since it appeared in 1992 and was shortlisted for that year's André Simon Memorial Fund Award.

The 30-Minute Cook was shortlisted for the Glenfiddich Award and for the Julia Child Award in the United States.

NIGEL SLATER

The 30-Minute Cook

The Best of the World's Quick Cooking

PHOTOGRAPHS BY KEVIN SUMMERS

ILLUSTRATIONS BY JULIET DALLAS-CONTE

WILEY

PENGUIN BOOKS

Published by the Penguin Group
Penguin Books Ltd, 27 Wrights Lane, London W8 5TZ, England
Penguin Books Australia Ltd, Ringwood, Victoria, Australia
Penguin Books Canada Ltd, 10 Alcorn Avenue, Toronto, Ontario, Canada M4V 3B2
Penguin Books (NZ) Ltd, 182–190 Wairau Road, Auckland 10, New Zealand

Penguin Books Ltd, Registered Offices: Harmondsworth, Middlesex, England

First published by Michael Joseph 1994
Published in Penguin Books 1996
10 9 8 7 6 5 4 3 2 1

Printed and bound in Great Britain by
Butler & Tanner Ltd, Frome and London

Distributed in the United States by
John Wiley & Sons, Inc.,
605 Third Avenue, New York, NY 10158–0012

Library of Congress Cataloging-in-Publication Data
A catalog entry for this title is available
from the Library of Congress
ISBN 0-470-23770-8

CONTENTS

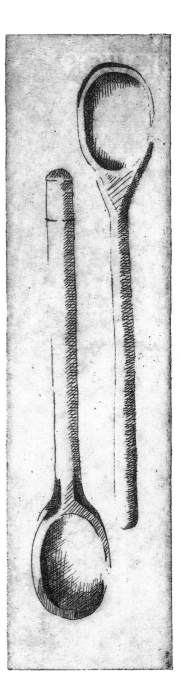

For Digger, Magrath and Poppy. Again.

ACKNOWLEDGEMENTS

This book was written in a short, energetic and hectic burst. In much the same way, in fact, that most daily cooking is done. That final hour or so before you get ready to go out, get the family to bed or collapse in front of the box after a day's work.

Louise Haines, my editor at Michael Joseph and whose idea it was that I should write a book in the first place, has worked not just on *The 30-Minute Cook*, but also on my previous two books. I cannot thank her enough for her patience, support and guidance through what has become a culinary trilogy. In particular for allowing the books to complement each other while maintaining their individual character and format. That she has suggested working with this tardy, chaotic and often batty writer on another, though quite different, book is nothing short of a miracle.

I want to thank Eleo Gordon at Penguin Books, Michael Pilgrim at *The Observer* and Delia Smith and Michael Wynn Jones for their continued support. Thanks, too, to Kevin Summers, Bob Eames and Juliet Dallas-Conte for making this a tempting, beautiful and, above all, practical book. Finally, thanks also to the authors and cooks who have let me use their recipes and ideas, and so freely given their advice, encouragement and time.

INTRODUCTION

This is the third of my fast food books, the other two being *Real Fast Food* and *Real Fast Puddings*. Whereas the other two were distinctly European, this third collection casts its net somewhat farther, taking in recipes from India, south-east Asia, north Africa, the Middle East and the further reaches of Europe. There is still a healthy clutch of recipes from Italy, France and Spain, though, to give a clearer picture of what the rest of the world eats when it comes home tired and hungry and demanding something good to eat pronto. Sorry, North America, but I had to draw the line somewhere.

At a rough guess, that now adds up to almost a thousand ideas for something quick and simple to make for supper that hasn't come out of a tin, ready made from the supermarket or hot from the take-away. But this is not haute cuisine. It is nothing more than a collection of recipes, reminders and possibilities that may interest you more than something from the chilled, prepared-food cabinet. The principle is that it is quite possible to make a meal for yourself in the time that it takes a cook-chill supper to heat up or the delivery boy to bring round a pizza.

The 30-Minute Cook is an eclectic collection to say the least. Though it is not by any means comprehensive. There are quick curries from India, spiced kebabs from Morocco and, of course, stir-fries from China. But there is much more too. Fish cakes from Thailand hot with fresh chillies, creamy Indian kormas, mild curries flecked with coriander leaf, charred, juicy grilled meats from north Africa crusty with spices, and herby, garlicky seafood from France. Anyone who does not fancy meat will have a good time too with risottos, quick couscous and tempura vegetables.

* *Real Fast Food* and *Real Fast Puddings* are available both in hardback published by Michael Joseph and in paperback published by Penguin Books.

Tricky one this. I make no claim to being an expert on the home cooking of China, India, Thailand, Morocco or even Britain. That said, I have tried to keep the recipes as close to the traditional ones as possible. The recipes have been begged, borrowed and occasionally stolen. I cannot thank enough those who have shared their recipes with me; where the ideas have come from other authors rather than friends I have credited them in the text or in the bibliography. Some of the recipes are my own versions of well-known classics. Some are completely original, and others are used with permission from other authors.

But those hidebound by purism may not be amused by my occasionally unorthodox methods or ingredients. Does it *really* matter that I eat my spiced lentils on naan bread with a knife and fork like beans on toast? Does it make the slightest difference if I choose to eat my Chinese noodles with a spoon and fork, Italian style, rather than dribbling juice down my chin and over the table using chopsticks?

If the answer is yes, then you may have bought the wrong book. If you are willing to take a broader, more relaxed view of it all, then we will probably stay friends. All that matters to me is that I have something on my plate that is good to eat. How I wish to cook and eat it is not an issue when the result is delicious. So you will find I have cut the odd corner here and there. I see nothing wrong with a little westernization of Eastern dishes as long as this doesn't mean losing the whole point of the dish. In other words, don't worry if you haven't got a wok.

A Word about Authenticity

About Accessibility

The range of 'ethnic' ingredients in the shops is dazzling. Anyone who hasn't looked beyond the Worcestershire sauce lately is in for a surprise. Bunches of green coriander, bottles of sweet, salty soy, whole and ground spices, matured vinegars, fresh curry pastes, chilled stocks and Eastern condiments are not new to those who use the big-name supermarkets. I think some of them deserve a round of applause for stocking mouth-popping chilli pastes, vivid red chilli peppers, bottles of fish sauce, bunches of pak choi and baby aubergines. It almost makes up for the tasteless tomatoes they palm us off with. Bored to tears with pasta, with pesto and pizza, I use these 'new' ingredients all the time. Knobs of lemony ginger root and peppery rocket are not the oddities they were three or four years ago, and end up in my shopping basket almost as often as lemons and basil. Though I wish more shops would stock kaffir lime leaves.

If purists blanch at some of my short cuts I hope they will at least understand the book's *raison d'être*. All I am attempting to do here is pass on a few ideas for spicing up your daily eating. I just think I have found something Indian, Chinese, Tunisian, Greek or Thai that is more exciting than chops and I am telling you about it. The fact that I haven't the time to wash my basmati rice for an hour under running water or make my own noodles is really neither here nor there when my only interest is to liven up the daily task of getting something on the table. Fish fingers can be awfully dull.

And Practicality

Most of the recipes are for two. I know more people who eat in twos than in fours. Except at the weekend. The recipes are easy to double up if you eat in fours; this is because they include none of the ingredients that cause trouble when multiplied, such as baking powder and gelatine. I have cooked most of the recipes in half an hour. It is a loose half hour, though, and those who live with a stopwatch in their hand may be disappointed from time to time. The cooking methods are as easy as you can get. There is nothing in the book beyond the scope of the committed non-cook, I promise.

Use the recipes as a starting-point for your own. If you get halfway through a recipe and think you have a better idea than me, then try it. It's called progress. I would hate the idea of anyone following my recipes slavishly. Just use them as a springboard for your own ideas. I have cooked all the recipes in the book, but have not tested them so rigorously that they have lost their heart and soul in the search for workability. You may find a few rough edges here and there.

Finally, I cannot emphasize just how much better food seems to taste if it is made by a relaxed cook. No one stands on ceremony in my kitchen. My favourite meals are still the ones that I eat with a fork, standing up in the kitchen with one eye on the telly. I never attempt too much. A 30-minute main dish with a salad and one veg is enough for me. If I have a whole hour then I will make a pudding too. Getting your noodles, naan, pastry and pasta out of a packet will help. So will buying your salads and vegetables ready washed. Pouring yourself a little drink as soon as you come home will help no end. In my book a relaxed cook is a good cook. When all is said and done, you are only making yourself something good to eat.

A QUICK COOK'S TOUR

Europe

The British kitchen has few recipes that you could honestly call fast food. If we are to eat something for supper that does not either (a) come out of a tin, (b) come ready made from the supermarket or (c) take an age to cook, then we really have to look across the water. But once we do, we are spoilt for choice.

Italian chicken breasts all savour and crunch from their Parmesan crust, a hot soup rich with prawns and mussels, salmon cooked with a cream sauce laced with aniseed-scented herbs are all yours in 30 minutes or less. So too are trout wrapped in prosciutto, pasta with asparagus and Parmesan (both from Italy) and pasta with sardines and saffron from Sicily. Turkey escalopes, now available neatly prepared from the supermarket, are given point when fried in butter with ham and slices of lemon that caramelize as they cook.

Greece offers souvlakia, crisply charred outside while still pink inside and a startling mint and Feta salad. Spain does the 30-minute cook proud with a salad of Serrano ham, rocket and melon that is tangy, refreshing and spicy all at once, liver pan-fried with mellow sherry vinegar and a wonderful dish of chicken with orange and mint.

France, suddenly closer than ever, has fast food to die for: chicken, tangy with a grainy mustard and vinegar sauce or smooth and rich with cider and cream. Brick-red fish soup and blissful potatoes cooked as slowly as they dare with butter and melted cheese. And that is without mentioning the flaky croissants oozing with cheese and smoky ham.

The Principles and Practicalities

The sauté pan, with its solid base and straight sides, is one of the most useful things in my kitchen. I use it almost daily. I can fry in it a trout in butter, an escalope of pork in oil, or simmer a risotto till thick and creamy. I can cook a sausage slowly or flash-fry a lamb steak. I think of this long-handled, high-sided frying-pan as Europe's answer to the wok. In my kitchen it is just as indispensable.

Much European fast food is deep fried – the *fritto misto* of Italy with its little fishes all crisp and golden, oysters for slapping between crisp French baguettes slathered in mayonnaise and little croquettes of cannellini beans. It is easy enough to do at home, and certainly produces some of the most delicious food imaginable.

Thailand

....

Thai cooking is robust, sassy and dazzling to the eye and to the palate. Thankfully, much of it is quick to cook. There is no compromise with Thai cooking – you either love its fresh, sometimes fiery, flavours or you don't. I love them. Quick cooks will delight in the Thai dishes that take no longer to cook than it takes to cook the rice that traditionally accompanies them.

A chicken curry, green with coriander and chillies and rich with coconut milk, is a favourite. Its mild piquant heat becomes addictive after a while. Thai chicken can also be stir-fried with garlic and *nam pla*, the salty fish sauce that is so much a part of Thai cooking. Fish is poached in a broth with refreshing lemon grass and fiery chillies, and rice is scented with heavenly basil. Even fish cakes, possibly the most popular Thai dish of all, are not out of the question for a quick supper with the help of a food processor.

At the heart of a Thai meal lies rice. A meal is simply not a meal without it. The rice is the sustenance, the point of the meal. All else is nothing more than a flavouring, a condiment if you like.

The Principle

Although I like rice, I am not fond of it enough to give it that sort of prominence in the meal. Sorry, Thailand. Of course, this gives rise to a problem. Thai food can be mouth-puckeringly hot. Eaten in small amounts with a great deal of rice this is fine. When the ratio is reversed, the mouthful becomes unpleasantly hot. Unless, of course, you have a palate like a rhinoceros. Consequently, some may find that the spicing in this book is a tad on the mild side for them. In which case you must tweak the chilli content of each recipe to suit yourself.

Generosity is part and parcel of Thai life. This extends to the table and in most cases even a simple supper will include several dishes from which to help yourself, presented all at once. However dazzling this may be, it is simply not the way I can eat, or wish to eat, on an everyday basis. It just doesn't work for me. I have assumed the same of the readers of *The 30-Minute Cook*. Therefore the Thai dishes included here are mostly those which fit comfortably into my own eating pattern. In other words, a single main dish you can eat with rice, rather than lots of highly spiced bits to pile on top of a rice mountain. It is the flavour, excitement and robustness of Thai cooking squeezed into my own simple eating style. Surely, there is no crime in that?

The Practicalities

You can use a wok for many of the recipes. Or a large frying-pan. A good supermarket should have almost everything you need, but there are a few exceptions. Namely, lemon grass and lime leaves. Both have a bright, clean citrus flavour very different from lemon or lime juice or even zest. There is a hint of spiciness to them. One or two more enterprising shops do carry lime leaves. A few more sell lemon grass. Often they come as a twee Thai package along with searingly hot bird's-eye chillies. Take this if that is all that is on offer. But it is only a matter of time before lime leaves, of which I am becoming inordinately fond, are as easy to find as coriander leaves, ginger and basil. Thai basil, incidentally, is not quite the same as the one we know. But the Italian stuff is close enough for me.

North Africa

I have an enormous soft spot for this part of the world. Morocco in particular. Its food must be some of the most fragrant in the world. The smells, the sounds and the flavours are like no other. The Medina in Marrakesh is a magical place; every corner you turn has a different smell – of Arab bread baking, a breeze heavy with rosewater, fresh mint or cinnamon, or a waft of hashish or jasmine. Almost best of all is the smell of meat being cooked on a charcoal brazier. It is these aromas that are the heart and soul of north African cooking.

Fast food in this part of the world relies on fish and meat that have been steeped in spices (cumin, chilli, paprika, saffron and turmeric) and aromatics (onion, lemon, garlic and olive oil), and then grilled till lightly charred yet succulent. Even twenty minutes in such a spice bath will turn a bland fillet of white fish into a lip-tingling scented morsel. Meat takes a little longer, but is still, I think, pertinent to this collection.

Think of chicken with slices of lemon and violet olives, a mouth-popping salad of lemon, parsley and onion or a delicately perfumed salad of grapefruit, carrot and rosewater. Or the Tunisian way with mackerel, which involves pushing a cumin-strong spice mix into its flesh before grilling it amber and black. This is all fast food.

Marinating is not something that need be done overnight. Small pieces of chicken or fish will take up the flavours quicker than that if time is of the essence. And for the purposes of this book it is. A slightly thicker marinade is often the answer, especially when it cooks to a thick crust around the food. Or, of course, you could simply steep the food for as long a time as you have. You may be surprised the effect even a quarter of an hour in a paste of onion, garlic, cumin and paprika has on the fish you have dashed in and bought on your way home. The one you were going to skip for the Sole Bonne Femme from the chilled cabinet. Until you had a better idea.

A quick dash round the supermarkets as they are about to close will still leave you with little that cannot be bought in any other European market. Beans and crème fraîche from France, peaches, prosciutto and Parmesan from Italy, olives and oranges from Spain and salty, tangy Feta from Greece seem like old friends now. And the prospects are even better. Though I wish someone here would stock proper French *lardons* for my frisée – *lardons* that turn golden and crisp and ooze enough fat with which to dress the salad.

The Principles and Practicalities

India
....

Indian cooking is not just about slow-simmered and intricately spiced casseroles. It has fast food too. Until I spent some time in India I was quite naïve about the daily cooking there, and was surprised that so much of it would be practical to the busy home cook in Britain.

Dal, which makes a deeply comforting supper with rice, fits as easily into the life of a 30-minute cook as Indian spiced kebabs marinated in cream and chilli. Many of the classic chicken dishes of India are suitable for the quick cook, whether fried with ochre spices, simmered in coconut milk, or stirred with cream and yoghurt and scattered with leaves of coriander; they are here. Fish too, with prawns grilled with yoghurt and chilli, fillets served in a spiced batter or dipped in yoghurt and a paste of green herbs and spices and fried till crisp.

Vegetable dishes are the vital spark of Indian cooking, and many can be made in minutes. Creamy heads of cauliflower with cumin or chilli or yoghurt and poppy seeds, crisp green broccoli spiced with crunchy mustard seeds, and green beans with ginger are as fast as you can get. Even vegetable korma scrapes in just in time.

The Principle

Indian cooking, whether simple or extravagant, relies on spices in one form or another. They are the blood in the veins of Indian cooking and provide the fragrance and flavour base for even the simplest dishes. Invariably a mixture of several, known as the masala, it can be as basic or as complicated as you wish. Ready-made masalas are available in the shops; most are good, some are very good, and they are extremely convenient. By good I mean aromatic and interesting. But in terms of fragrance and flavour it is better to spend five minutes mixing your own.

Almost all spices need to be roasted to release the volatile oils that are their flavour. Roasting spices is less hassle than you may think. It takes a matter of seconds and can be done in the pan you are about to cook in. Roast whole spices in a dry pan till fragrant, a matter of seconds, and then grind them in a pestle and mortar. I speed things up by using the coffee grinder. Forgetting to wipe it out after gives an interesting cup of coffee the next morning. If you are using ready-ground spices, add them to the onions and garlic shortly after they have softened.

We are well acquainted with many of India's intrinsic ingredients. Ginger, garlic and mustard have had a place in our kitchens for a long time, even if the mustard we know is in ground form rather than the seeds more prevalent there. Chillies are becoming easy to track down now, with the supermarkets offering a range of sizes and heat levels, and even pungent coriander leaf, to which I have recently become addicted, is in every decent green-grocer's.

The spices we know so well from our spice racks are no strangers to kitchens here, but the way they are used may be new to some. In India, brilliant yellow turmeric, rich rust-red chilli powder and earthy cumin are not left for months on the shelf in pretty pots losing all their joy. There they are ground as needed or bought ready-prepared but in small amounts to keep them fresh. Once ground, many spices lose their soul, particularly coriander seeds and chillies, so be ruthless with the spice rack and grind as you need.

The common cooking oil used is groundnut, which suits me fine, as that is what I use when olive is too strong a flavour. The ubiquitous ghee (basically butter that has had its milk solids skimmed off to stop it burning) I tend to replace with a knob of butter and a spoonful of oil. Those more orthodox than myself will jump at the prepared ghee available in Indian grocers' and more adventurous supermarkets.

For the sake of practicality, I have used virtually no ingredient in the book that isn't available in any good supermarket. So the heady scent of fresh fenugreek leaves that permeates almost every Indian kitchen is not included, on the grounds that the leaves are currently impossible to obtain outside the Indian quarter of the nearest major city. It will probably still surprise you just how many ingredients used daily in Indian cooking are in your cupboard anyway.

The Practicalities

China

....

Some of the tastiest fast food in the world comes from China. Sizzling chicken with mushrooms and noodles, crisp green beans shining with sesame oil and garlicky mushrooms spluttering from the pan are but three of the thousands of quick suppers the Chinese enjoy every day.

Chinese cooking, in its simplest form, is perhaps the easiest of all for a non-cook to pick up. The rules are few and simple. A stir-fry of crisp vegetables made savoury with soy and ginger demands nothing more of the cook than a little pluck to get the pan blisteringly hot and the ability to shake the pan and stir the food at the same time. Even I can do that.

For reasons of speed, I have concentrated on the stir-fry. In cooking terms it is truly a meal in minutes, though the preparation time should not be underestimated. In order to cook right through before the outside is overdone any stir-fry ingredient needs to be cut quite small. Bite-sized is as big as you dare go if the inside is to be fully cooked. But there is no need to go overboard and dice everything into dolly mixtures. Liquorice Allsorts will do.

There are few ingredients used in Chinese cooking that will be new to you. Soy sauce, garlic, ginger and coriander are now almost as well known as their British cousins, Worcestershire sauce, onions, mustard and parsley. Oyster and hoisin sauces may mean checking out the oriental shelf at the supermarket though, along with yellow bean paste, you can find them at most grocers' shops nowadays. They will probably be next to the Worcestershire sauce.

The Principle and the Wok

You don't need a wok to cook yourself a Chinese supper. But one will make life a lot easier. Its broad, round bottom and thin metal allow the heat to spread rapidly – in seconds rather than minutes – essential to Chinese cooking. It's not just for stir-frying; it can be used for deep-frying, boiling or steaming too. The investment is minimal, mine cost just a few pounds from Chinatown, it never sticks and I don't even have to wash it – just wiping it with a cloth keeps it in good condition. It works much better than some of the fancier, heavier examples I have used. I get on better with a one-handled thin wok; others find two handles a help, though I cannot see why. As I said before, you don't have to have one to cook Chinese. But it helps.

You can stir-fry almost anything, but particularly good are pork, chicken, green vegetables and mushrooms. They seem to work in harmony with the basic flavourings – garlic, ginger, spring onion and soy – that are the essence of quick Chinese cooking. But the fierce heat is the thing, and a little courage is needed as you add chopped chicken to smoking oil and the skin crackles and pops and spits back at you. But it is worth it. A dish of mushrooms and chicken with garlic, spring onions and ginger, and finished with soy sauce, is as good a fast supper as you will get anywhere.

The Practicalities

I tend to cook Chinese when I am on my own or perhaps when there are two of us. I usually make one dish, often stir-fried, which I eat as the only dish, possibly with rice but more often with a bowl of salad. Unorthodox I know. But who cares. The idea of fiddling about with more than one dish at once may be authentic but it is not my style. At least not for everyday eating.

And another thing, no matter what you do to a stir-fry, it is difficult to make anything that isn't perfectly enjoyable. It is amazing how garlic, spring onion, ginger and soy work together. Chinese cooking is a doddle. Unless, of course, you take it very seriously.

And a Word about the Middle East

....

There are a few recipes here with a Middle-Eastern flavour. They are mostly grills, spiced with the superb flavours of that region: saffron, cumin, yoghurt, lemon, pine nuts and mint among others.

Generally speaking, it is not a quick cuisine. Flavour in a traditional Middle-Eastern dish tends to build up, layer upon layer, over several hours. It is not, I think, a style of cooking to be hurried or to have its corners knocked off. That said, there is enough that is suitable for inclusion here: spiced grilled kebabs with butter and saffron, vegetable couscous and chicken with dried fruits, pine nuts and spices, to name but a few.

And South America

··········

I have spent far too little time in South America. The few recipes featured in this book from that part of the world are based on a small area (I only managed Bogotá, Medellín, Cartagena and a few small villages in the Andes this time round). Although interesting, the recipes should not be taken as the best from that enormous culinary area – only what I tasted and thought was good enough to include.

For me, the high spot of the cooking is the grains – such as bobbly quinoa – the *salsas*, lively with tomato and chilli, and the wonderful tropical fruits. These translate comfortably enough into my daily cooking. Quinoa is a lot easier to find nowadays, and tropical fruits can make the most refreshing, luxurious and instant of desserts. There are no special ingredients, cooking methods or equipment. Unless a bag of quinoa is beyond your local health food shop.

Salsas seem set to replace the sauce as we know it. Finely chopped tomatoes, avocadoes, mangoes or papaya, spiced with onion and chilli, and flecked through with coriander, are a speedy accompaniment to grills and fried dishes. They take but a few minutes and can be chopped while the principal dish is cooking. They are fresh, fun and require little more than a sharp knife. Hooray for the *salsa*.

A NOTE ON INGREDIENTS

Gloriously shiny, almost black vinegar with a sweet, deep mellow flavour. Made in and around Modena in northern Italy, it is matured in wooden casks for anything up to twenty years. It should, I think, be used with more discretion than it sometimes is, though even a teaspoon of it will turn a salad dressing into something special. Needless to say, you must pay for all those years of tender loving care. Ignore cut-price supermarket specials and go for broke, at least £12 at the time of writing.

Balsamic Vinegar

I honestly think I will never tire of the tender, sweet, peppery Italian basil that marries so well with tomatoes. It is a herb that holds a special magic, though only when strewn raw on salads or in pasta. It loses everything when cooked. But it is not the only basil. Thai basil, which they call *bai horapa*, is a slightly different variety, having small leaves, beautiful mauve and green stems and tasting of both sweet basil and aniseed. It is rarely found here, but use it if you come across it in Asian shops. Sweet basil makes a reasonable substitute.

Basil

Tiny, hard, dried soy beans that resemble something's droppings. They add a salty, musty tang to Chinese vegetable, seafood and poultry dishes. I rinse and chop mine before use, though real pros. apparently don't rinse theirs. Buy them from Chinese shops – they will keep indefinitely in the fridge.

Black Beans

When I say butter in a recipe you can take it that I mean unsalted.

Butter

By cardamoms I mean the little green ones, not the inferior white ones or the hairy brown ones. They take but a second to split; use your fingernail and shake and pick out the tiny black seeds. I use them in two ways, either whole (usually in a pilaf), in which case pick them out

Cardamoms

as you eat, or finely ground. A pestle and mortar is best and will do the job in one minute. Unless you fancy using the coffee grinder and doing several while you're at it. The fragrance is quite magical.

Chilli Sauce

Every cuisine has its own chilli sauce. They liven up even the most mundane of dishes, making food both comforting and uplifting. Some are a thick chilli purée while others are thin, made from a distillation of chillies and vinegar. In north Africa and the Middle East they have the fiery harissa, a thick dark red paste sold here in old-fashioned yellow and red tins. America has thin, hot tabasco, Italy has *crema piccante*, rich and thick and milder than some. *Sambal oelek* is the spiced chilli sauce from south-east Asia. In the recipes I generally refer to them by name. Occasionally I mention thick chilli sauce, by which I mean one of the bottled chilli tomato sauces available in delicatessens. And avoid any chilli sauce made in Vietnam. If you value your tastebuds and sinuses, that is.

Chillies

These have brought both fire and flavour to the world's cooking for thousands of years. Both dried and fresh, they are used in quantity almost everywhere but Europe. But we are catching on. Most greengrocers now manage at least one variety, with many of the large stores offering three or four, from the large mild Anaheim and the hotter Jalapeño to the blistering tiny Thai chillies that send me into floods of tears from two feet away. As a general rule, the smaller the hotter. Remove the seeds and the effect will be milder. I refer to large mild, medium hot, or small hot throughout the book. And red, which are generally riper and sweeter than the green. Practicality getting the better of authenticity.

Coconut Milk and Cream

Let's get one thing straight: coconut milk is not the thin opaque liquid that rattles around inside a coconut. Coconut milk is what you get when you mix grated coconut flesh with water. You can use fresh coconut. If you have all day. You can use desiccated coconut. If you're desperate. Or best of all, to my mind anyway, you can crumble one of those blocks of creamed coconut in warm water and use that. I don't know why I say crumble, the blocks are rock hard and you need a good strong knife to break them. I use half a 200g/7oz block of creamed coconut to 150ml/¼ pint water. Coconut cream is the thick pulp that rises to the top if you leave it to settle. Scoop it off and use in the recipes that call for coconut cream. Use the liquid underneath for cooking rice. It will not be thick enough for general use.

Coriander

With its fragile, pungent leaves similar in appearance to flat-leaf parsley, coriander is the most used herb in the world. You either like it or you don't. It is used constantly in Thai, Chinese, Indian and South American cooking. After initially thinking it tasted of washing-up liquid I became addicted to the stuff. Available in most good supermarkets and greengrocers'. Not to be confused with coriander seeds: same plant but totally different flavour. The leaves are a herb, the seeds are a spice. Confused?

Fish Sauce

The south-east Asian answer to soy sauce. More salty than fishy, it is called by different names all over the East, but best known here by the Thai name *nam pla*. I use *nuoc mam* from Vietnam. There is little difference in my book. But then, I am hardly an expert. You probably don't want to know that it is made by leaving fish in brine to ferment in the sun for months on end and then draining off the results. Available here from Asian grocers.

Galangal

Easy to find in Asian greengrocers'. Impossible to locate in British ones. 'Essential' to Thai cooking, you will find ginger a fair substitute for its slightly medicinal notes. It looks similar, though a little more pink and stripey. I have abandoned it altogether and use ginger every time.

Garlic

You will notice that I always squash, purée or slice garlic, but never chop it. This is one of my idiosyncracies. As much as I love the stuff, I have no stomach for the chopped clove. There is something about little nibs of garlic that gives me the most appalling tummy ache.

Ginger

Knobbly beige rhizome ubiquitous throughout the East. Its zingy, warm lemon notes are essential to Asian cooking. The spicy, citrus aroma of a freshly broken piece is one of the great smells of all time. Buy a firm, fat hand of it from the supermarket and keep it in the fridge for no longer than a fortnight, slicing off a knob or two as you need it. And you will need it in this book.

Hoisin Sauce

Thick, rich, shiny red-brown sauce used in China both as ingredient and condiment. Made from soya beans, vinegar, spices and sugar, it has unkindly and incorrectly been referred to as the Chinese answer to HP sauce. Though I wouldn't put the latter near my Peking Duck.

Kaffir Lime Leaves

The dark, shiny green leaves of the knobbly Kaffir lime. Used in Thai cooking for its fresh, spicy lime flavour that is more aromatic and less astringent than the zest or juice. Like bay leaves, you fish them out rather than eat them. An exciting addition to anyone's larder, they can be found in quite a few major supermarkets now. Try flavouring rice with them.

Lemon Grass

These long thin stems of lemony balm-like leaves are much more frequently available than they used to be. Most major supermarkets have a few sticks. Use its coarse, grey-green, fibrous stems to flavour Thai rice and clear soups.

Monosodium Glutamate

A natural salt found in, among other things, sugar beet, and used with gay abandon in Chinese restaurants to enhance the flavour of the food. About a quarter of a million tons is produced each year. As modern thinking suggests that it is unnecessary I have not included it in the recipes. I am not convinced that good fresh ingredients need their flavour 'enhanced' in this way. And anyway, it makes me fart.

Oyster Sauce

Originally from the coastal area of southern China, this thick, brown sauce is made from oysters and soy. Yet it is not at all fishy to taste and is used in cooking and as a condiment. Buy the most expensive.

Pancetta

I mention this Italian streaky bacon a lot. For my money it has a lot more going for it than most of the bacon you can buy. It has plenty of fat, sweet fat at that, and fries crisply when diced. I particularly salute the fact that you can buy it, green or smoked, in large lumps rather than sliced. But you may have to go to the deli for it. The silly old supermarkets tend to slice it like Parma ham.

Parsley

The shops are getting the message that flat-leaf parsley looks and tastes better than the curly sort. It is easier to find than it was, but use whatever you can find. As long as it is bright and bushy-tailed.

Rice Wine

Shaoxing wine is as much a part of Chinese cooking as soy or ginger. Yet this ancient wine, made from fermented rice, yeast and mineral water matured in cellars for several years, is not that easy to find here. This probably explains why even Chinese cooks substitute dry sherry instead.

Sesame Oil

Particularly greasy oil made from sesame seeds, usually added to Chinese food at the end of cooking. Even a little goes too far. And somehow the bottle always leaks.

Soy Sauce

Made from soya beans, flour and water fermented to produce the dark, salty brown liquid that seasons Chinese and Japanese cooking. There are two main types: light soy is the saltier, dark amber in colour and used in cooking; dark soy has been fermented longer, is shiny, almost black in colour and more mellow than light. Slightly thicker, it is used as a dipping sauce at the table. Shoyu, Japanese soy, is slightly sweeter, less salty and generally the one I use. Kikkoman brand is well known and easy to find.

Stock

The chilled fresh stocks in the supermarkets are sound, if a little dear. They are the ones I mean when I refer to stock in the recipes. Use them in preference to the salty powdered versions or cubes. If it really must be a stock cube, water it down with twice the amount of water it says on the packet. Even then it will probably taste like an emetic.

Tomato Passata

Purée of tomatoes sold in bottles or tetrapacks. Somewhere in consistency between juice and chopped tomatoes. A useful base for, say, pasta sauce.

Tomato Purée

You will notice a dearth of tomato purée in my books. With one or two exceptions, such as Bolognese sauce, I reckon it sounds the death knell to everything it touches. Its bullying presence ruined much cooking in the 1970s, when it featured in almost everything on the menu. I should know, I put some of it there.

Turmeric

Used in its fresh state in India, this brilliant yellow-ochre spice is used almost exclusively dried elsewhere. It will add a warm note and dazzling orange-yellow colour to your cooking. And your clothes, hands and teeth. It keeps well in ground form.

Yellow Bean Sauce

Also called yellow bean curd. A spicy and aromatic addition to Chinese cooking made from fermented yellow beans.

CHAPTER 1

Vegetables

Never has vegetable cookery been so exciting. There are two main reasons for this burst of green energy; the ever growing numbers of vegetarians who demand more and more interesting vegetable dishes and the enthusiasm the supermarkets and consumers have shown for Oriental, unusual and old-fashioned varieties of veg.

A quick glance at my local chain supermarkets and greengrocers reveals baby aubergines, red onions, corn cobs in their husks, fancy salad leaves, tiny earthy potatoes and hot-tasting greens from China. There are chillies from South America, organically grown baby carrots, and lemon grass, knobbly limes and ginger from Thailand. It is a truly international offering, and one that I have recently been making the most of.

Vegetables are a boon for the 30-minute cook. There are greens to stir-fry, juicy mushrooms to add to a curry and asparagus to grill. Sweet potatoes from Peru to bake, tomatoes from Italy to roast and a host of weird and wonderful mushrooms to stir-fry, curry and grill. Enough. Let's get on with it.

ASPARAGUS

Not the luxury it once was, but still a joy to eat. No matter where the imported spears come from, asparagus is still best in the summer months, from May to August. When the strawberries are ready too. Ignore everything you have read about tying it up in bundles and steaming it. Asparagus can be cooked lying down in simmering water in a large sauté pan or frying-pan. Just bring the water, enough to cover the spears when they are lying flat, to the boil, and then simmer till tender to the point of a knife. The timing will vary according to the age and thickness of your spears. Anything from 3 to 10 minutes.

Grilled Asparagus

For each person
•
8 asparagus spears, neither too fat nor pencil thin
light olive oil and butter
½ lemon

Asparagus cooked on the grill has a deep flavour, particularly if the stalks are allowed to singe a little. Choose spears about 1cm/½ inch in diameter.

There is no point in trimming the asparagus, as you will need something to hold it by. Lay the spears on the grill pan and heat the grill. Not too high, if you have a choice. Melt the butter in the oil over a low heat and then brush the spears all over. Cook the asparagus slowly, constantly brushing with the butter and oil. When the stalks are tender, their flesh browned in patches, serve them with the lemon and any butter and oil from the pan.

Dipped Asparagus

For each person
•
6 good thick asparagus spears
1 soft-boiled egg

Cook the asparagus in boiling water in a shallow pan till tender but not floppy. About 3–4 minutes. Maybe a little longer. Dip the spears into the egg as if they were soldiers of toast. Timing is of the essence here.

Baked Asparagus with Pancetta
············

Boil a bundle of asparagus until it is just tender. Drain carefully and lay the spears in a shallow, ovenproof china dish. Heat the oven to 200°C/400°F (gas mark 6). Melt a generous ounce (30g) butter in a shallow pan and fry a handful of diced pancetta, or French lardons, in it till golden. Tip them and the butter over the asparagus and then sprinkle with grated Parmesan – only lightly though. Bake for 10 minutes till the cheese has melted. For 2.

AUBERGINES

Inedibly dull when raw, the aubergine takes on a voluptuous and velvety texture with the application of oil and heat. I can think of few ingredients whose flavour changes so radically during cooking. Its dry, juiceless flesh soaks up olive oil like a sponge, turning the most boring vegetable on earth into a tender, succulent and sexy one. To the 30-minute cook, this convenient and easy-to-store vegetable, or fruit if you prefer, is a delight, offering untold versatility.

Yes, I like the aubergine, though I remain unconvinced of the need to salt it. Theoretically, to purge it of its bitter juices the aubergine is heavily salted and set in a colander to drain for an hour or so. Yet I have rarely come across a bitter aubergine. Not even the larger specimens, as big as a truncheon and almost as tough, have shown any sour notes at all. Perhaps modern hybrid strains have had the bitterness bred out of them.

Far more useful is to salt them so the flesh soaks up less oil when you fry it. Aubergines are serious drinkers and can empty a pan of your best olive oil in minutes. A brief blanching in boiling water will have the same effect as salting, though I rarely bother with that either, knowing the oil soaked up into an aubergine's flesh gives the fruit its unique sensual texture.

Young aubergines, shiny, plump and firm, are a friend to the cook with little time. They cook quickly when sliced into rings or cut lengthways into strips. Even halved, the cooking time is not long if you score the cut surface deeply with a knife before baking, grilling or sautéeing.

Italy, India and the Middle East have some marvellous ideas for the quick cook who wants to exploit the aubergine's tender flesh. Simple treatments, such as grilling with Parmesan or baking with onions and pine nuts, are often as sumptuous as the more time-consuming and better-known stuffed versions.

Goat's Cheese and Olive Aubergines

....

For 2

•

2 medium aubergines

6–8 tablespoons olive oil

100g/4oz green or black olive paste

225g/8oz soft goat's cheese

2 tablespoons grated Parmesan cheese

A salty, tangy plateful deeply redolent of the Mediterranean.

Wipe the aubergines and cut off the prickly stems. Slice each aubergine in half from stalk to thick end. Warm enough olive oil in a shallow pan to cover the base. Pop in the aubergines, cut side down, and cook over a low to moderate heat till the flesh is pale golden brown. As it soaks up the oil, add a little more.

Turn the aubergines over and cook until tender to the point of a knife, about 7–10 minutes. Remove and drain on kitchen paper.

Get the grill hot; spoon the olive paste on to the cut side of each aubergine. Slice the cheese into 1cm/½ inch rounds and place over the olive paste. Scatter the Parmesan over the top and place under the preheated grill till the goat's cheese softens and starts to melt and the Parmesan colours.

Pan-fried Garlic Aubergines

....

As it stands, this makes a fine accompaniment to almost anything. With a few intelligent additions, it can make a meal.

Cut the aubergine into cubes, no larger than 2.5cm/ 1 inch. Warm the olive oil in a frying-pan with the garlic, add the aubergines in one layer if you can, in two batches if you cannot, and cook them till golden on all sides. They should be tender in the middle. Scoop them out and drain on kitchen paper for a second or two before tipping into a warm serving dish and seasoning with coarse salt, fine pepper and the chopped parsley.

For 2
•
2 medium aubergines
4 tablespoons olive oil
2 cloves of garlic, squashed flat
a little coarsely chopped parsley

▶ *Serve with a dollop of thick yoghurt into which you have stirred both chopped coriander and grated fresh root ginger*

▶ *As you remove the aubergine from the pan replace it with a couple of large handfuls of washed and still wet spinach. Cook for a minute or maybe two, covered with a lid, till the leaves have wilted. Drain them in a colander and press out the moisture with a spoon, roughly chop and stir in the still-warm drained aubergines. Season with salt and pepper and serve with wedges of lemon*

Hot Aubergine and Cheese Sandwiches

For 2

•

2 large, fat aubergines

I clove of garlic, crushed with a little salt

100g/4oz Mozzarella cheese

4 tablespoons grated Parmesan cheese

a handful of basil leaves, about 20

plain flour

olive oil for frying

approximately 8 cocktail sticks

An idea from southern Italy via Valentina Harris. I have departed from Ms Harris's classic recipe by swapping Mozzarella and Parmesan for her Pecorino simply for the creaminess of the former when it melts, and I have shallow- rather than deep-fried my version. I have also omitted the small red chilli, finely chopped, which she adds to the cheese, though for no particular reason.

Cut the prickly stems from the top of the aubergines and slice them down their length, into pieces about 1cm/ ½ inch in thickness. You should have about 8. Bring a pan of water to the boil and drop in the aubergine slices. Blanch for 2 minutes, no longer, and lift them out. Drain and dry with kitchen paper.

Lay half of them flat and spread with the crushed garlic clove. Place thin slices of Mozzarella on each – it doesn't matter if there is some overlap. Scatter over the grated Parmesan and the basil. Season with coarsely ground black pepper.

Place the remaining aubergine slices on top and then secure each pair with the cocktail sticks. Thread them through both top and bottom slices thus holding the filling loosely in place. You will probably get away with two sticks, about 2.5cm/1 inch away from each short edge.

Dust each sandwich with flour and fry in shallow oil, over a medium heat, for roughly 4 minutes on each side. The cheese may ooze a little from the sides – just scoop it up with a palette knife and wipe it on the aubergines. Sprinkle lightly with salt and serve while hot.

Opposite Baked Aubergine Slices with Red Peppers and Pine Nuts (page 33)
Over, left Roast Sweetcorn (page 78); *right* Baked Sweet Potatoes with Chilli Butter (page 77)

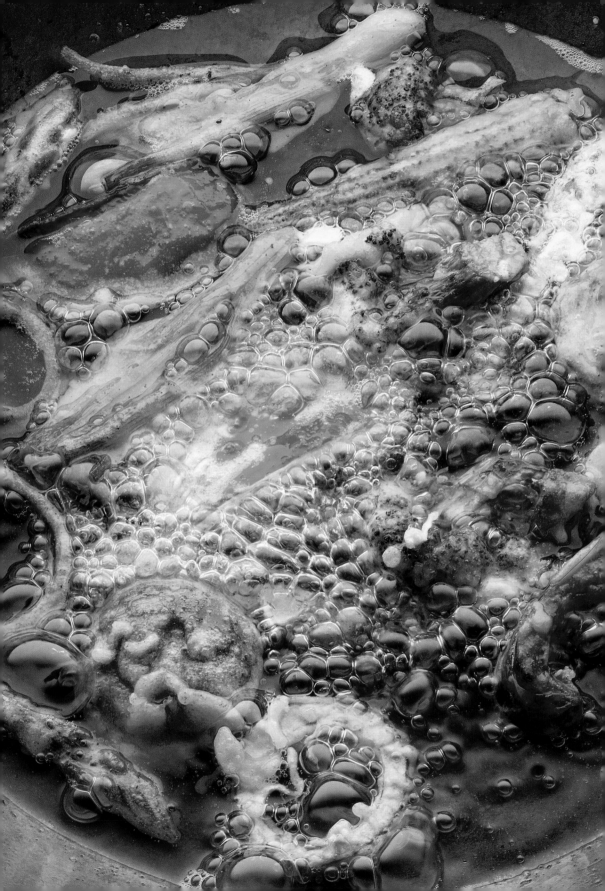

Baked Aubergine Slices

....

Photograph opposite page 32

Slices of melting baked aubergine with a somewhat Italian bent. At their most basic, with olive oil and thyme, they make a tender accompaniment to grilled fish or poultry. A little more imagination can turn them quite effortlessly into a main dish.

For 2
•
2 medium aubergines
100ml/4fl oz olive oil
thyme

Set the oven to 200°C/400°F (gas mark 6). Slice the aubergines about 1cm/½ inch thick. It does not matter whether you slice them into rounds or from stem lengthways. Brush a baking sheet with a little olive oil and arrange the slices on it in one layer. Brush the slices generously with olive oil. Sprinkle with a little thyme, though it should be fresh rather than dried, and then with some salt and coarsely ground pepper.

Bake till tender, about 15–20 minutes.

Spread lavishly with thick tomato sauce and a good sprinkling of Parmesan cheese, and return to the oven till bubbling.

With Tomato Sauce and Parmesan

Slather ready-made pesto sauce over the baked aubergines, with or without the thyme, and cover with thin slices of Mozzarella cheese. Season the cheese with pepper and a trickle of olive oil, and then grill till the cheese just melts. But no longer lest it toughens.

With Pesto and Mozzarella

Quarter, core and seed 2 red peppers and bake them with the aubergines as above. Dot over a few pine nuts and raisins, grill for a minute to colour the nuts and then scatter with torn mint leaves and coarsely ground black pepper. Serve with thick, cold yoghurt into which you have stirred some more chopped mint.

And with Red Peppers and Pine Nuts

Mixed Vegetable Tempura (page 86)

Some Quick Ways with an Aubergine

....

Breadcrumbed Aubergine

Slice the aubergine thinly, about 5mm/¼ inch I would say, and dip the slices into beaten egg and then into fine dry breadcrumbs. Press down firmly to make the crumbs stick (you can dip and crumb a second time if you wish), and fry in shallow oil until golden. Drain carefully and serve hot with garlic mayonnaise or tartare sauce. For 2.

Grilled Aubergine with Warm Mint Dressing

A lovely idea from Greece. Slice the aubergine thinly as above but from stem to thick end instead of into rounds. Brush copiously with olive oil and grill till tender, about 4 minutes on each side and not too close to the heat. Meanwhile, whizz up a dressing of extra virgin olive oil and lemon juice, and then stir in plenty of chopped mint and salt and pepper. Spoon the dressing over the warm aubergines and serve with crusty bread. Serves 2.

Indian Spiced Aubergine

For 2 people as a quick, mildly spiced stew to be eaten with warm Indian breads. Warm 2 tablespoons groundnut oil in a pan, and fry a medium onion, chopped, until it softens. Add a chopped green chilli pepper, and 1 large or 2 medium aubergines, cut into roughly 2.5cm/1 inch cubes. Cook for 5 minutes over a medium heat. Add 2 seeded and roughly chopped tomatoes, and stir in 175ml/6fl oz vegetable stock or water. Cook for 15 minutes until the aubergine is soft. Season with salt and pepper, a teaspoon of garam masala and a palmful of chopped coriander leaves. Stir in 100ml/4fl oz thick natural yoghurt as you serve. Serves 2.

BROCCOLI

I had become a bit bored with broccoli. Its presence had become ubiquitous, it tasted far too healthy for its own good and, curiously, even straight from the pot it was almost invariably cold. And yet a head of broccoli is such a splendid thing. The crunchy green stalks that cook to translucent, almost fluorescent, green, the tender heads of tight flower buds with a pleasant frilly texture in the mouth. And all those vitamins.

I suspect overkill was the problem, and also under-cooking. Like green beans, broccoli is often served under-cooked. Al dente is all very well (and I am the first to whinge about overcooked greens), but broccoli's flavour is so dull when the vegetable is blanched in boiling water instead of being properly cooked.

My interest has recently been rekindled by the reappearance of the sprouting variety. Beautiful clusters of fine green stems with purple heads. Tender and fine with crinkly sage-blue leaves, this is much more to my taste than the neat, tight bouquets wrapped in rubber bands and clingfilm. Granted, it is more seasonal and keeps for only a day or two, but to my mind the purple sprouting variety has as much charm as asparagus.

In the supermarket you are most likely to be offered clingfilm wrapped bunches. In which case, go for perky, snappy bunches. Nothing wilted, and nothing in flower. Ignore any that is yellow. It will stink when you get it home. Keeping better than most greens, a bunch of broccoli, tied and wrapped like a posy, offers much in terms of convenience.

SOME BROCCOLI STIR-FRIES

Chilli Broccoli

....

For 4, as a side dish

•

2 tablespoons groundnut oil

2 small red chilli peppers, seeded and chopped

1 medium onion, finely chopped

1 clove of garlic, sliced

450g/1lb broccoli, broken into large clusters

Punchy flavours. Bright colours.

Heat a wok and pour in the oil. As the oil starts to smoke throw in the chillies, onion and garlic. Turn down the heat immediately and cook over a low heat, stirring continuously, for 2 minutes.

When the onion is golden add the broccoli and fry for 5–7 minutes till the broccoli is bright in colour and tender to the point of a knife.

Broccoli with Parmesan

....

For 2, as an accompaniment

•

350g/12oz broccoli

100g/4oz Parmesan cheese

50g/2oz butter

A delightfully simple Italian idea that I first came across in Peter Graham's *Classic Cheese Cookery*. My version is less exacting than Mr Graham's, who ties his vegetables in bundles and cooks them like asparagus, and then sautées and bakes them. His way is perfection but the tender heads and stalks actually come to little harm in my rather cavalier method.

Simmer the broccoli in salted water till the stalks are tender, a matter of 5 minutes. Meanwhile, grate the Parmesan. If you have bought it ready grated, I hope the stuff you have is good. Some ready-grated cheese is about as interesting as sawdust.

Soften the butter – it should not be completely liquid. Drain the broccoli and put it into an ovenproof dish big enough to take it in one layer. Dot with the butter and sprinkle with grated Parmesan. Bake for 10 minutes or so in a preheated hot oven, 200°C/400°F (gas mark 6), until it is golden brown. I rather like it if the florets of broccoli have caught a little in the heat. But don't let it burn.

Broccoli with Ginger and Mustard Seeds

....

An Indian method that can be used for other similar vegetables such as cauliflower, spinach and spring greens.

Get a wok hot and heat the oil in it. Add the mustard seeds and when they start to pop and splutter, add the garlic, ginger and broccoli. Fry for 5 minutes over a high heat, stirring constantly. Add the garam masala, salt and some pepper. Stir the whole lot round, pour in a wineglass of water and cover with a lid. Simmer for a couple of minutes.

For 2, as an accompaniment
•

2 tablespoons groundnut oil

I teaspoon yellow mustard seeds

2 cloves of garlic, sliced

2.5cm/I inch knob of fresh root ginger, peeled and cut into matchsticks

350g/12oz broccoli florets, not too small

½ teaspoon garam masala

Purple Sprouting Broccoli and Eggs

....

Choose the youngest, tenderest, freshest sprouts of purple broccoli in the market. The dish, if you can call anything so simple by such a grand name, is only worth bothering with if the broccoli is amazingly new and crisp. Bring a pot of water, a deep one, to the boil. Salt it and add a handful of purple sprouting broccoli spears. Cook them till they are just tender, about 3 minutes, then whip them out and drain.

Have ready a nice boiled egg. It must be soft with a runny yolk. Dip the warm spears into the egg, like soldiers, and then finish the egg off with a teaspoon. For 1.

Broccoli with Oyster Sauce

....

For 2, as a side dish

•

350g/12oz broccoli
3 tablespoons groundnut oil
2 tablespoons oyster sauce

Similar method to that for Broccoli with Ginger and Mustard Seeds on page 37, but with a completely different flavour – mellow and savoury rather than bright and hot.

Split the broccoli into large florets, trimming the stalks if they are a bit thick. You can slice a piece off each to thin them to a point if you wish.

Heat 2 tablespoons of the oil in a hot wok. Fry the broccoli, over moderate heat, for 4–5 minutes, stirring and turning from time to time. When it is bright green and tender, pour over the remaining oil and the oyster sauce. Toss gently so as not to break the heads and heat for a minute before serving.

....

▶ B*roccoli responds well to frying over a high heat as long as it is moved around the pan regularly and the heat isn't so high that the tender heads burn before the stalks cook. A way round this is to cut the heads from the stalks and add them to the pan after the stalks show signs of becoming tender (i.e. you can slide a knife point into them effortlessly). I cannot honestly say I bother, preferring the contrast between crisp emerald green stalks and slightly softer dark green heads*

CABBAGE AND ORIENTAL GREENS

Supermarket shelves, market stalls and greengrocers now offer a wealth of lush green leaves, from heavily ridged and juicy Chinese cabbage, hot and spicy mustard greens, crunchy-stemmed pak choi and frilly curly kale to the crinkly Savoys, ice-hard drumhead and bronze-edged January King cabbages we know so well.

Each one is worth eating. The flavours are startlingly different, as anyone who has tried some of the offerings in Chinatown will testify. New favourites of mine are pak choi, sometimes known as Chinese celery cabbage because of its fleshy white stalks, and the mustard greens, a huge family of leaves mostly available from Chinese supermarkets. I am also fond of mitzuna, the spiky-leafed Japanese greens, but they are still a rare find.

The leaves fall into two main categories, the tender leaves such as Chinese cabbage (bok choi), pak choi and yellow-flowered choi sum, and the coarser-leaved varieties – the traditional cabbages such as the Savoy. With the exception of cooking time, which obviously decreases with the tenderness of the raw leaf, all the varieties are interchangeable. You can stir-fry any of them in the traditional Chinese manner, crunch them raw in salads or lightly steam them and drizzle with seasoned oil.

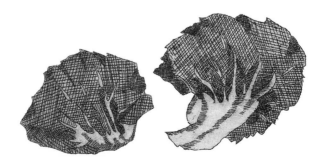

Creamed Cabbage

....

Use hard white cabbage.

Shred a small, hard, white cabbage. The shreds should be quite wide. Like pappardelle. Heat a large knob of butter with a tablespoon of nut oil (walnut or hazelnut) or olive if that is what you have, and fry the cabbage till it softens and becomes translucent; about 10 minutes. Stir in a small pot (about 100ml/4fl oz) double cream and season with salt and pepper. The pepper should be quite fine. For once. Simmer over a low heat for 2 minutes; then add a squeeze of lemon and serve. For 2.

Quick Spiced Cabbage

....

For 2

•

450g/1lb cabbage

2 tablespoons groundnut oil

2 medium onions, sliced into rings

½ teaspoon cumin seeds

¼ teaspoon chilli powder

1 teaspoon garam masala

lemon, to serve

Indian spiced greens. Use spring greens or any cabbage.

Cut the cabbage into long thin shreds, removing the tough stalks as you go. Heat the oil in a large frying-pan or wok. Add the onions and fry till limp and deep golden, about 10 minutes, stirring from time to time. Add the cumin seeds and cook over a medium heat for a further minute.

Throw in the cabbage. Fry at a moderate to high heat until the leaves are shiny and tender. They should brown slightly at the edges. Add salt, pepper, chilli and the garam masala. Fry for 3–4 minutes, constantly stirring, and then serve hot with wedges of lemon.

Cabbage with Fat
....

A glorious mélange of dark green leaves (Savoy, spring greens or January King) and rich poultry fat. Goose fat is available in tins from French delicatessens and occasionally butchers' shops.

Roll up the leaves and shred them, not too finely, with a large knife. Melt the goose fat in a deep frying-pan. When it is hot add the smoked bacon, cook for 2 minutes and then add the shredded leaves. They will spit and pop if they are still wet from washing.

Fry the leaves until they wilt and darken. They will shine with fat. Season with salt and pepper, and serve sizzling from the pan.

For 2
•
4 double handfuls of dark green leaves
3 tablespoons goose fat
75g/3oz smoked bacon, diced

Greens with Bacon and Chilli
....

Use dark or white cabbage, pak choi, Chinese cabbage (bok choi).

Roll up the leaves and stalks and shred them finely with a large knife. Dice the bacon and melt it over a high heat. If little fat runs from it, as often happens nowadays, then add some oil. Groundnut will do. When the fat or oil is hot and the bacon has started to colour, add the shredded greens. Cook for 5 minutes, less if the leaves are soft, stirring pretty much all the time. Sprinkle over the chilli flakes, cook for a minute more, season with salt and serve, as hot as you can.

For 2
•
6 handfuls of washed green leaves and fine stalks
100g/4oz fatty smoked bacon
I teaspoon dried chilli flakes

10-Minute Greens

....

Cabbage and Cheese

Steam shredded white cabbage till tender, drain and toss with cubes of blue cheese (Roquefort, Beenleigh Blue, Stilton, etc.), ground pepper and a little walnut oil.

Greens and Bacon

Stir-fry 100g/4oz fat unsmoked bacon, cut into thick strips, in a hot wok. Add a little oil if it sticks. When the fat is golden and the bacon sizzling, lift it out with a draining spoon, leaving the liquid fat behind. Add 350g/12oz chopped pak choi, Chinese cabbage or mustard greens and stir-fry for a minute in the fat. As they wilt, return the bacon to the pan and serve hot.

Garlic Choi

Slice a few heads of pak choi into large bite-sized pieces. Separate the crisp, fleshy white stalks from the soft green leaves. Heat a wok and pour in a couple of tablespoons of groundnut oil. Swish it round the wok, and when it is smoking hot add a tablespoon of chopped garlic. Quickly, so that it does not burn and become bitter, stir the garlic round the pan. As soon as it is golden brown (as opposed to brown brown), add the white pak choi. Stir continuously for 1 minute. Add the green leaves and a good pinch of salt and fry for a further minute. Serve while singing and hot.

Chinese Greens with Oyster Sauce

Cut any Chinese greens (yellow flowering mustard greens or pak choi) into 7.5cm/3 inch lengths. Blanch in boiling, salted water for 2–3 minutes, until the leaves and stems are bright and tender. Drain thoroughly and place on a hot dish. Mix 2 tablespoons groundnut oil with an equal amount of oyster sauce, and then tip over the steaming greens.

And Some 5-Minute Greens
············

Mix 2 tablespoons of oyster sauce with 1 of sesame oil and 1 of sugar. Pour it into a warm bowl and toss lightly blanched dark cabbage, mustard or Chinese greens in it.

With Oyster Sauce

Shred Brussels sprouts finely. A large knife is best for this. Then toss them in hot bacon fat with plump golden raisins.

With Bacon Fat

Dress freshly cooked and steaming hot cabbage with a mixture of softened butter, a little lemon juice and a sprinkling of toasted caraway seeds.

With Caraway

Toss freshly cooked cabbage with a mixture of grated orange zest, toasted pine nuts and chopped parsley.

With Orange

Pak choi can be split down the middle – by middle I mean from leaf to stalk – and steamed till tender, 4–6 minutes. Lift from the steamer and then anoint while still steaming with a mixture of soy sauce, rice wine and thinly sliced young garlic.

With Soy

Have a go at deep-fried 'seaweed'. Shred half a cabbage very, very finely with a large sharp knife. Fry the shreds in deep hot groundnut oil. Remove them as soon as they become crunchy (a matter of seconds), drain on kitchen paper and sprinkle with sugar.

Chinese-style

Fry last night's cooked cabbage in hot butter and a little garlic. Season it thoroughly and then stir in the remains of the gravy or pan juices from the roast. Serve piping hot.

Frugal-style

CARROTS

A raw carrot, crunched as I write, is a favourite afternoon snack. It stops me eating heavily buttered crumpets and the like. I will vote for carrots too when coarsely grated and spiced with other members of the same family, dill, coriander, parsley (a refreshing mixture that, grated carrot and chopped parsley) and caraway seeds. Where the carrot and I part company is when it is boiled.

Old carrots, by which I mean maincrop rather than tired, seem to have more flavour than the new baby varieties, even if the latter do still have their fluffy green tops on. Although in my book nutrition comes second to flavour and enjoyment, it is comforting to know that carrots are rich in beta carotene and many of the more important minerals. Like watercress, carrots actually taste as if they are good for you as you munch on them, hard from the fridge and wet from the cold tap.

The Turks have a pleasing way with carrots that involves frying them with mint and olive oil, while the Greeks bless them with mint and lemon juice. In Iran they are enriched with butter and sweet dates, though I find them sweet enough when spiced Indian-style with cumin seeds and lime.

The 30-minute cook will find the ready-washed carrots from the major stores a more realistic prospect than the mud-encrusted ones from the health-food shop. Though it is worth looking out for well-presented organically grown examples – there are plenty about, and they sometimes have a better flavour. They also tend to come with a splendid mane of green fronds, a good guide to the freshness of the carrot. And as for peeling, I cannot remember the last time I met a carrot that needed anything more than a mild scrub. It is worth remembering that many of the vitamins lie directly under the skin. Or so the experts tell me.

Turkish Carrots

....

Sharp tangy yoghurt is an appealing foil for the carrot's natural sweetness.

Cut the carrots into thick slices. You can keep them whole if you are using baby ones. Heat the olive oil in a frying-pan, add the carrots and cook slowly, over a low heat, for 15 minutes or until tender. They should not be soft, but should have a little bite left in them. Brown in patches is a plus.

Add the mint and yoghurt to the pan. Toss gently and then remove from the heat. The vegetables will be hot enough to warm the yoghurt without further cooking, which will curdle it. Serve warm.

For 4, as a side dish
•
450g/1lb carrots
2 tablespoons olive oil
2 tablespoons chopped mint
2 heaped tablespoons thick yoghurt

Carrots with Mustard Seeds

....

A hot version of Madhur Jaffrey's Gujerati carrot salad. For 4, as a side dish.

Heat 2 tablespoons groundnut or vegetable oil in a sauté or frying-pan. Add 350g/12oz small carrots or thickly sliced maincrop carrots and fry for 10–15 minutes over a medium heat till they are tender. Add a tablespoon of black mustard seeds, turn the heat up a little and cook for a few seconds until they start to pop. Squeeze a little lemon juice into the pan and serve hot.

Roast Carrots

....

If the oven is on anyway. For 2, as a side dish.

Slice half a pound of carrots thinly, about as thick as pound coins. Toss them in a little olive oil and season with coarsely ground black pepper, salt and chopped thyme leaves. Roast them in a preheated hot oven (200°C/400°F/gas mark 6) for 25 minutes till golden brown. Serve as an accompaniment to roast meat or poultry.

Carrots and Bacon

....

For 2, as a side dish

•

25g/1oz butter
450g/1lb small carrots
100g/4oz tiny bottled onions
100g/4oz smoked streaky bacon

Bacon is a joy with all root vegetables, especially the sweeter ones, carrots, parsnips and beetroot.

Melt the butter in a sauté pan. Keep the heat moderately high. Add the carrots, kept whole, and the baby onions. Dice the bacon and add it to the pan with a little salt and pepper when the vegetables are beginning to brown. Turn the heat to low, cover and cook for 25 minutes till all is golden and meltingly tender.

The Alternative to Boiled Carrots

....

If the carrots are a large variety then slice them, as thick or as thin as you like. Place them in a pan to which you have a tight-fitting lid. Pour in enough boiling water to come halfway up the carrots. Add a generous knob of butter and a healthy squeeze of lemon juice. Pop in a sprinkling of white sugar, and salt but no pepper. Simmer them gently until they are tender but offer a degree of resistance when you bite into them. The time will, of course, depend on how thinly you cut your carrots; 7–10 minutes should do it.

CAULIFLOWERS

The huge piles of cauliflowers, like fluffy white clouds, are a startling sight in my local street market on crisp winter mornings. Freshly cut, they are a difficult vegetable to beat for those who like crisp textures and strident flavours. A day too long, though, and they have an unspeakable smell that has put many off for life.

I like cauliflower served raw, snapped into bite-sized florets and smothered in thick Greek yoghurt and tiny blue-black poppy seeds. Fried quickly in hot oil with cumin seeds and chilli it can be worth eating too, and bound in a creamy parsley and ham sauce we may have found this particular vegetable's zenith.

Cauliflower with Crème Fraîche and Bacon

Cream in any form, double, soured or crème fraîche, has an affinity with cauliflower. Bacon or ham also.

Cut the bacon or pancetta into small dice, about the size of dolly mixtures. Fry in a shallow pan in their own fat if there is enough, or in a little butter if not. Bring a pan of water to the boil, salt it and cook the cauliflower in it for 4–5 minutes till almost tender. It should just resist the knife.

Drain the cauliflower and add it to the bacon. Stir in the crème fraîche and season with salt, pepper and a palmful of parsley. Bring slowly to the boil and then turn down the heat and simmer for a couple of minutes.

For 2, as a side dish
•
100g/4oz smoked bacon or pancetta
a little butter
1 medium cauliflower, broken into large florets
100ml/4fl oz crème fraîche
chopped parsley

▶ *I have made double quantities of this creamy, smoky vegetable dish before now, and eaten it as a main dish, with mashed potato*

Cauliflower with Yoghurt and Poppy Seeds

....

You hardly need a recipe for this. Break a crisp, creamy fleshed cauliflower into large florets. The pieces should be bite-sized. Little bits would be horrid. Season some thick Greek-style yoghurt with black pepper and beat it for a minute till it is creamy and smooth. Toss the cauliflower in the yoghurt and then sprinkle over a scattering of poppy seeds. Chopped parsley might be interesting.

Cumin and Chilli Cauliflower

....

For 2
•
350g/12oz cauliflower florets
1 tablespoon groundnut oil
1 teaspoon cumin seeds
3 tablespoons thick chilli sauce
2 tablespoons chopped coriander leaves

A spicy side order similar to a dish I was handed by mistake in India. My version is less spicy than the one I had there.

Cook the cauliflower florets in boiling salted water for 4–5 minutes until tender; they should still have some bite, though.

In a wok or frying-pan heat the oil and cook the cumin seeds in it till lightly toasted. They may pop and splutter. Add the drained cauliflower and the chilli sauce. Stir and fry for 1 minute. Salt and pepper it. Coriander it. Serve hot.

FENNEL

Fennel is a love it or hate it vegetable. I love it, especially for its delicate green-white crisp flesh and its characteristic aniseed flavour. As an accompaniment to main dishes, particularly fish, it needs nothing more than slicing thinly and dressing with a light olive oil and plenty of lemon juice and black pepper.

Stir-fried Fennel

....

Aniseed is a flavour well known in China. It comes principally from the beautiful spice star-anise, a hard, brown, star-shaped seed pod, and is either added whole for slow-cooked dishes or in ground form for quick cooking. The European sources of similar aniseed notes, fennel and tarragon, are rarely used in Chinese cooking, though fennel, crisp, white and mildly flavoured, lends itself particularly well to stir-frying and Chinese spicing.

Cut the fennel in half and then diagonally into thick pieces, and at an angle into long tapering slices. Blanch them in boiling water for 2 minutes. Drain thoroughly.

Heat a wok and then pour in the oil. When the oil is hot, but not blisteringly so, add the garlic, ginger and black beans, and stir-fry for a minute; then add the fennel. Fry for a further minute and pour in the rice wine or sherry. Sprinkle over a few drops of sesame oil and serve.

For 2, as an accompaniment
•
450g/1lb fennel bulbs
1 tablespoon groundnut oil
2 cloves of garlic, sliced
1 small knob of fresh root ginger, peeled and finely chopped
1 tablespoon black beans, rinsed and coarsely chopped
2 tablespoons rice wine or dry sherry
a little sesame oil

Fennel Baked with Butter and Parmesan

....

450g/1lb fennel bulbs

50g/2oz butter

50g/2oz freshly grated Parmesan cheese

Fennel is more at home in Italy. Although often baked for an hour or more with cheese and olive oil, I find it keeps its sparkling fresh flavour when blanched in boiling water and then baked for a shorter time.

Cut the fennel bulbs in half. Drop them into boiling water and simmer for 5–6 minutes, until slightly translucent. Drain and place in an ovenproof dish, cut edges up. Dot with butter, season with freshly ground pepper and top with the grated cheese. Bake in a preheated oven, 200°C/400°F (gas mark 6), for 20 minutes till golden, basting once with the buttery juices.

GREEN BEANS

The scarlet runner is still my favourite bean, though it has to be freshly picked to be really good. The supermarket versions I have eaten lately have lost some of their flavour. Farm shops seem to be a good bet. The round French *haricot vert* is probably the most popular bean now, though far from my first choice. Its principal plus is that it keeps its flavour and crispness better than most.

Look for beans that are crisp and cold to the touch. It is not enough to say that you should look for beans that snap smartly when bent. The point is that they must also be juicy inside. You only get to know this if you have ever grown your own. Some beans snap crisply even when they are old.

I love the smell of newly sliced runner beans almost more than the taste. I have recently seen them ready sliced in cellophane bags. It will take a lot to convince me that this is a bonus. It takes very little time to slice a few beans and the cut edges do tend to leak goodness. No, I can manage to slice a few beans. No matter how short of time I am.

There is a train of thought that says that beans should be blanched and served crisp. I disagree. However fresh and green they look on the plate, the flavour of an undercooked bean is bound to disappoint. I cannot count the number of nearly raw, virtually tasteless beans I have eaten in restaurants.

Beans need a decent time in the pot if they are to provide anything more than something for the teeth to crunch. They should, I venture to suggest, be slightly limp and if any restaurateur is reading this, they also need to be eaten really hot, not tepid. I reckon a good 8 minutes at a rolling boil.

▶ *The Chinese love the long thin 'yard long beans', a.k.a. Chinese pea or snake beans, which you can pick up here in long green coils at oriental greengrocers. I would like to taste such beans freshly picked. The ones I have bought have all been on the tough side, and as they are usually cut into short lengths for cooking anyway, I am not sure they have too much going for them*

Beans with Ginger

Beans Indian-style.

Bring 175ml/6fl oz water to the boil in a wok or shallow pan. Add the oil, beans, and a good pinch of salt, and simmer, covered, for 5 minutes. Remove the lid, add the ginger, chilli, sugar and coriander. Continue to cook, without the lid, for a minute or so.

For 2, as an accompaniment

•

2 tablespoons groundnut oil

450g/1lb green beans, cut into 2.5cm/1 inch lengths

1 tablespoon finely grated fresh root ginger

1 small red chili pepper, seeded and chopped

1 teaspoon sugar

2 tablespoons chopped coriander leaves

Green and Black Bean Stir-fry

....

For 2

•

225g/8oz green beans

1 tablespoon groundnut oil

2.5cm/1 inch knob of fresh root ginger, peeled

2 cloves of garlic, finely sliced

1 tablespoon black beans, rinsed and coarsely chopped

1 tablespoon chilli bean sauce

1 teaspoon sugar

100ml/4fl oz vegetable stock

2 tablespoons rice wine or dry sherry

Two beans, Chinese style.

Cut the green beans into 5cm/2 inch lengths. Heat a wok until it is really hot, add the oil and when that is hot too add the ginger and garlic. Stir-fry for 30 seconds, add the black beans and the chilli bean sauce. Fry for 30 seconds more and then add the green beans. Keep frying and stirring for a few seconds; then add the sugar and pour in the stock and rice wine or sherry. Cook for about 2 minutes with the heat up high, continuously stirring and frying, till the beans are bright green and tender. Serve.

Beans and Nuts

....

Almost every cuisine seems to have a recipe for marrying beans with nuts. The two work together, a lovely combination of flavours and textures.

Green Beans and Sesame Seeds

....

For 2

•

350g/12oz green beans

2 tablespoons sesame seeds

1 tablespoon dark soy sauce

1 tablespoon rice wine

A Japanese way.

Cook the beans in boiling salted water till tender, about 7–8 minutes. Put the sesame seeds into a dry frying-pan and roast them over a medium heat till they start to colour lightly. They will smell nutty and warm.

Mix the sesame seeds with the soy sauce and rice wine. Drain the beans and toss while still warm in the sesame dressing.

Green Beans and Almonds

············

A French way.

Cook the beans in boiling salted water for about 7–8 minutes and then drain them. Toss in melted butter – it should be sloppy rather than liquid – and scatter over a few almonds, flaked, that you have toasted golden.

Green Beans and Peanuts

············

And a Chinese way.

Cut the beans into 5cm/2 inch lengths. Heat a wok until it is really hot. Pour in the oil and wait till it just starts to smoke. Fry the shallots till golden, stirring all the time, then add the beans. Continue frying and stirring till the beans are green and tender. Add the peanuts, salt generously and fry for a minute more till the beans are golden. Serve hot.

For 2

•

225g/8oz green beans

2 tablespoons groundnut oil

3 shallots, finely sliced

75g/3oz unsalted peanuts

MUSHROOMS

Fine mushrooms do not come in tins. Fine mushrooms have firm, creamy beige tops with velvety, dark brown gills underneath. They need neither peeling nor brushing. A wipe with a damp thumb will remove any growing medium. Washing will turn them to wet sponge.

I am constantly amazed by the assortment of cultivated mushrooms at the supermarket: grey pleurottes softer than suede, canary yellow ones too, firm shaggy, organic brown chestnut mushrooms and the deep brown 'stuffing mushroom' as big as a saucer. In posh shops there are all manner of wonderful ones to try. It would be easy to get carried away. But this is above all a practical book, so I will confine myself to what you can expect at any decent greengrocer's.

I include the charming little button mushrooms, not for their flavour, which is lacking, but for their ability to soak up other flavours. Sauté them with cubes of smoked fatty bacon and some fresh sage and you will get my drift. Flat mushrooms as big as a plate, which turn up from time to time at the greengrocer's, I keep for grilling. Basted with butter and a little garlic there is no better supper.

I often pick up a punnet of mushrooms without thinking too hard about what I shall do with them when I get them home. There is not much in the cupboard that will not work with them to produce a first-class supper. Eggs for a mushroom omelette, rice for a risotto, spring onions and oyster sauce for a stir-fry, or lemon and Parmesan for the simplest of grills.

But there is more too. Mushrooms are used extensively in the East, sometimes special varieties such as the shiitake now available from many supermarkets and sometimes more everyday cup and button. The Thais make a sour, spicy soup with fresh oyster mushrooms, while the Chinese know that even inoffensive button mushrooms turn into flavoursome, savoury nuggets when stir-fried with garlic, ginger and soy sauce. So juicy and delectable do mushrooms become when tossed in hot oil and aromatics that I have included two stir-fries and a handful of ideas for things to throw into them. And as they lend themselves so well to spicy cooking I have included my lazy version of a mushroom curry too.

When buying mushrooms, either plain or fancy, check that they are dry. Mushrooms perspire heavily when wrapped in plastic, and will quickly turn soggy and rot. Porous brown paper bags are best for storing your buttons, chestnuts and oysters; some of the supermarkets even have special 'mushroom bags' now. They will keep in the salad crisper at the bottom of the fridge for a few days.

Mushroom Tart

....

Photograph opposite page 96

I have eaten two sublime mushroom tarts in my life; the first at a small hotel in Austria, high in the mountains in mid-autumn, and the second in Soho, at Alastair Little's eponymous restaurant. I doubt whether either included frozen puff pastry in their recipe, but I do in mine. White button mushrooms will yield little joy. Go for dark brown, medium-cupped mushrooms or huge field ones, sliced into wedges. Garlic, in this instance, is pretty much obligatory.

For 2
•
250g/9oz mushrooms, wiped
50g/2oz butter, softened but not melted
2 cloves of garlic, sliced
2 tablespoons chopped parsley
175g/6oz puff pastry, defrosted

Preheat the oven to 220°C/425°F (gas mark 7). Cut the mushrooms into bite-sized pieces, quarters for the small to medium cup variety, chunks for the big flat field mushrooms. Mix the butter with the garlic. Fry the mushrooms in a shallow pan with half the butter, adding a little more butter or olive oil if they have soaked it all up. Stir in the parsley.

On a lightly floured surface roll the pastry into a rectangle approximately 20 × 13cm/8 × 5 inches. Lift carefully on to a baking sheet. Using a sharp knife, score a smaller rectangle 4cm/1½ inches from the edge, cutting only halfway through the layer of pastry. Scoop the mushrooms from the pan and place them on the innermost rectangle, trying not to let them hang over the outer rim. Place in the hot oven and bake for 15 minutes till the pastry is risen. Dot with the remaining butter then close the door for another 5–7 minutes till the pastry is golden and the mushrooms sizzling. Serve straight from the oven, before the pastry has time to go soggy.

▶ *Puff pastry keeps in the freezer compartment of the fridge for weeks, and takes about an hour to thaw. Most of it is pretty good, particularly if somewhere along the line you can add a bit of butter, which will give it a better flavour. The garlic butter in which the mushrooms are cooked here will help the flavour of the pastry enormously. Chilled fresh puff pastry is good too, if your supermarket is up to stocking it*

Broccoli and Mushroom Stir-fry

....

For 2, as a main dish

•

**225g/8oz chestnut or large flat
mushrooms, wiped**

3 tablespoons groundnut oil

4 spring onions, chopped

2 large cloves of garlic, sliced

**225g/8oz broccoli stems and florets,
cut into bite-sized pieces**

2 tablespoons light soy sauce

**2 tablespoons rice wine or dry
sherry**

A classic Chinese stir-fry. Nothing fancy. Unless you want
to throw in some smarter mushrooms such as shiitake or
oyster. The best version of this I have yet made used big
black mushrooms (they had been around a day or two)
and a slice of lamb's liver, added with the mushrooms.

If you are using brown cup mushrooms, cut them into
quarters; if you have large flat ones, slice them about as
thick as pound coins. Heat a wok. Get it really quite hot
and then pour in the oil. Straight away add the spring
onions and cook till they wilt and turn dark green, a
minute or so; then add the garlic and cook for a minute
till dark golden brown.

Stir in the broccoli and fry for 2 minutes, stirring almost
continuously, till it turns vivid green. Add the mushrooms
with a little more oil if the broccoli has drunk it all. Fry
for 2 minutes then add the soy sauce and rice wine or
sherry. Fry and stir the whole lot for a minute or two till
the broccoli is tender and the mushrooms brown. Season
with freshly ground pepper. You won't need salt with all
that soy. Serve hot and sizzling from the pan.

Stir-fry of Four Mushrooms

....

Follow the above recipe but forget the broccoli. Increase
the mushrooms to 450g/1lb. Substitute some smooth grey
pleurottes (oyster mushrooms), some shiitake and some
brown chestnut mushrooms for some of the others. For
preference I would have fewer shiitake and more pleurottes. But mix them as you will. A little grated ginger
root would be an authentic enough addition, added after
the garlic has coloured.

Some Good Things to Add to a Mushroom Stir-fry
....

- shredded spring greens instead of the broccoli
- celery, sliced diagonally across the stem
- oyster sauce; replace half of the soy sauce with 2 tablespoons oyster sauce (oyster sauce has an affinity with both mushrooms and broccoli)
- chopped coriander leaves, at the end
- replace half the broccoli with shredded smoked chicken or cubes of smoked pork

Pan-fried Mushrooms
....

All manner of mushrooms respond well to being quickly fried in butter and olive oil. Use any mixture you like or just one variety. One of the most delicious versions was when I used only plump chestnut mushrooms. You cannot go wrong whatever combination you use. I use garlic here only to scent the cooking oil rather than as an ingredient. It would be easy to overpower the flavour of the mushrooms.

Separate the mushrooms into firm and fragile varieties. Without actually seeing your shopping basket I suggest button, shiitake and chestnut in one pile and soft oyster mushrooms, chanterelles or other fancy funghi in another.

Warm the oil in a sauté or deep frying-pan. Melt the butter in it. When it sizzles and foams add the firm mushrooms, halved or quartered as common sense suggests. Add the garlic and fry, stirring from time to time, over a moderate heat for 5 minutes. Stir in the fragile mushrooms and cook for a further 5 minutes. Don't overcook them. Season with parsley, lemon juice, salt and coarsely ground black pepper.

For 2
•
450g/1lb assorted mushrooms, wiped

2 tablespoons olive oil

50g/2oz butter

2 cloves of garlic, squashed flat

1 tablespoon chopped parsley

a little lemon juice

Spiced Mushrooms

....

For 2, with rice if you wish

•

4 tablespoons groundnut oil

2 medium onions, sliced into thin rounds

2 plump cloves of garlic, sliced

2.5cm/1 inch knob of fresh root ginger, peeled and grated

1 tablespoon ground coriander

1 teaspoon mild chilli powder

350g/12oz firm mushrooms, such as chestnut or large button, wiped

1 tablespoon tomato purée

225ml/8fl oz vegetable stock or water

4 tablespoons thick Greek-style yoghurt

1 tablespoon chopped coriander leaves

Mushrooms take well to Indian spicing. Coriander, in particular, either whole seeds or in ground form. They can even take a little chilli powder, providing you are not using fancy funghi, which would be a waste. For once, I use tomato purée, but here it has a purpose that could not be answered by using fresh tomatoes. It adds depth to the dish that chopped fresh ones cannot. I have suggested a mild chilli powder, but how much goes in is obviously up to you.

Warm the oil in a heavy-based pan over a medium heat and then fry the onions till golden. If the onions have browned slightly round the edges, it is all to the good. Stir in the garlic and grated ginger. Cook for a minute and then stir in the ground coriander and chilli powder. Fry for a minute more. Add the mushrooms and cook over a medium heat for 4–5 minutes till tender.

Add the tomato purée and stir in. Cook for a further minute and then stir in the stock or water. Cook for 5–6 minutes, covered, until thick and dark brown. If the mixture has not thickened by this time, boil hard to reduce the liquid. It should be a thick, spicy slush. At the last moment, partially stir in the yoghurt and sprinkle with chopped coriander.

Some 10-Minute Mushrooms

....

Deep-fried Mushrooms

I have never seen so many wild mushrooms in one place as at the open market at Vicenza, near Venice. Wooden boxes and wicker baskets piled high with mauve and fawn, chocolate brown and beige, dove grey and black funghi. Later that day I ate some of them deep-fried, some recognizable, others not, in a typical trattoria – its counter display piled high with baskets of grey, downy pleurottes and moss-covered porcini.

Wipe 450g/1lb mixed mushrooms and cut them into large bite-sized pieces. The smaller ones you can leave whole. Beat 3 eggs and season them with salt and black pepper. Dip the mushroom pieces first into the egg, then into fine, dry breadcrumbs (you can buy them in Italian grocers if you don't want to make your own). Fry in deep, hot oil for a minute or two till crisp and golden. Serve hot, with wedges of lemon. For 2.

Wipe and trim 450g/1lb of assorted mushrooms. Any variety is suitable. Cut 175g/6oz of smoked bacon – Italian pancetta would be good here – into dice. About the size of dolly mixtures. Chop up a handful of fresh green parsley, not too fine, and peel and chop a clove of garlic. Heat a little walnut or olive oil in a sauté pan, add the mushrooms, cut or sliced where necessary, the bacon, garlic, a little salt and half the parsley. Cover with a lid and cook on a gentle heat for 20 minutes till the mushrooms are tender. Grind over a little pepper and serve with the pan juices. For 2.

Mushrooms with Parsley and Ham

Or tarragon mushrooms. Wipe 350g/12oz mushrooms. Any variety will do. Even buttons this time. Cook them with a couple of crushed garlic cloves in 3 tablespoons olive oil for 7–10 minutes. Add the leaves from 3 healthy sprigs of tarragon. Add a little salt and some black pepper. Stir in 225ml/8fl oz double cream, or crème fraîche if you prefer, and warm slowly, almost to the boil. Season with freshly ground black pepper and salt. Something to be served on rounds of thick toast. For 2.

Champignons à l'Estragon

Big, velvet-gilled field mushrooms. As big as a beret. Brush them generously with olive oil. Put a knob of butter and a glug of oil in the upturned cup. Grind a little pepper and salt, and grill, slowly, on a low heat, constantly buttering and oiling till you have a gold, brown and black mushroom. As savoury and tender as a piece of steak.

Grilled Mushrooms

PARSNIPS

I can be terribly old-fashioned at times. For instance, I still believe that parsnips taste better after the first snap of frost and I am rather suspicious of those tiny ones that appear in the shops in the summer. I don't want parsnips in the summer; I want peas and runner beans. Parsnips are as much a part of autumn and winter as asparagus is of summer. And that, I'm afraid, is that.

The parsnip, creamy yellow tapered beauty that it is, is the queen of the root vegetables. Truth told, it is at its best cooked around the roast, covered with meat juices and the sticky bits from the pan. But it is still of interest to the quick cook. Thinly sliced, it makes a welcoming sauté with fatty bacon and a few nuts. Cut paper thin, you can even stir-fry it in unorthodox manner with walnut oil and parsley. The French feed their cattle with parsnips. Which is possibly why their meat tastes so good.

Buttered Parsnips with Bacon and Pine Nuts

....

For 2, as a side dish

•

450g/1lb parsnips, scrubbed or peeled

75g/3oz unsmoked bacon, diced

50g/2oz butter

caster sugar

25g/1oz pine nuts

If the skins are muddy or tough, then take a minute or two and peel them; otherwise a good scrubbing will suffice. A sweet-smelling, comforting sort of dish.

Slice the parsnips into quarters from stalk to thin end. Cut them in half lengthways if they are awkwardly long. Cook the bacon in the butter in a sauté pan for 2–3 minutes until the fat turns golden and then add the parsnips and the sugar. Brown their edges lightly in the fat and butter, and then turn down the heat, letting them simmer over a moderate heat for 20 minutes.

When the parsnips are tender and slightly sticky toss in the pine nuts and cook for a few minutes till golden. Serve hot.

Parsnip Mash with Brown Butter and Bacon

....

Peel a pound of parsnips. (It just isn't the same in metric.) Cut them into even-sized pieces and boil in salted water till tender. They should be soft but not fluffy. Drain them and return to the pan. Mash them thoroughly with an ounce or so of butter. Then pour in a little double cream and beat with a wooden spoon till light and fluffy. Add salt and pepper, and beat again. Cover with a butter wrapper or similar and then with a lid.

Put a couple of ounces of butter in a frying-pan. Dice 75g/3oz bacon, smoked or not, and fry it in the butter till it is golden. Just as the butter starts to smell nutty and turn brown, but before it burns, scoop the mash into a warm dish and pour over the brown butter and bacon. It will feed 2 generously as a side dish, though I have been known to eat it as a main course on my own.

Parsleyed Parsnips

....

A perfect partner for pork chops.

Slice the parsnips thinly. Heat the oils (the olive is there to stop the nut oil burning) in a wok. When they are hot, though far from smoking hot, add the parsnips. Fry them, stirring from time to time for 8–10 minutes, or until they are golden. Sprinkle them with chopped parsley and serve.

For 2, as a side dish

•

450g/1lb parsnips, scrubbed or peeled

2 tablespoons walnut oil

1 tablespoon olive oil

2 tablespoons chopped parsley

PEAS

There is good news on the pea front. After years of neglect in favour of the frozen variety, fresh peas have made a comeback of late. Even my local greengrocer has crates of tiny pea pods, from British growers in season, and from Egypt, France or Cyprus during the rest of the year. Some of the posher supermarkets have gone one step better for the quick cook – trays of fresh, shelled peas ready to cook.

Useful though these podless peas are, I do miss shelling the sweet, green peas from their pods when I am in a romantic mood and the sun is shining and I can sit in the shade with a net of peas and a colander, eating almost as many as I put in the pot.

I have never been a fan of the frozen pea. Sweet, yes, but where is the flavour? Lost, I presume, in the manufacturers' search for sweetness. But fresh ones in their pods are not really practical when you come home hungry at seven o'clock. Fresh, shelled ones are the answer if you can find them, though the French bottled ones can be good – the process seems to deepen their flavour.

Still, a packet of frozen peas is better than no peas at all. Keep them away from water, though, and cook them in olive oil, on a low heat for 10 minutes. The olive oil, particularly if it is a peppery one, will soften some of their intense sweetness, and give them a little more interest.

A Better Way with Peas

Put 225g/8oz shelled fresh peas, or frozen if you must, in a small saucepan with 4 tablespoons olive oil, a little salt and 2 tablespoons water. Bring to the boil and then turn down to a simmer. Give them 10 minutes, a little less if you are using frozen ones. For 2.

Peas with Lemon and Mint

....

Cook the peas as above, adding the mint and lemon. Grind over a little coarse black pepper as you serve.

For 2
•
4 tablespoons olive oil
225g/8oz shelled peas
2 sprigs of mint
juice of ½ lemon

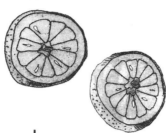

Peas, Potatoes and Fennel

....

An Italian way with peas. Mix equal amounts of freshly cooked peas, boiled tiny new potatoes and thinly shredded raw fennel. Pour over a little olive oil and even less white wine vinegar. Season with chopped mint and black pepper. Serve warm.

Pea and Artichoke Heart Stew

....

A light, fresh-tasting vegetable dish that works either as a meal in itself, perhaps a light lunch with bread and cheese to follow, or as an accompaniment to chicken or fish.

Warm the olive oil in a large, heavy pot and then add the garlic. Cook over a medium heat for 1 minute till fragrant. The garlic should not colour at all. Meanwhile, drain the artichoke hearts and cut them into quarters.

Add them to the pot with the lemon juice and the peas. Pop in the thyme and cook for 10 minutes. Season with salt and pepper and stir in half the parsley. Continue to cook for a further 3 minutes. Stir in the last of the parsley and serve in bowls with open-textured crusty bread.

For 2
•
100ml/4fl oz olive oil
4 large cloves of fresh young garlic, sliced
2 × 225g/8oz tins artichoke hearts
juice of ½ lemon
350g/12oz shelled peas
1 tablespoon chopped thyme
2 tablespoons chopped parsley

Peas with Olive Oil and Chillies

....

For 2, as an accompaniment

•

4 tablespoons extra virgin olive oil
225g/8oz shelled peas
I small onion, thinly sliced into rings
I small red chilli pepper, seeded and chopped
2 sprigs of mint

Bright green peas, emerald olive oil and little flecks of red chilli. A lively accompaniment for almost anything.

Put the oil into a heavy-based pan and add the peas with a tablespoon of water. Stir in the onion, the chilli and the mint, and simmer for 10–12 minutes, shaking the pan from time to time.

Use as an accompaniment or as a sauce for pasta shells.

Peas and Ham

....

Simmer fresh, shelled peas with a little butter or olive oil and a few drops of water till they are tender. Stir in a handful of chopped parsley. The herb should not be chopped too fine. Divide between two plates and serve with thinly sliced Parma ham. The peas, the parsley and ham make a delightful marriage.

Pea and Pink Grapefruit Salad

....

I know this sounds odd, but the slight tartness of the fruit is fun with the sweet peas. Simmer 225g/8oz shelled peas in 3 tablespoons olive oil and a tablespoon water for 7–8 minutes. Tip the lot into a cold bowl. Peel and cut a pink grapefruit into segments. Finely shred a handful of crisp (Cos) lettuce leaves. Mix, season and serve.

Opposite Chinese Noodles with Chicken and Mushrooms (page 148)
Over, left Red Lentils with Turmeric and Mustard Seeds (page 238); *right* Sausage and Bean Hotpot (page 196)

POTATOES

Regular readers will know of my deep fondness for the potato. It is almost an addiction. I make no secret of the fact that I find it one of the most enjoyable things there is to eat. I love its simplicity, versatility and flavour. And its ability to soothe and sustain. But it is the little things that are important, the crisp sticky edges of a roast potato that has stuck to the roasting tin, the first forkful of creamy buttery mash, or the crisp bite of a barely cooked Jersey Royal. These are the important things, not elaborate recipes for layered potato and scallop terrines.

I have dealt at reasonable length with the subject in *Real Fast Food*. I have written several articles about potatoes and photographed them a hundred times, but I still know very little about them. My bible is Lindsey Bareham's *In Praise of the Potato*, and if the quality of a cookbook can be judged by its splattered pages then this is a very special book indeed.

The versatility of the new potato has only recently dawned upon me. I had previously held these tiny, nutty, thin-skinned potatoes in so much esteem that I blindly followed everyone else's advice that they should only be boiled with mint and anointed with butter and herbs. I have only recently dared to roast them, in a hot oven with olive oil and butter, or cut them into quarters and cook them slowly in obscenely rich goose fat. Or bake them as I would a whopper. Or sauté them slowly with herbs and dripping. Stuff foie gras and caviar – give me potatoes.

My local greengrocer stocks two maincrop varieties, one of which always seems to be King Edwards from some country or another, and often three new potatoes. From time to time he will have waxy, salad varieties such as Pink Fir Apple or Charlotte. My supermarket concentrates on maincrop, i.e. old potatoes, having three

Pappardelle with Mozzarella, Grilled Peppers and Olives (page 110)

varieties and sometimes more, with just one new potato. There are literally hundreds of varieties of potato. Pitiful really that this is a somewhat typical offering.

Most potatoes come in plastic bags nowadays. This is not necessarily a good thing. These ready-washed potatoes do save time, but tend to taste and keep less well than those from the greengrocer with their light covering of earth. That is not to say they should be caked in soil – I'll not pay good money for mud – but the vegetables do keep better in the dark and unwashed. Nature's way, I guess.

One alternative is to remove the potatoes from the plastic bag when you come home and transfer them to a paper carrier. But I am sure I am not the only person who hates unpacking the shopping, so this is unlikely, except in the most organized of homes. My advice is to buy small quantities of loose potatoes from the greengrocer. Old or new. And then keep them in a cool dark place. But not the fridge, which will spoil their flavour.

Roast Jersey Royals

For 2–4, as an accompaniment

450g/1lb new potatoes
25g/1oz butter
1 tablespoon olive oil

You need not use Jerseys, the delicious kidney-shaped new potatoes, for this. Any new potato will do, but I tried this idea with Royals and they were unbelievably buttery and succulent.

Rinse or wipe the potatoes. But you must be gentle. Place them in a small roasting tin with the butter and the oil. Season with salt. Place over a moderately high heat on top of the stove and cook for 5 minutes, tossing them round in the pan. When the skins have coloured a little put them in a preheated hot oven 200°C/400°F (gas mark 6), and roast for 20 minutes. They are ready when tender to the point of a knife, buttery and slightly wrinkled. Serve hot.

Roast New Potatoes with Mushrooms and Breadcrumbs

....

Put the new potatoes, which you will of course have wiped thoroughly, into a roasting tin. Squeeze over the lemon juice and scatter on the thyme leaves. Pour in the oil and place the tin over a moderate heat for 4–5 minutes, shaking the pan from time to time. Add the mushrooms and toss them gently with the potatoes; then season with salt and pepper. Roast in a preheated hot oven, 200°C/400°F (gas mark 6), scattering over the crumbs after 10 minutes. All should be tender and golden after about 20–25 minutes.

For 2

•

450g/1lb new potatoes

juice of ½ lemon

2 teaspoons chopped thyme

1 tablespoon olive oil

100g/4oz small mushrooms, wiped and halved

4 tablespoons dry breadcrumbs

Pan-fried New Potatoes with Pancetta and Sage

....

Six cloves of garlic to a pound of tiny potatoes sounds excessive. It isn't. Slowly pan-fried, the garlic takes on a soft, sweet richness. Use bacon if pancetta eludes you. Veggies can leave it out altogether.

Wipe the new potatoes and cut them in half.

Pour the olive oil into a sauté pan and place over a moderate heat. When it is quite hot add the potato halves, the garlic, sage and the pancetta. Fry until the bacon fat and the potatoes are light gold in colour, then season with salt and pepper, and cook over a low to medium heat for 20 minutes or so. The dish is ready when the potatoes are golden brown and buttery and the garlic is soft within. Each diner should split the skin of the garlic cloves and scrape out the creamy flesh, spreading a dab on each potato as they eat.

For 2

•

450g/1lb new potatoes

3 tablespoons olive oil

6 plump cloves of garlic

3 sage leaves, torn into shreds

75g/3oz pancetta, diced

Tartafin

....

For 2, with the accompaniments below

•

450g/1lb waxy potatoes

2 cloves of garlic

2 tablespoons olive oil

50g/2oz butter

100g/4oz semi-soft or easy-melting cheese, such as Gruyère, Port-Salut, Camembert, Taleggio or, for authenticity, Reblochon

I have been cooking potatoes in olive oil and then topping them with cheese for years. It is one of the simplest and most delicious suppers I can think of. I have used Italian Taleggio, French Cantal and Swiss Gruyère, and even goat's cheese on one occasion, to melt over the tender potatoes. What I did not know until recently is that it is a traditional French recipe, from Normandy. It was Thane Prince who put me straight, in her column in the *Telegraph*, when she published a version of this dish which she had found on a trip to Normandy, where they use Reblochon – a creamy local cheese.

Scrub the potatoes and slice them thinly, no thicker than pound coins. Peel and slice the garlic and cook it slowly, in a large sauté pan, in the olive oil and butter till fragrant and pale gold.

Lay the potatoes in the pan, cover with a lid and cook over a low heat for 20 minutes till you can push a sharp knife through the layers with little resistance. They should be quite soft and buttery.

Slice the cheese and lay on top of the potatoes. Cover and cook again for a couple of minutes till the cheese has just started to melt. Eat immediately.

....

▶ *When served with sliced charcuterie, gherkins, olives and bread, this is one thing I would rather eat than almost anything else*

New Potatoes and Goose Fat

....

Oh bliss! Cut 450g/1lb new potatoes in half. Cook them for 25 minutes in 4 tablespoons goose fat, which is available in tins from smart food shops, over a medium to low heat. Salt, pepper, 4 whole peeled garlic cloves and chopped thyme leaves should be added after 5 minutes or so. Serve when melting and tender.

▶ *New potatoes will cook to buttery tenderness in boiling salted water in 12–20 minutes depending on their size and variety. I cook them whole so that they don't become waterlogged. Whole ones will bake or roast in 20–25 minutes. I usually halve or quarter them if they are very big, so that they cook more quickly and, more importantly, their cut sides roast to a succulent pale gold. Only a fool would peel them*

Mash (Slob's Version)

....

A somewhat casual version of the fashionable potato, olive oil and cream mash.

Rub off the flakiest of the potato skins. Drop the potatoes into boiling salted water. Simmer, partially covered, until tender to the point of a knife, about 15–20 minutes depending on their variety and size. Drain thoroughly and place on a heated serving plate. With a large fork, crush the potatoes roughly, like lumpy mash, drizzle with olive oil and then add dollops of crème fraîche. It will melt over the hot, squashed potatoes. Be generous with the salt.

For 2

•

450g/1lb new potatoes

1 tablespoon extra virgin olive oil

2 tablespoons crème fraîche

Bacon-fat Mash

....

Save the melted fat and juices from the breakfast bacon and stir into mashed potatoes in place of (or even as well as) butter for a glorious treat. Make sure that the fat is hot when you add it. Serve with stir-fried cabbage.

Cheese Mash

....

Boil 450g/1lb new potatoes in boiling salted water till tender. Drain. Put them on a plate. Mash with a fork, skins and all. Smother with butter. And grated Gruyère or Cheddar cheese. And freshly ground pepper. Scatter rocket leaves on top. Or basil. Eat while hot, helping the cheese to melt by pushing it into the hot buttery potato with your fork. For 2.

Steamed New Potatoes with Chervil

....

Chervil comes in neat little packs from the supermarkets. It has a faint aniseed flavour and is really quite charming. Steam the tiniest of new potatoes in a colander over boiling water till tender. Use a steamer if you have one. Split each cooked potato by pinching it with your fingers. A tea towel will help avoid burnt paws. Drizzle over lightly beaten, seasoned yoghurt and sprinkle over chopped chervil.

More 30-Minute Potatoes

....

New potatoes, boiled till tender and then finished in a sauté pan with crème fraîche and chopped tarragon leaves.

Sautéed

New potatoes baked for 30 minutes in a preheated hot oven, 200°C/400°F (gas mark 6), till the skins are crisp, and then split and buttered.

Baked

This blissful Irish dish should be made with potatoes boiled in their skins, which are then peeled and mashed. I love the robustness of this cheat's version, though it will not please potato purists. Choose half-a-dozen floury, thin-skinned potatoes. Cut them into large chunks and cook for 20 minutes in boiling salted water. Drain and mash with a potato masher and then beat in melted butter, about 75g/3oz, or perhaps a bit more, and half-a-dozen spring onions, finely chopped, and salt and pepper. The resulting mash will have tiny flakes of potato skin, but will be really none the worse for it. For 2.

Cheat's Champ

A Colombian dish gleaned from Lindsey Bareham's potato book. Boil 700g/1½lb waxy potatoes in their skins. Drain and cut into chunks (you can peel them if the skins are a bother to you). Meanwhile, soften a medium onion in 25g/1oz butter. Add 2 large tomatoes, chopped (you can skin these too if you wish) and cook for 5 minutes, stirring. Add salt and pepper. Stir in 150ml/¼ pint double cream and 100g/4oz grated Cheddar cheese. Pour the sauce over the potatoes, adding further cheese and some fresh white breadcrumbs, and grilling if you wish. For 2.

Papas Chorreadas

Cut a pound (450g) new potatoes into thick coins. Put them into a sauté pan, season with salt and pepper, then add 50g/2oz good dripping. You can use butter if you want. But not marg. Don't use that for anything. Add 5 tablespoons water, cover with greaseproof paper, a tight lid and cook over a moderate heat for 25 minutes. For 2.

Scottish Stovies

SPINACH

The flavour trapped in the lush dark leaves of the spinach plant makes it the most sought-after of all vegetables. Which other member of the family can boast that it is used to flavour the most basic of pasta doughs and yet appears as the star turn in the *Treize Desserts* of the traditional Provençal Christmas Eve feast? In Italy a purée of its leaves is used to flavour bread the colour of the national flag (tomato providing the orange), while in India it was considered good enough by the King of Nepal to be offered to T'ai Tsung, the T'ang emperor, as the finest vegetable the country had. To the Arabs it is the prince of vegetables.

Spinach responds better than any other vegetable to quick cooking. Nothing is to be gained in terms of flavour or interest by long cooking, while a 'flash in the pan' will preserve both its taste and looks. Indian cooks spice it with butter made fragrant by cumin, ginger, cloves and fennel. Although theirs is a coarser type more akin to chard. The Chinese, who use a soft-leaved, subtly flavoured variety, fire it in a hot wok with garlic and the hottest of chillies, while the Italians may well mix the cooked leaves with shallot, butter and cheese, and fry the result.

A word about frozen spinach. I always get in a bit of a mess with those blocks of washed, chopped and cooked spinach leaves, invariably ending up with a blackened sludge surrounding a block of green ice. I have had better luck with the infuriatingly difficult to locate bags of individually frozen leaves. They thaw in minutes and the flavour is good. But I cannot say I get much for my money.

When buying spinach, listen to the leaves as you rummage through them. If they squeak, buy them. It means that they are perky and freshly picked. They will have a bounce to them. Supermarket shoppers will benefit from the neatly packed, ready-washed, baby leaves – shaped like little hearts on tiny tender stalks.

Fragrant Spinach

....

Indians talk of spinach (variously *saag, sag* or *sak*) with a good deal of enthusiasm. Certainly I have seen it in the relatively lush Goan markets, though it is far from an everyday commodity elsewhere. Spinach needs copious water during its short growing period. Although *palak*, the coarse, heavily veined spinach I have encountered there, is a different leaf to the bags of ready prepared baby leaves on our supermarket shelves, the recipes translate happily enough.

Wash the spinach and remove the toughest stalks. Plunge the leaves into boiling water for 30 seconds, no longer, and then drain. Warm two-thirds of the butter or ghee in a high-sided frying-pan, sauté pan or whatever, and add the ginger and chilli. Cook over a low heat till both are soft (about 5 minutes). Meanwhile, grind the whole spices and add them to the pan. Cook till their fragrance rises – it is a curious warming perfume – and then add the spinach. Cook for a minute over a slightly higher, medium heat.

Melt the remaining butter in a small pan, add the garam masala and let it foam. Divide the spinach and its pan juices between two plates (or offer it in a separate dish) and then tip over the foaming spice butter. Squeeze a little lemon juice over the spinach and eat while hot and fragrant.

For 2, as a side dish (though I have eaten it as a main dish with rice before now)

•

4 large double handfuls of spinach (about a pound)

75g/3oz butter or ghee

2.5cm/1 inch knob of fresh root ginger, peeled and grated

1 small, hot green chilli pepper, seeded and chopped

½ teaspoon each of cumin seeds, mustard seeds and fennel seeds

½ teaspoon garam masala

lemon juice

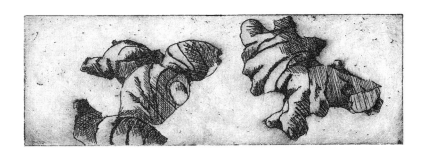

Creamed Spiced Spinach

....

For 2–3, as a side dish

•

75g/3oz butter

½ teaspoon mustard seeds

½ teaspoon cumin seeds

1 teaspoon sugar

1 small, hot red chilli pepper, seeded and chopped

about 450g/1lb spinach, washed, tough stalks removed

50g/2oz shelled almonds or pistachios

75ml/3fl oz double cream

India again, this time where the green leaf meets spices, nuts and cream. An elegant and aromatic accompaniment to almost anything.

Melt the butter in a large pan over moderate heat. Add the mustard and cumin seeds. When the mustard seeds start to pop, stir in the sugar and the chilli and cook for 2 minutes while you roughly chop the spinach. Take care that the spiced butter does not darken; if it looks at all ominous, remove it from the heat at once.

Add the chopped spinach to the pan, cover with a lid and cook for a good 5 minutes, tossing occasionally. Warm the nuts under the grill, or toast them in a dry pan. Stir the cream into the spinach and its juices, season with salt, scatter over the warm nuts and serve.

....

▶ *Cream and butter will soften spinach's tart astringency in minutes. Cook your greens as you wish, either with or without water. Warm a little cream or butter in a shallow pan and add the cooked, drained spinach. Heat gently, then season (salt, pepper, parsley, lemon juice, freshly grated nutmeg, whatever) and serve*

Spinach with Bacon and Mustard Dressing

....

For 2, as a side dish

•

4 handfuls of young spinach leaves

100/4oz smoked streaky bacon, cut into 5mm/¼ inch dice

6 tablespoons extra virgin olive oil

1 tablespoon white wine vinegar

1 tablespoon Dijon mustard

Mustard has an uplifting effect on spinach. Stir a blob of mild French mustard into the dressing for a spinach salad and you will see what I mean. Lemon juice has much the same effect, but is less subtle. Bacon's salty tang, too, is a happy partner to spinach leaves' overwhelming wholesomeness. As a side dish for, say, grilled chicken or duck, or as a light lunch accompanied by rice.

Wash the spinach leaves, unless they come from one of

those supermarket bags that says 'ready washed', and pick out any tough stalks. But leave a few – they are only unpleasant in large amounts.

Fry the bacon till crisp, in its own fat if there is enough (there probably won't be), or in a tablespoon of the oil. Place the salad leaves in a bowl, lift the bacon from the pan with a draining spoon and add to the spinach.

Pour the rest of the oil into the pan (don't be tempted to discard the tasty bacon fat), turn the heat to low and stir in the wine vinegar and mustard, and some black pepper. Bring slowly to the boil but remove from the heat just as it gets there. Whisk constantly with a hand whisk or a fork. Tip the hot dressing over the spinach and bacon, and serve.

Some Quick Ways with Spinach

....

Spinach Gravy

Almost too good to be true. Get the jug of gravy from last Sunday's roast out of the fridge. Warm it gently in a shallow pan. Mix a little arrowroot or cornflour with cold water to make a smooth paste and stir it into the bubbling gravy. Stir until it starts to thicken and then add enough very lightly cooked spinach to soak up most of the gravy. Serve with sausages, liver or rice or noodles.

Stir-fried Spinach

Heat a large wok till it starts to smoke, add 2 tablespoons groundnut oil and then add 3 juicy cloves of garlic, thinly sliced. They will colour quickly, and you should let them go brown like the Chinese do. But not dark enough to turn them bitter. Quickly add a good 450g/1lb spinach, washed and with its toughest stalks removed. Fry the spinach and garlic, constantly moving them round the hot pan (do not let it cool down), for 2–3 minutes. Pour in a tablespoon of light soy sauce and grind over some black pepper. A side dish, for 2–3.

Spanish Spinach

Plump up a handful of raisins or little golden sultanas in a cupful of boiling water. Wash 450g/1lb spinach (quantities are not really that important), and remove the coarsest stems. They tend to get stuck in your teeth if you don't. While the leaves are still wet dump them in a large saucepan and cover with a lid. Cook over a high heat for a couple of minutes, shake the pan and then cook for a further minute. Add a little more water if they look dry. Take off the lid and lift the bottom leaves up to the top. Cover and cook again. When the spinach has wilted, drain and roughly chop it. There is no need to be too particular about this. Heat 2 tablespoons oil, any oil, in a large pan. The one you cooked the spinach in will do. Cook a sliced clove of garlic till golden, add a fistful of pine nuts, the plumped-up raisins and the spinach. Season and cook for 2 minutes. Enough for 2.

SWEET POTATOES

The quintessential autumn supper in our house is sausages, proper ones from the butcher, and a baked sweet potato. If you have never had one let me tempt you by saying that inside their thin earthy skin is sweet, glowing orange flesh that has a charming nuttiness to it. Buttered generously, their flesh mashed with a fork as you eat, they are among the most seductive of vegetables.

Timing is tricky. I have known medium-sized potatoes take anything from thirty minutes to an hour. Real whoppers take for ever. But they are still of interest to the quick cook who can throw them in the oven and then get on with other things.

Sweet potatoes are stocked by most supermarkets and greengrocers. Take care, though – they can sometimes work out rather expensive. You will probably get scolded for doing this, but it is worth scraping a little of the skin away with your nail – if the flesh underneath is orange, then buy them, if it is white, don't. White sweet potatoes tend to be more fibrous and rather sugary.

Baked Sweet Potatoes with Chilli Butter
....

Photograph between pages 32 and 33

Unlike our own King Edwards, sweet potatoes tend to leak a sugary juice when they are baked. At its best, it just makes the base of the potato sweet and honeyed. Left too long, it will drip over, forming huge charred balloons on the bottom of the oven. So cook them on a baking sheet, speared with a skewer to speed them up, for about an hour.

Meanwhile, cut a medium-sized mild red chilli pepper in half and scrape out the seeds and the white membrane. You will have removed the fiercest of its heat, but there will be enough there to interest. Chop the flesh finely. Soften, rather than melt, 50g/2oz butter and fold in the chopped chilli. You can add a little chopped coriander leaf if you like. It will make the potato feel more at home. Split the cooked potato in half, slather on the chilli butter and eat while hot.

SWEETCORN

I like my sweetcorn served on the cob, hot, dripping with butter, its sweet juices dribbling down my chin and fingers. Roasted, boiled, grilled or barbecued, it lives up to the promise of its name, and is satisfying enough for a light lunch or supper with a bowl of soup alongside. Cook it as soon as you get home, serve it straight from the pan and don't be British with the butter.

Buy your sweetcorn from a shop with a high turnover. Check that the cobs are firm with absolutely no dis-coloured kernels. They should be a creamy yellow. If you have a choice, go for cobs that are still protected by their papery green husks. Ignore anything that looks less than spanking fresh. Gardeners tell me that this is a vegetable that, once picked, loses its joy by the minute. Sweetcorn waits for no one.

Roast Sweetcorn

Photograph between pages 32 and 33

....

Peel back the husks, if they have not been removed at source, and pull away the long silky threads. Lay each cob on a rectangle of foil, butter it generously and grind over some black pepper. Pull the foil up around the cob and scrunch the edges to seal. Bake in a preheated hot oven, 220°C/425°F (gas mark 7), till tender, about 30 minutes.

TOMATOES

Come summer, the British grow some wonderful tomatoes. Full of juice and not too sweet. But most of them are gardener's tomatoes, and never reach the shops. I have eaten even better fruits in Italy and France, knobbly and scarred, touched by the blazing sun and grown outdoors amidst other vegetables, though I am not convinced they travel well. And I still think the best way to eat a good tomato is to munch it like an apple, with the juice running down your chin.

Summer would not be the same without decent tomatoes to bite into. My favourite are those that are not red all over, but tinged slightly orange round the stalk, even speckled with green. These are not too sweet, having that snap of acidity that I find so important in a tomato. Around the Mediterranean it is easy to find such fruits, with a balance of sweetness and acidity, and with a deep, rich tomato flavour. Market stalls in summer and autumn are piled high with knobbly, misshapen, ridged tomatoes that smell almost as delicious as they taste and leak copious amounts of juice when they are cut. These are worth buying.

Out of season, I will go so far as to suggest you don't buy tomatoes. You don't need them. There are plenty of other good things about. Leave the supermarkets with their wishy-washy, bland, fluffy, tasteless toms. Wait till summer.

Some of the major supermarkets have invested a great deal of time and effort in finding decent out-of-season tomatoes. I think they have failed. No matter what country they import them from, which variety they plant or what technology they use to grow them, they invariably fail to come up with anything of interest. The best you can say is that they are red enough to kid us into thinking they taste of something. My advice is to forget them.

A good tomato can be a thing of joy. Sniff it: if it does not smell then it will have little taste. The best test is to tweak the stalk: if the fruit smells good then buy it. But most shops guard against such shoppers, and pack their tomatoes away in plastic cases. Who can blame them?

Tiny tomatoes, labelled Gardener's Delight, are aptly named, and to be recommended. Especially if they are very slightly under-ripe. They are good to snack on, though tiresome in a salad. Interesting large salad tomatoes are more difficult to track down. But a tasty one, rich with juice, jelly and crunchy seeds is worth the hunt.

• Check that the tomatoes are not over-ripe when you buy them. You will have tomato soup in your bag by the time you get home
• Ripen tomatoes in the airing cupboard or on the window-sill, though they won't be the same as those ripened on the vine
• If you are cooking with less than brilliant tomatoes a little sugar and lemon juice may perk them up
• As will a dose of tomato ketchup
• Generally speaking, the more ridged and gnarled the fruit, the more interesting it will be. Rather like us

Tomato and Olive Tarts

....

These crisp, savoury tarts make a delightful outdoor summer lunch, especially with a bowl of green salad into which you have tossed some lightly cooked French beans. A bottle of rosé would not go down badly either. Use frozen puff pastry squares, and bottled pesto instead of the olive paste if you prefer.

Set the oven to 240°C/450°F (gas mark 8). Put a large baking sheet in the oven to get hot. Cut the pastry into 2 equal pieces. On a lightly floured surface roll out each one large enough to cut a 18cm/7 inch round from it. Use a plate as a cutting guide.

Prick each circle of pastry 4–5 times with a fork so that the pastry does not puff up in the middle and tip the tomatoes off. Put a tablespoon of olive paste, or pesto, in the middle of each piece of pastry and spread it within 2.5cm/1 inch of the edge.

Slice the tomatoes thinly, but not paper thin, and place on top of the olive paste, overlapping them slightly. Brush the tomatoes and the bare pastry edge with half of the oil. Grind over a little black pepper and sprinkle with salt.

Lift the hot baking sheet from the oven and carefully slide the tarts on to it, using a large flat fish slice, or better still, the flat bottom from a steel tart ring. Bake the tarts in the hot oven for 15 minutes till dark golden brown. Snip or tear the basil leaves into little pieces and drop into the remaining oil. Remove the tarts from the oven, brush with the basil oil and eat while still crisp and warm.

Makes 2 tarts

•

150g/5oz defrosted puff pastry

2 tablespoons green or black olive paste or pesto

4 medium, ripe tomatoes

2 tablespoons extra virgin olive oil

8 or so basil leaves

Roast Tomatoes with Basil and Olive Dressing

....

For 4, as a light lunch or starter
•
8 large (but not beefsteak) ripe tomatoes
olive oil

For the dressing:
•
3 tablespoons extra virgin olive oil
1 tablespoon red wine vinegar
10 basil leaves, shredded
12 stoned black olives, roughly chopped

The point of this hot salad is the accompanying juices. Provide good bread, white not brown, crusty not soft, to mop them up.

Get the oven really hot, 230°C/450°F (gas mark 8). Slice the tomatoes in half across their circumference. Place them snugly in a roasting tin and drizzle with olive oil. A couple of tablespoons will do. Grind over a generous amount of black pepper.

Roast the tomatoes for 25 minutes until meltingly tender. If the edges have charred slightly, it is all to the good. Beat together the dressing ingredients. Take the tomatoes out of the oven and serve on warm plates, spooning over any liquid from the roasting tin. Pour over the dressing while the tomatoes are still hot and eat with crusty bread.

A Tomato Plate

....

If you come across an assortment of tomatoes, round, oval and squat, yellow, scarlet and orange, tiny and pear- or cherry-shaped, or perhaps as big your hand, then buy a few of each.

Slice them as you will, then jumble them artfully on a large platter. Something rustic and jolly or plain white porcelain. Mix 4 tablespoons olive oil with half as much balsamic vinegar and a little salt and coarse pepper. Sprinkle the harlequin mixture with the dressing and let it sit for a while before you eat it.

Spiced Tomatoes

....

A quick Indian-inspired supper dish. Tart tomatoes and warm spices to mop up with warm naan.

Warm the oil or butter in a shallow pan. Add the coriander, fennel seeds, cumin and garlic, and fry till fragrant and sizzling, taking care not to burn them. Add the chilli powder and fry for a few seconds. Quarter the tomatoes and add them to the spiced butter with a handful of chopped coriander leaves. Cook for 5 minutes till the tomatoes soften and give some of their juice to the pan. Add salt and pepper to taste and eat with warm naan.

For 2
•
3 tablespoons groundnut oil or butter
1 teaspoon ground coriander
1 teaspoon fennel seeds
2 teaspoons ground cumin
3 cloves of garlic, sliced
1 teaspoon mild chilli powder
8 medium tomatoes
chopped coriander leaves

Tomatoes for Lunch

....

You have found some really fine-flavoured tomatoes. They smell and taste wonderful. Put them into a salad bowl on the table outside in the sun. You can lay a piece of muslin over them to keep off the flies if you want. Leave them in the sun for a good half an hour; the warmth will concentrate their flavour.

Eat them in the sun with a soft, bloomy goat's cheese, a handful of black olives and lumps of crisp, white floury bread such as ciabatta to soak up the sweet, tart juice.

Tomatoes with Mozzarella and Breadcrumbs

....

For 4, as a main dish

•

12 plum tomatoes

175g/6oz fresh breadcrumbs

8 anchovy fillets, rinsed, dried and chopped

2 plump cloves of garlic, crushed

a handful of parsley, chopped

1 ball of Mozzarella cheese, finely diced

6 tablespoons olive oil

Plum tomatoes often have more to offer in terms of flavour than other varieties. They also tend to hold their shape better than most, as anyone who has made a sauce with tinned tomatoes will testify. This recipe pushes the 30-minute cook to the limit. It takes about 40.

Preheat the oven to 220°C/425°F (gas mark 7). Slice the tomatoes in half lengthways and scoop the seeds into a bowl. Place the tomatoes skin side down in a roasting tin so that they nudge up to each other. Mix the tomato scoopings with the breadcrumbs, anchovy fillets, garlic, parsley, Mozzarella and 2 tablespoons of the olive oil.

Season with black pepper and salt, and then pile the filling into the tomato halves. Pour over the remaining olive oil. Bake in the preheated oven for 25 minutes, until the filling is golden.

Panzanella

....

A quick and substantial Italian salad. The ratio of ingredients is not important. This is not really a dish that needs precise measurements. I include them only to guide the inexperienced cook. Use more tomatoes and less cucumber if you prefer, or use spring onions, if you cannot find a large one sweet enough. I have fond memories of making this salad for lunch at a villa in the hills outside Florence. A gloriously bright day, we sat on the terrace, enjoying salad and sunshine, drinking a little too much for our own good.

Tear the bread into bite-sized pieces. Try to make each piece a contrast of crisp crust and soft crumb. Toast the bread pieces in a hot oven till lightly golden. You can grill them if you prefer.

Cut the tomatoes into roughly bite-sized pieces, taking care not to let their juice escape. Put them into a large bowl. Add the cubed cucumber. Slice the onion very finely. It must be a sweet one. Add to the salad bowl. Mix the parsley, vinegar, oil and basil leaves with a generous seasoning of sea salt and pepper, and then pour into the salad bowl.

Add the toasted bread and gently toss together the ingredients. Leave for not more than 10 minutes before serving.

For 2, as a main salad

•

4 slices of country bread

6 ripe, sweet tomatoes

½ cucumber, cubed

1 sweet red onion, peeled

a small bunch of flat-leaf parsley, roughly chopped

2 tablespoons red wine vinegar

5 tablespoons extra virgin olive oil

8 basil leaves, shredded

....

▶ *Use this recipe as a base for your own versions. Add any of the following, as the mood takes you: chopped rinsed anchovies, rinsed capers, rocket leaves, stoned black olives, blanched green beans, shredded red and yellow peppers, a little chopped chilli and chopped coriander leaves*

Photograph opposite page 33

Mixed Vegetable Tempura

....

For 2

•

200ml/7fl oz water

I egg

100g/4oz plain flour

50g/2oz cornflour

½ teaspoon salt

450g/1lb assorted vegetables, broccoli and cauliflower florets, strips of red pepper, baby Thai sweetcorn, thinly sliced onions, spring onions, etc.

groundnut oil for deep-frying

lemon wedges, to serve

Tempura batters are gossamer-thin, light and crisp, at times seeming almost non-existent. The batter recipe below is that of Rick Stein, who owns the Seafood Restaurant in Padstow. It is one of the few recipes I have come across that actually manages not to disintegrate into the cooking oil. It is typical of Mr Stein's well-judged cooking.

Chill the water and the egg. Whisk together all the batter ingredients just before dipping the food. The batter should only just be amalgamated, so that a few small lumps of flour are still apparent.

Get a pan of oil hot. If you are organized enough to have a kitchen thermometer the oil should register about 190°C/375°F. Dip the vegetables into the batter, then into the hot oil. Cook them until golden, turning from time to time with a fork. They will probably bob back up again but keep trying. Cook them for a couple of minutes on each side. Drain on kitchen paper and eat straight away, with lemon.

Salsa

....

For 2

•

I small red onion, finely diced

450g/1lb ripe tomatoes, cored, seeded and finely chopped

2 Jalapeño or serrano chilli peppers, seeded and finely diced

2 tablespoons chopped coriander leaves

juice of ½ lime

What a great name for a quick, sassy sauce with lively bright flavours and gay colours. The salsa is the 30-minute cook's answer to the sauce. Serve it with anything: grilled fish and chicken, spicy kebabs, sausages or just with pitta as a snack.

The rules are few. Ultra-fresh, ripe ingredients, fine chopping but not so fine it turns to slush, and eat soon after making. In my book, an all-purpose salsa such as this should be both refreshing with tomatoes and mouth-popping with lime and chillies. The quantities are not gospel.

Toss the ingredients gently together and eat while still fun.

Add any of the following to the basic tomato salsa:

- Red peppers, seeded and diced
- Cucumber, diced
- Basil leaves, chopped
- Avocado (Hass for preference), peeled and diced, taking great care not to crush it. A very slightly under-ripe avocado is best
- Mango, peeled, stoned and diced. Add the juice too
- Pineapple, peeled and diced
- Mint leaves, chopped
- Spring onions, instead of the red onions, diced
- A tablespoon of extra virgin olive oil
- Salt
- Fennel, finely chopped, including some of the feathery fronds
- Melon, any variety, peeled, seeded and chopped
- Papaya, peeled, seeded and diced

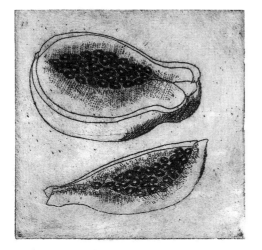

Mixed Vegetable Korma

....

For 2, with rice or naan

•

50g/2oz butter

2 medium onions (red ones if possible), sliced

3 cloves of garlic, crushed

4cm/1½ inch knob of fresh root ginger, grated

1 teaspoon ground cumin

1 tablespoon ground coriander

seeds from 6 green cardamom pods, lightly crushed

½ teaspoon ground turmeric

½ teaspoon chilli powder

2 bay leaves

freshly ground black pepper

1 medium potato, cut into 2.5cm/ 1 inch cubes

1 small aubergine, cut into 2.5cm/ 1 inch cubes

100g/4oz mushrooms, thickly sliced

75g/3oz green beans, cut in half

50g/2oz cashews or almonds

150ml/5fl oz yoghurt

150ml/5fl oz double cream

½ teaspoon garam masala

1 tablespoon chopped coriander leaves

Fragrant, mild and creamy. Also the longest list of ingredients in the book, but you will probably find most of them in the house anyway. The vegetables are suggestions rather than gospel. Use what you have to make up about the same weight.

Melt the butter in a heavy-bottomed pan, add the onions and cook for about 6 minutes until soft and golden. Add the garlic and ginger and cook for 2 minutes, then add the spices, bay leaves and a good grinding of black pepper. Cook for a few seconds, then add the vegetables: potato first, then the aubergine and mushrooms and lastly the beans. Stir in the nuts and 200ml/ 7fl oz water. Stir well and continue cooking for 15 minutes.

Mix the yoghurt and cream and stir into the korma, then simmer for 4 minutes. Do not boil, unless you want a ghastly curdled mess. Scatter over the garam masala and the coriander. Eat with pilaf or naan.

CHAPTER 2

Salads

I often make a meal of a salad. I have a large white French porcelain bowl, the rim of which curves out gracefully. It has seen a salad almost every day for years. I shall drop it one day. It will be the end of an era.

You need add very little to a simple salad to turn it into a meal. Crumbly white Feta cheese and large crisp croûtons turn a tomato and spinach salad into a substantial enough supper dish if there is pudding to follow. A smattering of crisp bacon and half an avocado will declare a spinach salad a light lunch, as will Cheddar cheese tossed in a bowl of red leaves and mushrooms. Even the lightest of ingredients, such as rocket leaves and melon, take on a robust and satisfying nature when a slice or two of Parma ham is introduced.

Mushrooms, quickly sautéed in butter and garlic, are especially good dumped on a plate of salad leaves. As are pan-fried tomatoes when scattered with capers and served astride a bowl of cooked French beans, olives and Little Gem lettuce. Wine, bread and something for pudding are all that is required.

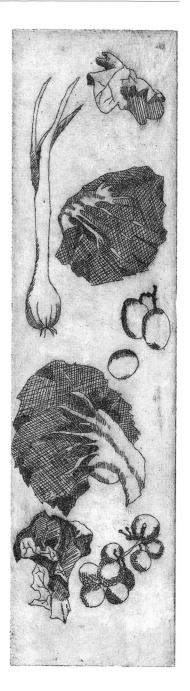

Green Salad

············

Occasionally I like a true 'green salad', consisting of nothing more than crisp lettuce and sliced cucumber in a mild vinaigrette. It suits cold poached salmon and mayonnaise like nothing else. But it is not what I want to eat every day.

My daily salad – I sometimes think I would die without it – consists of whatever is green and whatever is best at the time. This means tiny tender spinach leaves, lemony sorrel, soft-leafed lettuce and spicy rocket in summer and crunchy white cabbage, celery, Iceberg lettuce and chicory in the winter. But it depends on what is around. Sometimes I buy a ready-washed and bagged salad mesclun from the supermarket, though it wilts quickly and should be eaten on the same day.

In winter I have returned from my local street market with nothing more than hard white cabbage and imported beans, yet in October I have staggered home laden with oak-leafed lettuces, flaming radicchios and delightfully bitter chicory. Watercress is a constant. Mustard and cress (or whatever they call it now) makes a salad summery. Sometimes you can be spoilt for choice. Anything is fair game, but texture is important. A salad of cabbage, celery and chicory is hard going on the teeth, providing too much to chew on, yet a soft-leafed lettuce, *mâche* and sorrel salad leaves you wanting.

It can be fun to make a salad with just one or two ingredients. Sometimes these can be the most successful. Particularly if the bowl contains baby leaves tossed through with herbs. I try to include a herb in my daily green salad, and have tried most over the years. Tarragon and basil are favourites, though even the simplest salad seems to improve immeasurably with a freckling of bright green parsley.

A Few Good Things to Add to a Green Salad

....

• Parmesan cheese, grated or shaved (use the vegetable peeler); add after the dressing
• Croûtons – toss small cubes of bread in olive oil and scatter on a baking sheet. Bake in a hot oven for 8–10 minutes
• Nuts – almonds, walnuts, hazelnuts and cashews – provide a good crunch. Toast them first, rub off the flakiest of the skins and toss with the dressing
• Wedges of cheese – almost any cheese will turn a green salad into a substantial meal. Cut into bite-sized cubes and toss with the leaves. Semi-hard British cheeses are particularly suitable. A farmhouse Caerphilly with baby lettuce, watercress and sprouted seeds is a favourite
• Tinned flageolet beans. Rinsed in a sieve with plenty of cold running water and lots of chopped parsley
• Anchovies. Rinse and dry; then roughly chop. Add to the dressing with chopped parsley and basil

The heart of a good salad is the dressing. Don't be tempted by the supermarket ready-made dressings. Many of them contain vinegar that is too harsh, herbs that are dried and oil that is not the best. Even the smartest supermarkets, known for their food, offer nothing that isn't hideously sweet or unspeakably bland. So make your own. It won't take a minute.

This one is a mild dressing that will not fight with any additions to the leaves such as cheese or anchovies.

Mix the oil and vinegar with a fork or small whisk and season to taste with salt and freshly ground black pepper.

A Classic Dressing for Green Salad

25ml/1fl oz red wine vinegar
150ml/5fl oz extra virgin olive oil

Lettuce, Herbs and Spicy Leaves

....

Give two large double handfuls of lettuce leaves per person. Baby leaves are the most interesting, having both tenderness and a crunch to them. Add chopped parsley, and tarragon, chervil or basil. Toss with a few spicy leaves, rocket, nasturtium or watercress, and a few spoons of dressing. Use as an accompaniment to almost anything.

Bitter Leaves and Muscat Grapes

....

Wash two double handfuls of watercress, spinach, chicory, radicchio and rocket leaves per person. Use one, two or all of them. Add a handful of sweet muscat grapes, and half the amount of walnuts, toasted under a grill till fragrant. Dress with the basic dressing to which you have added a couple of tablespoons of orange juice. The bitter leaves, orange dressing and sweet grapes will be fun with a mild main dish, such as a risotto or pilaf.

Frisée, Lettuce and Cannellini Beans

....

Rinse a 400g/14oz tin of cannellini beans in a sieve under running water. Tear the frisée and lettuce (a couple of handfuls of each) into bite-sized pieces. Remember that frisée is inclined to be difficult to eat politely if the pieces are too large. Make the basic dressing on page 91, adding a tablespoon of chopped parsley and a little mustard. Toss all together gently.

Watercress, Chicory and Blue Cheese

....

For each bunch of watercress you will need a good firm, plump head of white chicory and about 100g/4oz Stilton, Roquefort, Gorgonzola or Cashel Blue cheese. Wash the leaves well and remove and discard the toughest stalks. Toss the leaves and cheese, cut or broken into chunks, with the basic vinaigrette, to which you have added a few toasted walnuts and some fat, sweet grapes.

Chinese Leaves, Avocado and Orange Salad

....

A refreshing salad. Good for mopping up the juices on the plate from a pork chop.

Slice the head of Chinese leaves across the diameter. Separate the pieces and wash in a sieve under running water for a few seconds. Drain. Prepare the fruit. Cut off the peel and bitter white pith. Slice the fruit in half from stem to navel, then slice thinly, though not by any means paper thin. Catch the juice that runs from the fruit in a salad bowl. You should manage a couple of tablespoons of it.

Peel and slice the avocado thickly. It falls into mush if you slice it too thin. Add the vinegar, shallot, oil and chopped herbs to the dressing. Whisk till it thickens slightly and then toss gently with the Chinese leaves, fruit and avocado. Set aside for no longer than 10 minutes before eating. This is a salad where crunchy textures and refreshing tastes are paramount.

Serves 4, as a side salad

•

½ large head of Chinese leaves

I large, yellow-fleshed grapefruit

2 small oranges, or I large one

I ripe **Hass** avocado

For the dressing:

2 tablespoons juice from the grapefruit

I tablespoon white wine vinegar

I shallot, finely chopped

3 tablespoons fruity olive oil

I tablespoon coriander leaves, finely chopped

I tablespoon chopped flat-leaf parsley

Goat's Cheese and Fruit

....

For 2

•

2 handfuls of fresh fruits, see below

½ teaspoon balsamic or sherry vinegar

1 teaspoon lemon juice

1 tablespoon olive oil

1 teaspoon walnut oil

2 slices of baguette or sourdough bread, 1cm/½ inch thick

a little olive oil

2 ripe *crottins* (goat's cheeses), approximately 5cm/2 inches high and across

An ambrosial mixture of soft goat's cheese, warm from the grill, crisp French bread and ripe fruits. A lovely plate of tart and sweet fruits and sexy, melting cheese.

Prepare the fruit, as below. Mix together the balsamic or sherry vinegar, lemon juice, oils and a little salt and pepper. Toss the fruit in the dressing and spoon on to two plates.

Sprinkle the slices of baguette or sourdough with olive oil and then toast under a hot grill on one side till golden. Place a goat's cheese on top of each uncooked side and grill till the cheese is soft and melting inside, but try to catch it before it bursts. Place the grilled goat's cheese in the middle of the fruit and serve immediately.

The Fruits. Strawberries, blackberries and raspberries are good used in this way, as are plums, peaches and nectarines. But only if they are truly ripe. Melon, particularly the glowing salmon-coloured Charentais variety, is successful; needless to say, bananas and pineapple are not. Best of all, though, are pears, really ripe ones, figs and sweet muscat grapes.

Cut the larger fruits, melon, pears, peaches and plums, into large bite-sized pieces. Any smaller and you will have a mess. The berries can go in as they are unless they include large strawberries that need halving or quartering.

....

▶ *The most sublime version ever was when I had loganberries, muscat grapes, blackberries and figs, tossed in the above dressing but made with hazelnut rather than walnut oil*

Red Leaves, Mushrooms and Cheddar Salad

....

Of course, you can use other cheeses: Camembert or Bonchester cut into soft dice would be good, or perhaps a blue cheese.

Slice the mushrooms and toss in a bowl with the garlic, parsley, vinegar, oil and lemon juice. Set aside for 15–20 minutes.

Tear the salad leaves into bite-sized pieces. Make sure that they are not too small, otherwise they will go wet in the dressing. Cut the Cheddar into thin strips. You can do this with a vegetable peeler in seconds. Toss gently with the leaves, mushrooms, a little salt and pepper and the dressing, and eat immediately with crusty bread.

For 2, as a light lunch or supper

•

125g/5oz chestnut or large button mushrooms

I plump clove of garlic, crushed to a paste

2 tablespoons chopped flat-leaf parsley

I tablespoon balsamic vinegar

75ml/3fl oz olive oil

juice of ½ lemon

6 double handfuls of red salad leaves; radicchio, red-tipped chicory, oak leaf, etc.

100g/4oz farmhouse Cheddar cheese

Warm Salad of Potatoes, Prosciutto and Parsley

....

For 2

•

12 medium, waxy potatoes, wiped clean

3 slices of prosciutto

2 teaspoons red wine vinegar

2 tablespoons extra virgin olive oil

3 tablespoons roughly chopped flat-leaf parsley

1 shallot, or 2 spring onions, finely chopped

Bacon, something smoked and cooked just long enough to go slightly crisp, is a fine substitute for the prosciutto if Parma ham eludes you.

Boil the potatoes in salted water till tender to the point of a knife. Roll the slices of prosciutto tightly and slice them into thin shreds, about 1cm/½ inch wide. Drop them into a salad bowl. Add the vinegar, oil, parsley and shallot or spring onions, and then season with salt and freshly ground pepper.

When the potatoes are tender, drain them and cut in quarters. Stir them immediately with the dressing so that the warm potato soaks up the dressing. Set aside for 10 minutes or so before eating.

....

▶ *If you are using bacon, grill or fry it till crisp and then chop it into small pieces. You will need 4 rashers of smoked streaky*

Opposite Mushroom Tart (page 55)
Over, left Toasted Croissants with Mushrooms, Onions and Melted Cheese (page 242); *right* Nectarines with Ricotta and Prosciutto (page 243)

Prosciutto with Melon and Rocket

....

The tang of Parma ham, or Spanish Serrano if you prefer, is a masterful match for ripe golden melon and fiery rocket leaves. A light, fruity olive oil, perhaps from the south of France would be better here than a pungent heavy one.

Slice the melon in half and scoop out the seeds over a bowl to catch the sweet, luscious juices. Scoop out the flesh of the melon in large bite-sized pieces. You can use a melon-baller if you have such a thing. If not, a teaspoon will do. Try not to make the pieces too small, which would make the salad wet. (There is a lot of juice in a melon.) Drop the bits into the bowl with the juices.

Tear the rocket leaves slightly if they are a bit big, though most are small enough to leave whole. The big ones can be terribly bitter. Drop them in with the melon. Shred the prosciutto thinly. But not so thinly that you can't see what it is. Add to the melon and rocket.

Mix the vinegar and the olive oil with some freshly ground black pepper. You won't need the salt. Toss the dressing and salad very carefully, so as not to smash the ripe melon, and eat immediately.

For 2, as a light lunch or supper
•
a ripe small melon, about 450g/1lb in weight
75g/3oz rocket leaves
75g/3oz prosciutto, thinly sliced
1 tablespoon white wine vinegar
3 tablespoons extra virgin olive oil

....

▶ **A**ny melon will work here as long as it is sweet. Honey sweet. And juicy. Charentais would be an extravagant but very beautiful alternative to the soft golden-green honey-dew. Just use whatever is around, as long as it is ripe

Grilled Lamb with Onions and Spices (page 173)

Some Simple Salads

....

Peach and Black Pepper

Slice perfect, lusciously ripe peaches and season them lightly with coarsely ground black pepper and lime juice. The peaches must be truly ripe and dripping with juice, which combines with the lime and pepper to make a simple dressing. Serve with grilled chicken.

Lemon, Onion and Parsley

A startling salad from Morocco. Peel a ripe lemon, making sure to remove all its bitter pith. Dice the flesh and then toss it with finely chopped sweet onion, a little salt, coarsely chopped flat-leaf parsley and 4 diced ripe tomatoes. Anoint with olive oil. Serve with fish.

Carrot, Grapefruit and Orange-flower Water

Still in Morocco. Grate a pound of carrots. Or 450g if you are metrically inclined. Use the coarse side of the grater so that the shreds still have some crunch. Toss them with the juice of a pink grapefruit, a little salt, a pinch of icing sugar and 2 tablespoons orange-flower water. Chill and serve.

Rocket, Parmesan and Raw Mushroom

Slice raw mushrooms – they can be quite small and young – fairly thinly. Toss them with a dressing of olive oil, balsamic vinegar and chopped parsley. Leave them for 15 minutes and then toss gently with small rocket leaves. Add shavings of Parmesan and serve. This is one of those salads that could be eaten as a main dish. Unlike the one above.

Tomato and Basil

Sweet, slightly tart tomatoes. Olive oil. Shredded basil. That's it. Oh, and some crusty bread for the juices.

Chicken, Orange and Watercress

Cold roast, or better still poached, chicken tossed with slices of peeled sweet orange and sprigs of peppery watercress. Dress with an orange juice and olive oil dressing, and chopped coriander leaves.

Shred the runner beans and blanch them for a minute in boiling water. A minute, that is all. Drain them and while they are still hot douse them with a light fruity olive oil and a squeeze of lemon.

Runner Bean, Lemon and Olive Oil

The saltiness of the bacon and Feta cheese is toned down by the mealy broad beans. Cook the shelled beans in salted water till tender, about 10 minutes, and then drain and toss them with hot, crisp grilled bacon and roughly chopped and crumbled Feta cheese. Good with a beer.

Broad Bean, Bacon and Feta

Peel and cube a mango. Beat 175ml/6fl oz yoghurt with a fork until it becomes thin and creamy. Add a small, hot, chopped and seeded chilli, 2 tablespoons finely chopped mint leaves, a scant teaspoon of curry powder and a little salt. Beat till the curry powder has virtually dissolved in the yoghurt. Toss with the mango. A lovely accompaniment to grilled poultry or fish.

Spiced Mango

I love sausage and potato suppers. Bangers and mash, sausage and chips, bubble and squeak, and the like. This warm salad – I use the term somewhat loosely – has almost as much comfort value. The chicken stock cube is important, a good home-made chicken stock just wouldn't be the same here.

Cut the potatoes into thickish slices. Mix the stock cube with enough water to come halfway up the potatoes in a saucepan. Put the butter in with the potatoes and the stock. Cook for 10–15 minutes till the potatoes are very tender. They will be even better if they have broken up a bit. (What you might normally call a disaster.) Fry the sausages till golden brown and black in patches. Put the potatoes on a large plate with their cooking juices, scatter with chopped parsley and serve the sausages on top.

Hot Potato and Sausage Salad

450g/1lb potatoes, peeled or not
a chicken stock cube
50g/2oz butter
4 fat butcher's sausages
chopped parsley

Thai Chicken Salad

....

A substantial supper for 2

•

1 large (or 2 smaller), boned chicken or duck breast

olive oil

4 tablespoons lime juice

2 tablespoons fish sauce (*nam pla***)**

1 tablespoon light soy sauce

4 tablespoons groundnut oil

a little sesame oil

1 teaspoon sugar

1 garlic clove, finely sliced

1 tablespoon chopped mint

½ cucumber, peeled

1 large carrot, scrubbed

small handful coriander leaves

1 hot red chilli pepper, seeded and cut into fine shreds

1 red onion, finely chopped

2 handfuls of bean sprouts, washed

Refreshing, hot, spicy and crisp; and versatile. Swap the sliced, crisp, skinned chicken for duck, pork belly, squid or prawns if you wish.

Grill the chicken or duck breast, brushed with a little oil and seasoned with salt and pepper, till tender. The skin should be crisp. You can sauté it if you prefer. Slice into 1cm/ ½ inch strips.

While the chicken is grilling, mix the lime juice, *nam pla*, soy and groundnut oil. Stir in a shake or two of sesame oil. Go easy as it is inclined to overpower everything else. Stir in the sugar, garlic and the chopped mint. Season with freshly ground black pepper. No salt.

Slice the cucumber and carrot finely. A vegetable peeler will be ten times quicker than a knife. Just run the peeler up or down the vegetables, shaving off long thin slices. It's quite fun actually. In a large bowl, toss the dressing with the cucumber and carrot shavings, the coriander and chilli, the onion and the bean sprouts. Toss in the chicken or duck. Serve immediately.

CHAPTER 3

Pasta and Noodles

The British have developed a penchant for pasta. And not before time. Long silky ribbons, sauce-hogging shells and plump, filling dumplings have been known throughout Asia and the Mediterranean for thousands of years. Quite why it took us so long to take them up is a mystery.

Pasta dough is, after all, little more than flour and water with the addition of oil or eggs and sometimes both. Yet it makes one of the quickest, simplest and most satisfying suppers imaginable. The soft, comforting dough responds as well to the creamy, cheesy sauces of Italy as it does to the pungent garlic and soy flavours of China or the pure, clear broths of Japan. Pasta's bland doughiness is just as successful a base for searing hot chillies as it is for melting, creamy Mascarpone. To describe pasta as versatile must be the understatement of the century.

I never seem to tire of pasta, eating it several times a week, either with the hot, clean flavours of the East or the sassy sauces of Italy. Anything salty will make pasta sing. Anchovies from the Med or *nam pla* fish sauce from Thailand, grainy Italian Parmesan or Japanese soy sauce, olives

from Greece and goat's cheese from France.

Real Fast Food has an abundant pasta chapter. *The 30-Minute Cook* casts a wider net and hauls in the noodles of the East and also includes the hot, salty, spicy and sour flavours I have recently grown to love; the coriander, soy, chilli, ginger and lemon grass, and ingredients from elsewhere such as chorizo, sauerkraut, Tabasco and black beans.

• Pasta and noodles need lots of water in which to cook. Otherwise they will stick together. Allow, if you have a pan big enough, 4.5 litres/8 pints water per 450g/1lb pasta. And be generous with the salt, about ½ teaspoon per litre (2.2 pints)

• The pasta is cooked when it is done to your liking. I prefer slightly chewy pasta, with a bit of a spring in its step. So I generally cook dried egg pasta for about 9 minutes, noodles (made with soft flour) for 4–5. Japanese noodles are done within 3–4 minutes. But if you prefer your pasta a little softer, then cook it for slightly longer. It's your supper, after all

• It is very difficult to make a pasta dish that isn't good to eat. Noodles of any sort are surprisingly forgiving of the unclassical approach to cooking. The only real crimes being serious overcooking or under-saucing

10-MINUTE PASTA

The two most effective 'sauces' for pasta are olive oil and cream. They both lubricate the dough, but in different ways, the oil giving a clean, fresh texture and the cream offering a more soothing, luxurious result. Although they are, of course, interchangeable, I tend to think of olive oil sauces for the summer, reserving the creamier recipes for autumn and winter. The choice, as always, is yours.

Olive Oil

....

Olive oil is the simplest of lubricants for cooked pasta, and works well enough if the oil is the best. By the best I mean the one you like. If supper is to be this simple then both elements must be spot on; the pasta should be well made, use an egg pasta, and not even slightly overcooked. It must be firm and slightly tacky. The olive oil I use for such a dish would be a rather peppery extra virgin. Rather green and new with a bite to it. It is one of the occasions I get out the smartest oil I have. Something estate bottled and absurdly expensive.

To Which You Can Add Any of the Following

- *Garlic*. Young garlic, that means the white, green and pink variety sold in the spring and summer. It will still have its thick stalk and a subtle smell. Peel the cloves – the skin will be soft rather than flaky – and slice them thinly. Toss them with the oil and pasta
- *Herbs*. Fresh herbs and olive oil give a clean fresh taste to a bowl of noodles. I find that a mixture is fine, but the best results come from a mix of half parsley and half of one other herb. Basil, parsley and olive oil is very fragrant, but try others in place of the basil; the aniseed herbs work well: tarragon, fennel fronds or chervil. Or try something peppery like watercress, nasturtiums or rocket

- *Preserves.* Sun-dried tomatoes in oil, posh, bottled mushrooms, artichokes and olives can all be sliced or chopped and stirred into a bowl of steaming hot, drained pasta
- *Cheese.* Parmesan or Pecorino cheese, grated or cut into shavings with a potato peeler. Feta cheese, crumbled and tossed with fresh mint, or goat's cheese, the softer the better, either sliced thinly or cut into chunks

Cream

....

Cream offers the cook a luscious, rich sauce for pasta in minutes. Use double, single or the more piquant crème fraîche, but the best results will be from fresh cream, unpasteurized if you can lay your hands on it, rather than that which has been heat-treated. Check the small print and avoid anything labelled UHT; it has been heated to a temperature that turns it thin, grey and tasteless.

A 10-Minute Cream Sauce for Pasta

....

Heat the cream in a small, heavy-based pan until it starts to bubble. Turn down the heat so that it simmers gently rather than boils. Add the butter and let it cook for 10 minutes or so while the pasta is cooking. Drain the pasta, return it to the pan and then pour over the reduced cream. Season with salt, freshly ground pepper and any of the following.

- *Bacon, Prosciutto or Ham.* Any cured pork product seems to be a good partner for pasta. Stir shredded prosciutto, crisply fried bacon or chopped cooked ham into the cream and toss with pasta. I would say that a good handful of parsley will make all the difference, as it does in *Jambon Persillé*, or boiled ham with parsley sauce
- *Mushrooms.* While the pasta is boiling and the cream is simmering, sauté some mushrooms. Button or chestnut mushrooms are probably preferable to big black ones. Wild funghi, chanterelles, ceps or oyster mushrooms would turn your simple supper into a feast. Cook in butter till tender and then toss them into the pasta and cream
- *Cheese.* As soon as the cream and pasta are mixed add either grated Parmesan, in generous amounts, or cubed Stilton, Roquefort or Gorgonzola, soft goat's cheese or Brie or Camembert. Semi-hard cheeses are less successful because they need a little more heat to melt. For my money the *ménage à trois* of hot pasta, cream and blue cheese is unbeatable

225ml/8fl oz double cream

a large knob (about 25g/1oz) of butter

30-MINUTE PASTA

Relax. You have a full half hour.

Pasta with Asparagus and Parmesan
....

For 2
•

350g/12oz asparagus
275g/10oz dried pasta
50g/2oz butter
2 cloves of young garlic, sliced
1 tablespoon lemon juice
grated Parmesan cheese

Perky green asparagus and young white garlic, gentle flavours for a summer lunch dish. Any pasta is suitable, with tubular or cupped shapes slightly easier to eat with asparagus spears than the ribbon varieties.

Put a large pan of water to boil. Cut the asparagus into 5cm/2 inch lengths. The water is actually for the pasta but the asparagus gets a quick dip in it first. When it comes to the boil add salt and the asparagus. Boil for 2 minutes and then scoop out with a perforated strainer or whatever.

Cook the pasta in the water till tender, about 7–10 minutes depending on the shape. Meanwhile, melt the butter in a shallow pan over a medium heat. Do not let it brown. If it starts to colour, add a spoonful of oil. Add the drained asparagus and cook for 3 minutes with the garlic. Add the lemon juice.

Drain the pasta, toss it with the asparagus, butter, garlic and lemon. Season with pepper and hand round the Parmesan cheese at the table.

Pasta with Roast Garlic, Mushrooms and Cream

....

A pleasing dish of mellow flavours. Compare the rich, mellow flavours of this method with the brighter cleaner tastes of the Chinese version, also with mushrooms and garlic, on page 114.

Drop the garlic cloves into a small saucepan of boiling water. Blanch them for 4 minutes, by which time they will be paler in colour and will have softened a little. Melt 25g/1oz of the butter in a shallow pan with half of the olive oil. Fish out the garlic with a draining spoon, pop the cloves out of their skins (it's easier than before they are cooked) and drop them into the oil and butter. Cover. Cook over a very low heat for 15 minutes, in which time they should turn golden and sweet.

After 15 minutes' cooking add the remaining butter and the olive oil to the pan. Stir in the mushrooms and replace the lid. Cook over a low heat for 7–10 minutes. Meanwhile, simmer the cream over a low heat to reduce it slightly. Use the pan in which you blanched the garlic, but throw out the water first. Put the pasta into a large pan of boiling salted water and cook till tender.

When the pasta is ready, after 9–10 minutes' boiling, drain and return it to the pan. Pour in the cream and the mushrooms and garlic. Season with salt and freshly ground pepper, add the parsley and stir gently. Serve hot.

For 2

•

8 fat cloves of garlic

75g/3oz butter

100ml/4fl oz olive oil

100g/4oz small mushrooms, halved or quartered

225ml/8fl oz double cream

225g/8oz dried pappardelle

roughly chopped parsley

Pasta with Sardines

....

For 2

•

225g/8oz tinned sardines in olive oil

75g/3oz fennel bulbs, with long stalks and lush fronds

275g/10oz thin dried pasta, such as bucatini or spaghetti

1 medium onion, chopped

4 tablespoons olive oil

2 pinches of saffron threads

4 tablespoons pine nuts

3 tablespoons sultanas, plumped in water for 15 minutes

4 anchovy fillets, rinsed and chopped

Fast food from Sicily. The Sicilians have easy access to fresh sardines, but this classic recipe works well enough with tinned. But it is probably best not to serve it to a Sicilian. The traditional version in Mary Taylor Simeti's magnificent, fascinating book, *Sicilian Food* contains wild fennel greens, which are thinner, more tender versions of the white crisp vegetable we know as fennel. But thin stalks and fronds from a young bulb make a respectable substitute.

Rinse the sardines, carefully so that they do not crumble, and set aside. Cut the feathery fronds from the fennel and slice the stalks and bulb very finely. Put on a large pot of water to boil. Cook the fennel slices in it for 4 minutes and then lift out with a slotted spoon. Bring back to the boil and add salt and the pasta.

Cook the onion in the olive oil until translucent and soft. Add the saffron, pine nuts, sultanas and anchovies, and cook over a low heat for 5 minutes; then add the sardines and fennel and its fronds. Cook for a further 2 minutes, trying not to smash the sardines too much. Drain the pasta and toss with the sardines, sultana and pine nut sauce. Check the seasoning – it may want pepper – and serve.

Pappardelle with Cheese and Ham

Rich, unctuous and straightforward. A simple and sumptuous supper with a frisée or rocket salad alongside.

Cook the noodles in plenty of boiling salted water. Melt the butter in a shallow pan and fry the ham in it till golden. Over a low heat, add the cheese, cut into cubes; let it melt slowly and then stir in the cream. Let it get warm.

Drain the pasta, toss it gently with the cheesy, creamy sauce and then fold in the Parmesan. Serve with a crisp green salad, with a clean, bright-tasting dressing.

For 2

•

275g/10oz dried noodles, wide pappardelle for preference

25g/1oz butter

75g/3oz smoked ham, or prosciutto, cut into small cubes

150g/5oz ripe Gorgonzola, Dolcelatte, or other creamy cheese

75ml/3fl oz single cream

2 tablespoons grated Parmesan cheese

Penne with Artichokes and Parmesan

I love those rather expensive baby artichokes that you can buy by the pound in Italian delis. They make a sensational partner for pasta with lots of parsley and Parmesan.

Cook the pasta as usual. It will take about 10 minutes in deep boiling salted water. Drain the artichokes of their vegetable oil and cut them in half (most of them are in half anyway, so they will be in quarters now). Drain the pasta, toss it with the artichokes, olive oil, parsley and Parmesan.

For 2

•

275g/10oz dried penne (or any other shaped pasta)

350g/12oz marinated, bottled baby artichokes

2 tablespoons olive oil

a handful of coarsely chopped parsley

4 tablespoons grated Parmesan cheese

Pappardelle with Mozzarella, Grilled Peppers and Olives

....

Photograph opposite page 65

For 2

•

225g/8oz dried pappardelle

3 bottled red and yellow peppers (they usually come in halves, in which case you need 6)

6 tablespoons extra virgin olive oil

juice of ½ lemon

I tablespoon capers, rinsed

chopped flat-leaf parsley

4 anchovy fillets, rinsed and chopped

6 tablespoons fresh breadcrumbs

50g/2oz butter

I ball of Mozzarella cheese, cubed

a handful of stoned black olives

The contrast between the tender noodles and crisp bread-crumbs is what makes this dish for me. The dressing is a piquant mixture of lemon, capers and olives and makes the whole thing sing.

Cook the pappardelle in boiling salted water for about 10 minutes till tender. It should be slightly tacky, not slimy.

Meanwhile, rinse the bottled pepper pieces under a running tap to remove their bottling liquid. Cut them into strips and place in a grill pan. Drizzle them with half of the olive oil and grill till sizzling. Pour the juices from the pan into a bowl. Beat in the remaining olive oil with a fork or small hand whisk and add the lemon juice, capers, parsley and anchovies, and season with black pepper.

Cook the breadcrumbs in the butter in a shallow pan. They should turn golden within 5 minutes or so. Stir them so as not to let them burn. Drain the pasta and return to the pan. Toss with the golden crumbs, grilled peppers, Mozzarella cheese, olives, and dressing. Serve warm, rather than hot.

A WORD ABOUT NOODLES

Let's not be precious. There is not a lot of difference between Japanese or Chinese noodles and Italian ones. If you have access to a Chinese supermarket then use fresh. If not, use dried – they are very good. If you are unfettered by tradition then use Italian fettucine or spaghetti. No one will notice. No one will care. Unless they are purists, in which case you would do well to serve the proper thing. Otherwise they will only talk about you afterwards.

Buying and Cooking Noodles

Noodles are made with the local staple grain, which may be rice, wheat or buckwheat. They are also made from mung-bean or potato flour. I confess to being a wheat noodle person. Rice noodles are excluded from this collection because they need an hour's soaking before use. And transparent cellophane noodles, which are made from mung-bean flour, are excluded because I don't like them. And it is my book.

Noodles are made from flour and water, though eggs are added in many cases to enrich the simple dough. They can be bought fresh, in Chinese supermarkets or, more popularly, dried. Egg noodles are the most popular. Bought fresh they have a delightful silky feel, and will keep for a couple of days in the fridge. More common are dried noodles. Sold in cellophane packs, they are usually split into compressed cakes, and you should allow one per person, unless the cakes are very small. Because such noodles are made with soft flour rather than the hard durum wheat used for fine Italian pasta, they cook very quickly. Fresh or dried need 5–6 minutes' cooking, about half that of dried Italian hard-wheat pasta.

Japanese noodles, thin, flat buckwheat *soba*, fine white wheat flour *somen*, and wider flat *udon*, are becoming easier to find here. You will find them in neatly packed rectangles in varying shades of beige labelled with beautiful, uncomprehensible hieroglyphics. A boon for the fast cook as they take barely 3 minutes to cook. Use them as you would any other ribbon pasta.

Noodle Soup

....

For 2

•

100g/4oz dried egg noodles

4 spring onions

600ml/1 pint good chicken or vegetable stock

Sssshhhllllllppp.

Cook the noodles in boiling water for 4 minutes or until tender rather than soft. Drain and drop into cold water, which will keep them from sticking together.

Cut the spring onions diagonally into 5cm/2 inch lengths. Pour the stock into a saucepan and bring gently to the boil. Season with salt and pepper, and stir in the spring onions. Simmer for 2 minutes and then drop in the drained noodles. Let them heat through in the seasoned stock for 2 minutes and eat immediately.

Another Noodle Soup

....

225g/8oz dried egg noodles

600ml/1 pint good vegetable or chicken stock

2 tablespoons dark soy sauce

1 teaspoon sugar

1 tablespoon rice wine or medium-dry sherry

1 tablespoon chopped coriander leaves

A more elaborate version of the simple soup above. If you can call the addition of soy sauce, sugar and sherry elaborate. Double the weight of noodles if you are using fresh.

Cook the noodles until tender in boiling water, about 4–5 minutes. Drain and drop into cold water.

Mix the stock, soy, sugar and wine or sherry. Bring gently to the boil in a saucepan. Season with pepper. Add the noodles and heat for 2 minutes. Pour into bowls, add the coriander leaves and eat while hot.

A Few Good Things to Drop into Your Noodle Soup

....

• Shredded chicken. Cut cold roast chicken into thin shreds, easier to do with the fingers than the knife
• Shredded spinach. Wash the leaves thoroughly. Roll them tightly and shred very finely with a large knife. Stir in at the last minute

• Green beans. Lightly cooked green beans, cut into manageable slices. Once cooked toss them with a little grated fresh root ginger
• More dark soy sauce
• Cooked peeled prawns. Choose small ones, sauté them quickly in a little oil and garlic and then drain and chop roughly. Stir them in as you eat

Noodles, Chicken, Black Beans and Oyster Sauce

....

A substantial supper dish of golden noodles, red pepper and black beans. The chicken can be replaced by mushrooms if you prefer. Use the large chestnut type, quartered into fat little nuggets or sliced thickly. You may need to use a little more oil due to the mushrooms' natural thirst.

Cook the noodles till tender, 4–5 minutes, rinse and drain.

Slice the chicken into thick pieces. Heat the oil in a wok, add the ginger, garlic and black beans, and fry, stirring constantly, for 1 minute. Add the chicken slices and the red pepper. Cook over a high heat until the chicken is golden and then add the soy, oyster sauce and as much chilli sauce as you fancy.

Stir-fry for 2 minutes, by which time the chicken should be cooked through and the pepper bright and soft. Blend the cornflour with 3 tablespoons water to a smooth viscous paste and stir it into the pan. Add the noodles and let the whole thing cook for 2–3 minutes over a medium heat till the sauce is thickened. Eat immediately while hot.

For 2
•
225g/8oz dried egg noodles
450g/1lb chicken breast, boned but skin on
4 tablespoons groundnut oil
2.5cm/1 inch knob of fresh root ginger, peeled and chopped
2 cloves of garlic, sliced
1 tablespoon black beans, rinsed and chopped
1 red pepper, seeded and thinly sliced
2 tablespoons light soy sauce
2 tablespoons oyster sauce
1–2 teaspoons chilli sauce
1 tablespoon cornflour

Stir-fried Noodles

....

For 2

•

225g/8oz dried egg noodles

4 tablespoons groundnut oil

6 spring onions, coarsely chopped

2.5cm/1 inch knob of fresh root ginger, peeled and chopped

3 cloves of garlic, sliced

100g/4oz button mushrooms, halved

225g/8oz bean shoots, rinsed

2 tablespoons oyster sauce

1 tablespoon rice wine or dry sherry

soy sauce, to serve

Classic Chinese in 10 minutes.

Cook the noodles in boiling water till tender, about 4–5 minutes, then drain. Let cold water run through them to stop them sticking together. Set aside.

Heat a large wok and pour in the oil. As soon as the oil is hot, but not so hot that it starts smoking, add the spring onions, ginger and garlic. Cook over a fierce heat, stirring to prevent them burning, for a minute or so. You will know when they are ready because the garlic will be a warm nut brown and the onions will have wilted.

Add the mushrooms, cook for a minute, and then add the bean shoots and noodles, and stir-fry for a minute. Pour in the oyster sauce and wine or sherry. Still over a high heat, fry for 2 minutes, but no longer than it takes for the bean shoots to cook (they should barely start to wilt). Sprinkle with soy – more or less depending on your taste – and serve.

Fish

I eat less meat as each year goes by. Fish, on the other hand, is a major source of interest to me, and fits perfectly into the life of a 30-minute cook.

Every cuisine has its fast fish recipes. Thai cooks marinate white fish in lime, chillies and sugar to give a sweet-sour effect, north Africa ones rub cumin and lemon into mackerel and char-grill it, while Indian cooks deep-fry it in a spiced batter.

In the recipes that follow I have been deliberately vague about which fish you can use for each recipe. It doesn't really matter whether the fillets you curry with coconut, chillies and lime leaves are haddock, cod or hake. Each will be slightly different in taste and texture, but will cook in a similar way. The choice is yours.

Where I think it is important, I have made it clear which variety is most suited to a particular recipe. But only if I think you will not like the result made with another type of fish. I am not going to suggest that you cook Dover sole with garlic and ginger if the delicate flavour of the fish will be outdone by the spicing. Of course you could, but I am not going to be the guy who recommends it to you.

Buying Fish

I have suggested before that you use your fishmonger to the full. He will be happy to do the horrid bits for you. His range of fish is likely to be head and shoulders above that of the average superstore, though you will have to wait five minutes while he prepares your chosen fish. Alternatively, you can scoop up a packet of neatly trimmed and smartly packaged fresh fish from the store. Neat and clean, if a little clinical.

A Quick Fish Soup

....

Photograph between pages 128 and 129

For 2

•

1 shallot, finely chopped

2 cloves of garlic, squashed flat

1 tablespoon olive oil

3 tomatoes, seeded and chopped

bay leaf

425ml/¾ pint hot fish stock (or at a pinch, water)

100g/4oz boned white fish (cod, skate or hake)

8 small clams, cleaned and sorted

8 mussels in their shells, cleaned and sorted

100g/4oz shelled prawns

1 teaspoon saffron strands

flat-leaf parsley, if you like

The mention of fish soup puts the fear of God into some cooks. Perhaps it's the fear of cod. French fish soups often rely on the crunching of shellfish carcasses and the puréeing of the flesh within, making the whole thing rich and deeply satisfying. But an enormous hassle. Needless to say, a fine fish soup can be made in minutes. Especially if you have bought a carton of fish stock from the supermarket. The recipe that follows is of the fragrant broth with shellfish variety, rather than a creamy purée.

Cook the shallot and garlic in the olive oil till soft and just turning gold. Add the tomatoes, bay leaf and fish stock or water. Bring to the boil. Turn the heat down to a simmer and add the fish; 4 or 5 minutes later add the clams, simmer for 2 minutes, add the mussels and prawns, and stir in the saffron strands. Cook for a further couple of minutes till the mussels and clams have opened.

Taste the broth – it may need salt and pepper. Throw out the bay leaf. Add some chopped parsley if you have some; it will add freshness and make the colours sing. Serve hot, spooning broth, fish and shellfish into large, warm bowls. Offer bread for dunking.

A Quicker Fish Soup

....

This is a bit of a cheat, but I've been doing it for years and no one has ever noticed. I could name a few restaurants that...

Open a 400g/14oz tin of fish soup – any brand will do, they all seem to be much of a muchness. (The stuff in bottles is a different story.) Tip into a saucepan with an equal quantity of bought fresh fish stock. Add 100g/4oz defrosted prawns, the same of squid rings, a pinch of saffron threads and a good slug of brandy. Bring the whole lot to the boil and then turn the heat down.

Make some croûtes by toasting slices of baguette, spreading them with red pesto from a jar and covering them with grated cheese (any type will do). Tip the soup into warm bowls and float the cheese croûtes on top. Eat piping hot, sinking the croûtes till the bread goes soggy and the cheese melts into the soup. Enough for two as a principal dish.

Poached Skate with Thai Flavours and Its Broth

....

Photograph opposite page 128

For 2

•

2 skate wings

a lime, sliced thinly

2 kaffir lime leaves

2 cloves of garlic, squashed flat

2 hot red chilli peppers

2.5cm/1 inch knob of fresh root ginger, peeled

2 spring onions, chopped

1 stalk of lemon grass, bruised

8 black peppercorns

chopped coriander leaves

dark soy sauce

A soothing way to eat a meaty wing of skate, served with a gently aromatic broth made interesting by some of the signature notes of Thai cooking: coriander, ginger, lemon grass and chilli. It does not have to be skate, I am sure a hunk of hake would be fine too, but the gelatinous texture of the skate seems to make the broth even more comforting. Serve with bread.

Place the skate wings in a large shallow pan such as a straight-sided frying-pan. Pour over enough cold water just to cover and add the lime slices and leaves, squashed garlic cloves, chilli peppers, the ginger cut into coins, the spring onions (both green and white bits) and the lemon grass. Season with peppercorns and a little salt.

Bring slowly to the boil over a medium heat, turn the heat down and leave to simmer – shudder is probably a better word – for 10–15 minutes, or until the fish has firmed up. Don't overcook it – the fish is ready when opaque, wobbly and easy to break into strands with a fork.

Sprinkle with fresh coriander leaves and shake in a little soy sauce to taste. Serve in an old-fashioned soup plate or similar deep-rimmed plate with some of its poaching liquor. Drink the sustaining, aromatic broth first and then attack the fish.

Thai Green Fish Curry

....

A green curry from Thailand, rich with coconut and fragrant with basil and coriander. Keep the heat low, though it may still curdle a little. That is its nature. You can use a ready-made curry paste but your own will be fresher tasting and can be made in a couple of minutes. You can use a few slices of lime instead of the lime leaves at a push but they aren't really the same and leaves are not so difficult to find. Two out of three of my local supermarkets have them.

Cut the fish into large bite-sized pieces. Don't cut it too small, no matter how small you may think your mouth is. Cut the creamed coconut into chunks and dissolve it in 300ml/½ pint hot water. Bring the coconut milk gently to the boil, in a heavy-based saucepan, stirring almost constantly. Stir in the curry paste and turn down to a gentle simmer.

Add the pieces of fish, the lime leaves, a good pinch of salt, and the fish sauce. Simmer gently for 12 minutes, until the fish is cooked. Taste for seasoning – you may like to add more salt. Scatter over the chopped coriander and basil leaves and serve, with rice if you wish.

For 2, with rice

•

450g/1lb fish steaks or thick fillets

1 × 200g/7oz block of creamed coconut

3 tablespoons green curry paste (page 144)

6 kaffir lime leaves

1 teaspoon fish sauce (*nam pla*)

1 tablespoon chopped coriander leaves

2 tablespoons chopped basil leaves

Photograph opposite page 129

Herbed Salmon with Garlic Cream Sauce

....

For 2

•

450g/1lb salmon fillets, about 2.5cm/1 inch thick

6 tablespoons chopped herbs: tarragon, chervil, dill and parsley

50g/2oz butter

1 clove of garlic, squashed flat

4 tablespoons crème fraîche, double cream or even Mascarpone cheese

lemon juice

French chefs have an affinity with fish, butter and cream that I occasionally aspire to. This is a simplified version of the sort of herby, buttery, creamy sauce that is often served with fish in France. Little boiled potatoes, complete with their tender skins, would be my choice of accompaniment. And a few green beans.

Cut the salmon fillets into pieces across their width, about 4cm/1.5 inches wide. Scatter the chopped herbs on a plate and roll the salmon pieces in them, pressing down on them to make them adhere to the fish.

Melt the butter in a shallow pan over a medium heat and add the garlic. When the butter starts to foam, place the herbed fingers of fish into the pan. Cook for 2–3 minutes or just until the fish becomes opaque. By now the butter will be slightly brown in parts and fizzing wildly. Stir in the crème, cream or whatever and leave to melt into the butter. Season with black pepper, and salt if you wish.

Just before you scoop the fish out of the pan squeeze a little lemon juice into the sauce: it will lift its flavour and prevent the sauce from becoming cloying.

Grilled Mackerel

....

Although I have yet to visit the country, I have encountered a number of references to a cumin-spiced fish dish from Tunisia that takes barely 15 minutes to prepare. I first came across Hout Mechoui made with mackerel – the authors suggest also conger eel and red mullet – in a very favourite book, *Plats du Jour* by Patience Gray and Primrose Boyd, a collection of recipes that has been in constant use in my kitchen for years. This is my slightly adapted version of that good recipe.

Make sure that the fish are thoroughly cleaned – the fishmonger may have missed a bit. Rinse them anyway. Lay the fish down on the grill pan and make half-a-dozen slashes along each one.

Mix the cumin with a little coarsely ground black pepper and some salt. Spread over the fish, smoothing it down into the slashes. Set the fish under a moderately hot grill, not too close to the heat. Mix together the remaining ingredients and baste the fish every few minutes, turning once. Watch carefully that the fish does not burn.

Cook until the fish are cooked right through and the skins a handsome mixture of silver, gold and black. About 6–7 minutes on each side, depending on the size of your fish. Serve with the wonderful pan juices, and plenty of crusty bread to mop them up.

For 2

•

2 fat, glistening mackerel
2 teaspoons ground cumin
3 tablespoons olive oil
2 tablespoons lemon juice
2 cloves of garlic, crushed to a paste
½ teaspoon cayenne pepper

▶ *Other versions I suspect less accurate (though I may be wrong) add a few tablespoons of water to the above mixture, giving a less concentrated spice paste*

Fried Fish in the Moroccan Style

....

For 2

•

100ml/4fl oz olive oil

2 tablespoons chopped coriander leaves

juice of ½ lemon

1 teaspoon mild chilli powder

2 teaspoons ground cumin

2 cloves of garlic, finely crushed with a little salt

½ teaspoon black peppercorns, finely crushed

450g/1lb white fish, filleted

plain flour

I find Moroccans the most generous of people. Even the guy who robbed me of my belt in the street gave me his old one in its place. Actually, his was better, having that beautiful chestnut patina that only comes with years of wear; mine was cheap and new. They will share their recipes too.

Mix half the olive oil with the coriander, lemon juice, chilli, cumin and garlic. Add the peppercorns. Put the fish fillets flat into a shallow dish and rub them with the spice marinade. Leave them for as long as you have; 15 minutes will do, but 30 is better.

Heat the remaining olive oil in a frying-pan. Remove the fish from the marinade, shake it to remove any excess oil and roll it in flour. Fry immediately in the hot oil till crisp and golden, a matter of 3–4 minutes, turning once. Drain and season generously with salt. Serve with lemon and a leaf or tomato salad.

Spiced Fried Fish

....

For 2

•

450g/1lb white fish, boned and filleted

2 limes

2 plump cloves of garlic, sliced

1 teaspoon ground cumin

1 teaspoon mild curry powder

½ teaspoon mild chilli powder

75g/3oz chick-pea flour

groundnut oil for frying

Which fish would I like for lunch? The choice was set out for me on top of a rusty oil drum in the Indian sun, though the fish was still wet, fresh and bright-eyed. The whole fish was then coated in chick-pea flour and spices and fried golden. Scattered with coriander and garnished with a wedge of lime, it was served on a battered tin plate that had seen more lunches than I had. What follows is an approximation of that lunch – one of many, it so happened – utilizing user-friendly filleted fish to free you from the irritation of skin and bones.

Cut the fish into 2.5cm/1 inch wide strips. Place in a shallow dish. Squeeze over the juice of one of the limes and toss the fish in it gently. Add all the other ingredients except the remaining lime and the oil and toss again.

Heat the oil in a pan. About 1cm/½ inch deep will do. When the oil is really hot (test it with a cube of bread), add the floured and spiced fish, shaking off any surplus flour. Fry till pale gold and crisp: a matter of 2 minutes or so. Lift out the fish, drain for a few seconds on kitchen paper and then pile on to plates. Serve with the extra lime, cut in half from stem to tip.

Trout Saltimbocca

....

Trout needs a bit of help nowadays. It has lost much of its joy now that it is so intensively farmed, yet it still jumps into people's shopping baskets at an alarming rate. Here is a way to lift it from its doldrums, based on the traditional Italian way with veal, though inspired by the brilliant Alastair Little, who uses red mullet.

Cut the butter in two and cut one half into 4 thin slices. Lay a slice of Parma ham flat on the table, place a slice of butter in the middle, then put one of the trout fillets on top. Roll up the fish in the ham, place a sage leaf over the loose end and secure with a cocktail stick.

Season the flour with salt and pepper. Heat a thin layer of oil in a frying-pan. Dust each parcel thoroughly with flour. Place, butter side down, in the pan and cook for about 3 minutes, till the ham is crisp. Turn over with the help of a fish slice, and cook for a further 2 minutes.

Remove to a hot plate. Tip the juices from the pan. Melt the remaining butter over a high heat and, as soon as it starts to froth, add the lemon juice and a little salt and pepper. Pour the hot, frothing seasoned butter over the fish and serve immediately.

For 2, with new potatoes and salad
•
75g/3oz cold butter
4 large slices of Parma ham
2 large trout, weighing about 450g/1lb each, filleted
4 large sage leaves
a little plain flour
groundnut oil for frying
juice of 1 lemon

Two Fried Fishes

....

Tali Machchi – Fish in Batter, Indian-Style

For 2

•

450g/1lb white fish fillets

2 tablespoons lime juice

3 tablespoons plain flour

3 tablespoons chick-pea flour

1 teaspoon garam masala

½ teaspoon ground turmeric

1 teaspoon chilli powder

1 egg, beaten

groundnut oil for frying

Place the fish fillets in a dish and squeeze over the lime juice. Season the flours with the garam masala, turmeric and chilli.

Put the beaten egg in a bowl and dip the fish fillets first into the egg, then into the spiced flour. Fry in deep, hot oil till golden, about 3–4 minutes, maybe less. Serve with lime.

White Fish Tempura – Fish in Batter, Japanese Style

For 2

•

1 large egg

225ml/8fl oz ice-cold water

100g/4oz plain flour

a good pinch of bicarbonate of soda

350g/12oz white fish, scallops, squid, prawns, etc., cut into large bite-sized pieces

a little plain flour

groundnut oil for frying

dark soy sauce for serving

Make the batter. Break the egg into a bowl and whisk in the cold water. It really must be ice cold. Don't ask me why, I only know that it must be so. Add the flour and the bicarbonate of soda at the same time, in one swoosh. Beat very lightly about half-a-dozen times. It will be lumpy. You will think you have failed. You haven't, it will be lighter this way.

Dust the fish with the second lot of flour seasoned with salt and pepper. Dip each piece into the batter and then into deep, hot oil. Fry for 1–2 minutes till very pale gold and crisp. The batter will puff up in bubbles and be almost non-existent. Serve with soy sauce for dipping.

A Handful of Good Things to Do with a Fish Fillet

....

You have been to the fishmonger's and bought a fat, juicy fillet or two of fish. It may have been cod, with its large and juicy flakes, or creamy hake or haddock. Perhaps you have splashed out and bought something more unusual. Whatever, in an everyday sense, most fish tend to cook in the same time. (Although perfectionists and purists will probably take a little more care.) And can be treated in similar fashion.

Sautéed, with Butter and Lemon

Still my favourite way to cook a piece of fish. Dust lightly with plain flour that you have seasoned with salt and black pepper. Fry gently in butter to which you have added a tablespoon of oil. Cook for about 4 minutes on each side. Serve with lemon, in thick wedges.

Spiced and Sautéed

Cut the fillets into thick strips about 2.5cm/1 inch wide. Dust the fish with plain flour to which you have added salt and a little curry powder. Fry in butter and oil as above over a gentle heat.

An Italian Way

Blanch about 225g/8oz spinach, which you have washed well, in boiling water. Lift out, drain and chop. Mix with a little grated nutmeg, 3 tablespoons double cream and 50g/2oz grated Parmesan. (Use Cheddar or Gruyère for a different texture.) Grill two fillets of fish for 3 minutes on each side and then top with cheese and spinach. Return to the grill till golden.

An Indian Way

Based on a Madhur Jaffrey idea. Whizz a good handful (about 50g/2oz) of coriander leaves, 1 plump, mild, chopped and seeded chilli pepper, 3 peeled garlic cloves, salt, a tablespoon each of water and lemon juice in a blender. Dip the fillets into yoghurt – you will need about 100ml/4fl oz for 2 thick fillets cut into 5cm/2 inch strips – and then into the green paste. Fry in hot groundnut oil for 3 minutes on each side. Serve with lime.

Grilled Fish with Chermoula

....

For 2

•

450g/1lb white fish fillets, cut into 3cm/1½ inch cubes

2 cloves of garlic, crushed with 1 teaspoon of salt

1 small onion, very finely chopped

a handful of flat-leaf parsley, chopped

2 tablespoons coriander leaves, chopped

1 teaspoon coriander seeds, ground

a good pinch of powdered saffron

1 teaspoon paprika

½ teaspoon chilli flakes

juice of 1 lemon

4 tablespoons olive oil

bay leaves

lemon or lime slices

Classic Moroccan spicing. This time for fish.

Place the cubes of fish in a shallow dish. Mix together the remaining ingredients. Toss this *chermoula* with the fillets and leave for as long as you can. If possible overnight, if not, for at least an hour or two. Though I have reduced it to 20 minutes before now.

Thread the fish on to 4 skewers. You can add a bay leaf and a lemon or lime slice now and again. It won't do a great deal for the taste but will smell quite magical. Cook under a preheated hot grill for 3–4 minutes per side. Get the fish quite close to the heat so that it chars slightly in places while remaining juicy inside. Pull away a flake of fish to see if it is cooked.

Serve with rice, salad or new potatoes. Though couscous would be more traditional.

Baked Hake

....

For 2

•

4 pieces of hake or haddock, each weighing about 100g/4oz

juice of 1 lemon

2 thick slices of bread, crusts removed

a handful of flat-leaf parsley

2 plump cloves of garlic, peeled

olive oil

good mayonnaise, to serve

A popular Spanish way with hake, a favourite fish of theirs. Though haddock will do, or pretty much anything else for that matter.

Put the oven on. Set it at 220°C/425°F (gas mark 7). Put the fish into a dish. An ovenproof one. Squeeze over the lemon juice. Sprinkle with salt. Set aside.

Throw the bread, parsley and garlic into a food processor. Whizz to crumbs. Tip in any excess lemon from the fish dish. Drizzle with olive oil. Cover the fish with the crumbs. When the oven has reached the right temperature, put the fish in and bake. Give it about 20 minutes. Serve with the mayo.

Shellfish

One late autumn evening a friend and I turned up in a hotel restaurant just outside Ravenna. There was something slightly sinister about the place that we couldn't quite put our finger on. But the food was good and we were hungry. There were only two of us even though the kitchen seemed to think we were twenty. Dinner was a feast, but absurdly simple.

Plate after plate of shellfish, much of it diminutive enough to eat with a pin (they gave us what looked suspiciously like hatpins), arrived until the table was piled high. We scoffed the lot with bread and white wine. It occurred to me that this was probably the most delicious seafood I had ever eaten, yet there was no butter, cream, herbs, spices or wine. Except in our glasses. I often think of this meal when I am offered some fancy-nancy shellfish dish in a restaurant here, when all I really want are some winkles and a pin.

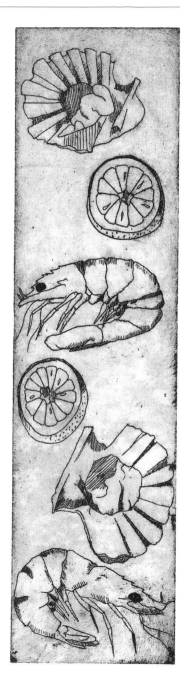

PRAWNS

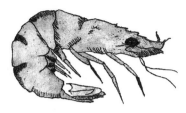

Ignoring the bagged frozen jobbies, which I dealt with in *Real Fast Food*, the prawn offers a few possibilities to the 30-minute cook. Most involve grilling over (preferably) hot coals or more likely under a domestic grill. Sucking my fingers while eating grilled prawns in their shells is a great treat. (Or anyone else's for that matter.)

Even the most enticing fishmonger's display will offer frozen, rather than fresh, prawns. This is apparently because prawns deteriorate so quickly that it is the only practical way to sell them. If you are lucky you may find a supply of grey, uncooked prawns. Fishmongers who offer such things are to be cherished.

Even the fresh ones must be fresh, if you know what I mean. Don't bother to ask, the proprietor is hardly likely to tell you the truth unless they came in a few hours ago. And he may skin and fillet you into the bargain. If the prawns are moving you are in luck. Sniff them. Prawns should smell of the sea rather than of fish, and they should look plump and wet. The smell will tell you instantly if they are not worth buying.

Cooking Fresh Prawns in a Pot

You will need a heavy-bottomed casserole dish and the prawns. Nothing else. Place the dish on the heat, a moderate one will do, rinse the prawns but do not shake them dry. Add the wet prawns to the pan and slam on the lid. Let them cook in their own salty steam for 7–8 minutes, by which time they will have changed from a dull, rather transparent grey to a pretty salmon pink.

Let the prawns cool a little. When they are just slightly too hot to handle serve them with napkins and a bowl of wobbly, yellow mayonnaise. Peel the prawns with your fingers, dipping each one in the mayo.

Cooking Fresh Prawns under the Grill

You will need about 350g/12oz prawns for two people. They must be plump and in their shells. You can skewer

Opposite Poached Skate with Thai Flavours and Its Broth (page 118)
Over, left Thai Crab Cakes (page 136); *right* A Quick Fish Soup (page 116)

them if you wish but I see little point. Lay the prawns flat on the grill pan, cook them over, or under, a high heat till pink for 3–4 minutes.

Eat them while they are hot with a little softened, warmed butter. Dip each hot prawn in the butter, sprinkling a little salt, peeling and sucking as you go.

Grilled Prawns in Yoghurt and Lime

············

Goa, or at least parts of it, is pretty much my idea of paradise. Especially out of season. Anywhere that has tall palms, long beaches with only me on them and straw huts to sleep in is my kind of place. They can still be found if you know when and where to go. But I am not going to tell you. I can stand any number of lazy days in the sand and sea and long, stoned evenings interrupted only by supper. The seafood is good too. I probably ate more prawns in a few weeks than I usually eat in years. The price has a lot to do with it. A few rupees buys what would cost a few quid back home. My fishmonger has cooked (pink) and uncooked (grey) prawns, though he is one of the few, so I usually have to make do with cooked. A not-too-expensive treat if you munch a filling naan, warmed under the grill, at the same time.

Thread the prawns on to long stainless steel or wooden skewers. It won't take long and will save time later, when you come to turn them. Mix together all the other ingredients with a teaspoon or so of salt and lay the skewered prawns in it. Leave them there for 15 minutes, or longer if you have time.

Get the grill hot – use either one of those grill pans that sit on top of the gas or an overhead grill. Remove the prawns from the marinade (some of the gunge will come with them) and cook them on each side for 4

For 2

•

450g/1lb large (but not huge) prawns in their shells

2.5cm/1 inch knob of fresh root ginger, grated on the coarse side of the grater

2 cloves of garlic, crushed to a paste

1 teaspoon garam masala

½ teaspoon chilli powder

1 tablespoon ground coriander

grated zest of a lime (use the fine side of the grater)

1 tablespoon lime juice

100ml/4fl oz thick yoghurt

Herbed Salmon with Garlic Cream Sauce (page 120)

minutes. It is worth remembering that they are already cooked (if they were pink), so the cooking time is very short. The prawns are ready when they have caught a little on the grill and are juicy inside their shells.

Remove the prawns from their spears as you eat, sucking the shells clean before peeling them back to get at the juicy meat within.

SCALLOPS

The secret is not to overcook them. It is a question of seconds rather than minutes. Pan-fried in hot butter a halved scallop will be ready to eat in a minute, that is, 30 seconds on each side. Grilling takes a little longer: 4 minutes should be enough for a whole scallop. Disobey at your expense.

I remain unconvinced of the qualities of frozen scallops. Though I am sure I have eaten them in restaurants without knowing. And no doubt in restaurants that should know better. My local fishmonger has fresh scallops glistening on the ice on his counter. They quiver on their shells like little white and coral coloured jellies and cost, at the time of writing, about £10 a pound. That is about a pound each. And worst of all, they do not benefit from padding out with other ingredients. If it is scallops you want, then you simply have to shell out for them.

Scallops and Bacon

For 2

3 rashers of smoked bacon
6 large scallops
cocktail sticks or toothpicks
soft, but not melted, butter
chopped flat-leaf parsley

It is difficult to think of anything more succulent than a fat scallop grilled in bacon. The two combine to produce a truly scrumptious mouthful.

Get the grill hot. Cut the rashers of bacon in half to give six short pieces. Lay each rasher flat on a chopping board and stretch each one so that it is long and very thin. The trick to doing this is to hold one end of the rasher and then stretch it away from you with a knife, running the blade along the rasher to stretch it.

Roll up each scallop and its coral in a rasher of bacon and secure the rasher on the scallop with a cocktail stick. Brush each scallop thickly with soft butter and grill for 3–4 minutes on either side till the bacon fat is golden. Scatter over parsley and serve. The few meagre, savoury juices in the pan are quite sublime.

Pan-fried Scallops with Buttered Breadcrumbs

....

Nothing complements a scallop like golden buttery bread-crumbs. You know very well I mean home-made crumbs (it takes 30 seconds in the blender) rather those ghastly day-glo orange things you find in packets. To my mind, fried breadcrumbs freckled with chopped parsley provide a far more interesting partner for the scallop than the classical treatment of creamy sauces.

Remove the orange beak of coral from each scallop. It takes less time to cook so is best added later. Slice each scallop in half to give six round pieces. Warm half the butter and oil in a frying- or sauté pan. When it sizzles add the breadcrumbs, cook for 4–5 minutes over a mod-erate heat till they are golden, stirring from time to time so that they do not burn.

In a second pan, warm the remaining butter and add the garlic. Cook over a moderate heat for a minute, and then scoop out the garlic and add the scallop slices. Fry quickly for 30 seconds, no longer, on each side. Any longer and they will toughen. Almost as soon as you have turned them, add the corals and tip the golden breadcrumbs from their pan into the scallops. Add the parsley and serve. Wedges of lemon would complete the story.

For 2

•

6 large scallops

50g/2oz butter

3 tablespoons extra virgin olive oil

50g/2oz fresh white breadcrumbs

1 plump clove of garlic, squashed flat

2 tablespoons chopped flat-leaf parsley

lemon, to serve

OYSTERS

The very essence of the sea in one wobbly, salty, slippery mouthful. Unless you are a dab hand with the oyster knife, ask your fishmonger to open their tightly sealed grey shells for you. Or risk a nasty cut. Allow six per person, or less if there is much to follow.

On the Shell

• Mash 3 finely chopped shallots and 2 tablespoons chopped flat-leaf parsley with 50g/2oz butter. Season with pepper and divide between 12 opened oysters. Grill them till the butter bubbles, about 4 minutes.

• Chop a good handful of fresh herbs, parsley, watercress (yes, I know it's not strictly a herb), aniseedy chervil and fennel fronds with 2 shallots. Beat in 50g/2oz butter and some pepper. Divide the herb butter between the oysters and sprinkle over a little Pernod. Grill till bubbling, about 5 minutes.

• Squeeze a little lemon juice on each opened oyster. Drizzle with melted butter and a few fresh breadcrumbs. Bake in a hot oven till bubbling, about 6 minutes.

Shelled

• Wrap each oyster in a rasher of streaky bacon and secure with a cocktail stick. Grill for 3 minutes, and then turn and grill for a further 2 till sizzling and the bacon fat has turned golden.

• Pour as much of the juice from 12 oysters as you can into a pan. Do this through a sieve to catch any bits of shell. Drop the oysters into the pan and cook over a medium heat for 3 minutes. Add almost 50g/2oz butter and 75ml/3fl oz double cream to the pan, bring to the boil, but turn down the heat just before it gets there. Sprinkle with parsley and serve.

• Roll the oysters in plain flour to which you have added a little salt, black pepper and cayenne. Fry them in hot butter for 2 minutes and then eat them with mayonnaise and a crisp baguette.

SQUID

Seafood you can actually get your teeth into. I first met squid in Greece, shining brilliant white on my plate on a blue stone table overlooking the sea. True, it doesn't taste quite the same without salt on my lips and sand in my toes (and everywhere else for that matter), but squid still has much going for it.

Supermarkets generally stock squid rings with a coating of batter. These are not so bad if you put plenty of salt on them, but better still are the naked rings, which need nothing more than lightly flouring and frying in hot oil. Generosity with the lemon is to be recommended.

Stir-fried Squid

....

For 2

•

1 teaspoon Szechwan peppercorns

1 tablespoon groundnut oil

2 spring onions, finely chopped

2.5cm/1 inch knob of fresh root ginger, peeled and cut into shreds

4 cloves of garlic, sliced

1 small hot red chilli pepper, seeded and finely chopped

350g/12oz cleaned squid, sliced into rings

1 tablespoon rice wine or dry sherry

2 tablespoons dark soy sauce

2 tablespoons chilli bean sauce

1 heaped teaspoon tomato purée

1 teaspoon sugar

sprinkling of sesame oil

A classic Szechwan sauce, this time for squid. The fish is not so delicately flavoured that it cannot cope with the garlic, soy, chilli-bean paste and chillies that this cuisine holds so dear.

Heat a wok over a medium heat and roast the Szechwan peppercorns till they are fragrant, about 2 minutes. Whizz them to a powder in a spice or coffee mill.

Wipe the wok thoroughly. The residue of pepper will burn and spoil the dish if you don't. Add the oil when the wok is hot and stir-fry the spring onions, ginger, garlic and chilli for a few seconds. Add the squid, and stir-fry for 1 minute. You will see it tighten up immediately it hits the hot oil.

Add the remaining ingredients except the sesame oil. Stir-fry for 2 minutes till the sauce has coated the squid and the whole lot is highly fragrant and hot. Sprinkle over a little sesame oil and eat hot and sizzling.

▶ *No Chinese ingredients in the cupboard?*
Coat the same quantity of squid in flour. A little salt and pepper will help no end. When the squid is lightly coated fry it in hot oil, whip it out as soon as it is golden and eat hot with lemon and a tub of garlic mayonnaise

WHELKS

You have bought some whelks or winkles out of curiosity and soaked them overnight in cold water. They can be good when dropped into boiling water and simmered for a couple of minutes, drained and the nugget of flesh picked out with a pin. Though they don't taste the same at home as they do when there is a tang of salt in the air. Like at the end of the pier. Brown bread and butter, cut thin, is the traditional accompaniment.

MUSSELS

I have eaten some very fancy dishes based on mussels. None of them was worth the trouble, except perhaps mussel soup. For my money, the tastiest way with mussels is to cook them in a sealed casserole in their own steam, and then to suck the wobbly orange flesh from the salty shells. Allow a kilo between two people if that is all there is, and plenty of very crisp baguette.

You can add finely chopped shallots (2), chopped tarragon and parsley (1 tablespoon each) and a glass of wine if you like. Though the juices, which are quite delectable, may need sieving to remove the grit. You can even stir in a spoonful of cream if richness is what you want. Just make sure the mussels are fresh – they should sink when dumped in a sink of ice-cold water (if they float chuck them overboard) – and that you cook them only until their shells open. Which will probably be about 3 minutes or so. You will have to peep.

Thai Crab Cakes
....

Photograph between pages 128 and 129

For 2, with rice and a salad

•

450g/1lb crab meat, thawed

6 kaffir lime leaves, finely chopped, or 1 stalk of lemon grass, finely chopped

1 teaspoon fish sauce (nam pla)

a fistful of coriander leaves

2 heaped tablespoons mayonnaise

2 small hot red chilli peppers, roughly chopped

3 spring onions, roughly chopped

75g/3oz fresh white breadcrumbs

oil for deep-frying

The spicy citrus notes of the kaffir lime leaves or lemon grass, heat from the chillies and the pungent scent of the coriander leaves are what makes these little fish cakes so extraordinarily addictive. Use only the freshest and greenest of the lemon grass, ruthlessly discarding the outer leaves which are sometimes dry. You *can* make the crab cakes without the lime leaves or lemon grass, of course, but they really won't be the same.

Throw the lot except the oil into a food processor and whizz till mixed. Don't whizz to a sludge. You can mix it by hand if you wish, but chop the chillies, onions and coriander leaves finely. Chill for 15 minutes, or longer if you have the time.

Shape the mixture with your hands into flat patties about 5cm/2 inches in diameter. That will be about 12. Dust them with a little flour, then fry them in shallow hot oil until crisp, about 3–4 minutes on each side.

▶ *If you like your crab cakes as hot as the Thais do, either add another chilli or add a few to the cooking oil. About 4 should do it*

CHAPTER 6

Chicken, Game and Other Good Things

The world's favourite meat. Quick curried chicken from India, a Chinese stir-fry with mushrooms and soy, Parmesan-crusted chicken from Italy and a spiced nutty grill from Egypt. They are all possible in 30 minutes, and they are all here, along with a Viennese recipe rich with cream and paprika, a recipe I found in Marrakesh with olives and lemons and a coconut and coriander version from Goa. I cannot tell you the number of times I have picked up a packet of free-range chicken thighs and a bottle of wine on the way home, not knowing what I would do with it till I got into the kitchen.

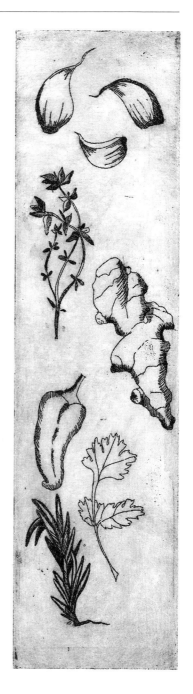

Buying Poultry

I implore you to buy free-range poultry rather than the unlabelled, intensively farmed type. The texture is firmer and more interesting, the flavour richer and the eating quality altogether more enjoyable.

There is also the knowledge, and for me this counts a great deal, that the bird I am eating has enjoyed a certain quality of life sadly denied to the majority of poultry.

I have seen both methods of chicken production. Free range nowadays is rarely the kind I was brought up with, the chickens running round the farmyard pecking at grass, wild flowers, corn and the potato peelings the farmer's wife put out for them. That, I am afraid, has pretty much gone for ever. Modern free range generally allows (there are a few cheats) the birds access to both grassland and shelter. The birds have the choice of pellet-type poultry feed or foraging for themselves in the vegetation. In many cases there is corn for them to peck at too. They are not fed growth hormones or antibiotics, and they are not packed in body to body fifteen thousand to a shed in the same way as intensively farmed birds. And if the chicken pieces you buy are unlabelled then that is how they will have been produced.

And have you ever tried making stock from the bones of intensively farmed birds? You might as well use dishwater as the liquid you get from their weak, brittle bones. With free-range birds your broth will be rich and wholesome and it will set to a golden wobbly jelly. If I cannot convince you of the rewards of buying traditionally reared poultry then I recommend you pick up a copy of Frances Bissell's *Real Meat Cookbook*, in which she puts forward a much stronger case.

Choosing the Right Cut

You cannot roast a chicken in 30 minutes. Unless it's a poussin, which I consider such a poor, tasteless little thing as to be not worth turning on the oven for. All the recipes that follow are for chicken pieces, the joints that you buy at the butcher's or, in emergency, at the supermarket. These are the practical answer for those who want a chicken dinner in half an hour. It is worth bearing in mind that butchers' cuts are normally from larger birds than the supermarket's, and free range generally larger still.

Whole legs

These L-shaped cuts include both the thigh and the drumstick. They will cook in 30 minutes, and have the mixed blessing of being on the bone. I say mixed blessing because although I suspect the flavour of meat cooked on the bone to be better, they do take longer to cook. They are large joints, particularly free-range legs from the butcher, and are the very devil to cook through to the bone.

Thighs

Buy the ones on the bone. These short, thick cuts of brown meat offer good eating, with plenty of flavour, a little fat to baste the meat as it cooks, and are often sold at a reasonable price. They also fit neatly in a baking dish, which is more than you can say for a whole leg. Good for grilling, pan-frying and flash-roasting.

Drumsticks

Hopeless for grilling as the thin end dries out before the thick end is ready. Good flavour, though, and with the added advantage of being easy to pick up and gnaw.

Breasts

The majority of these are sold off the bone. I remain unconvinced that this is a good thing, as they offer little enough in the way of succulence as it is, and are famous for drying out as they cook. Perhaps the best cut for poaching in stock for summer eating. Generally considered to be the best meat on the bird and sold at a premium, though to my mind extremely overrated in terms of flavour. If I am having a roast chicken, I eat the legs and wings and give the breast meat to the cat.

Supremes

These are the breast joints with their fillet attached. Huge hunks of white meat, the fillets have a habit of falling off, or worse, concealing the fact that the rest of the cut is not quite cooked. My advice is to tear them off and make a stroganoff with them tomorrow.

Fillets

These are the long, flat flaps of meat attached to the breast. Some supermarkets are selling packs of them at keen prices. A lean cut that cooks quickly. Ideal for flash-frying. The quickest cooking of all chicken cuts.

Wings

Juicy, scrunchy little morsels that most people waste by boiling up for stock. True, you do need quite a few per person but they are as cheap as can be. Get to the supermarket early, though, as they never stock enough and word is getting round. They have a delightful habit of going sticky, crunchy and chewy when roasted. Cooked with olive oil, lemon and garlic till golden, these are the best bits of all. Especially where the points stick to the roasting pan. Strictly for those who are not too grand to lick their fingers.

A Word about Buying Skinless Chicken Breasts

Don't. Can there be anything more joyless than a supermarket shrink-wrapped tray of skinned chicken breasts? Sitting in their pretty blue polystyrene tray like a row of newly born rodents. No skin to hold in the juices, no skin to baste the meat as it cooks, no skin to go crisp and char deliciously at the edges. Sure, there's no fat either, but if it's fat-free cooking you're after then you have bought the wrong book.

A Few Good Things to Eat with Chicken

....

• spinach leaves, cooked in a covered pan with a little lemon juice till they wilt, about 1 minute, and then drizzled with olive oil
• fresh peas (you can buy them ready shelled in some chain stores), simmered in butter and olive oil, and then tossed with chopped parsley and tarragon
• a bowl of baby green leaves, the sort that come ready washed in cellophane bags from the supermarket
• boiled white rice into which you have stirred butter, parsley, almonds and golden raisins
• the Slob's Version of Mash on page 69
• radicchio, sliced in half and brushed with olive oil, and then grilled
• broad beans, cooked for 7–8 minutes in butter and olive oil, and then tossed with chopped parsley and black pepper

- buttered noodles
- breadcrumbs, fresh and white, cooked in a frying-pan with melted butter till golden, about 10 minutes
- sliced mushrooms, sautéed in butter till tender with a teaspoon of ground coriander
- couscous, soaked for 15 minutes in an equal amount of water, and then rubbed through your fingers to separate the grains: bake, covered with foil, for 15–20 minutes, and then stir in a large knob of butter and a handful of salted cashew nuts
- raw fennel, sliced almost paper thin and then tossed with a mixture of lemon juice, olive oil and black pepper; be more generous with the oil than you would be for a salad dressing

The 30-Minute Roast Chicken

....

I said earlier that you cannot roast a chicken in 30 minutes. But you can roast *some* chicken in 30 minutes. (Thirty-five actually, but let's not fall out over 5 minutes.)

Heat the oven to 225°C/425°F (gas mark 7). Heat the butter and oil in an ovenproof dish such as a large Le Creuset or a roasting tin and sauté the chicken pieces and potatoes till the skin is golden, about 3 minutes on each side. The tin should be large enough for the pieces not to touch. Scatter over the herbes de Provence and squeeze over the lemon. By all means add a clove or two of garlic if you like. Grind over some salt and pepper. Put the chicken into the oven and roast for 30 minutes, basting once with the pan juices. Remove the chicken to a warm dish and put back into the oven.

Pour off half the butter and oil from the roasting tin, slosh in the glass of wine, place the dish on the heat and boil for 2 minutes. Season with salt and pepper and pour over the chicken. Serve with crusty bread and a salad to mop up the buttery, winy juices.

For 2
•
50g/2oz butter

I tablespoon olive oil

4 large chicken pieces on the bone, breasts, thighs, etc.

8 new potatoes, cut in half

I scant tablespoon herbes de Provence

½ lemon

I–2 cloves of garlic, if you like

a wineglass of dry white wine

Flash-fried Moroccan Chicken

Photograph opposite page 193

....

For 2

•

350g/12oz chicken fillets or boned pieces

I fresh red chilli pepper, seeded and finely chopped

I teaspoon crushed dried chilli pepper

2 cloves of garlic, finely chopped

juice of ½ lemon

2 tablespoons olive oil

I teaspoon ground cinnamon

2 tablespoons sultanas or raisins

2 tablespoons pine nuts

I tablespoon chopped mint

I love dusk in Marrakesh. I love the cacophony of sounds and smells as the musicians start and local lads set up their stalls of food, freshly squeezed juices and other good offerings. Some of their cauldrons look (and probably are) sinister, but others are tempting enough. A chicken leg, grilled over coals and smothered with raisins, pine nuts and a mind-blowing quantity of garlic is one of the best things I have eaten there. A bowl of dishwater flavoured with chilli the worst. This is my somewhat wimpish version of the former.

Place the chicken pieces in a shallow dish. Mix together the fresh and dried chillies, garlic, lemon, half the olive oil, cinnamon, sultanas or raisins and pine nuts, and then pour over the chicken. Leave for 20 minutes or so. An hour would be better if you have it.

Heat the remaining oil in a shallow pan; when it sizzles add the chicken pieces. Cook over high heat till golden brown and then turn them over and cook the other side. Pour in the marinade ingredients and bring to the boil, season with salt and pepper, and scatter over the mint. Serve hot with its pan juices.

• In the street I ate this with bread, but couscous would be my first choice here, the quick-cooking variety. For this amount of chicken I suggest 225g/8oz couscous, soaked for 15 minutes in cold water and then seasoned with salt and black pepper and steamed in a colander (a few grains will escape into the cooking water, but no matter) for 15 minutes. Fluff up with a fork and stir in a generous knob of butter before serving

• A plate of sliced oranges drizzled with olive oil and dusted with coarsely ground black pepper and a hint (and I mean a hint) of ground cinnamon, would be another choice

Stir-fried Chicken

....

Chop. Chop. Hot pan. Stir. Fry. Stir. Fry.

Prepare all the ingredients. You won't have time to chop as you cook. Shred the chicken into thin strips. Cut the broccoli into florets or top and tail the mange-tout. Slice the garlic thinly. Shred the ginger. Mix together the sauce ingredients. Get all the other ingredients out of the cupboard.

Put the chicken breast into a small bowl. Mix with the soy, wine or sherry, egg white and cornflour. Stir. It may go a little lumpy, but no matter. Set aside for 10 minutes. Get the wok hot, or a big frying-pan, it doesn't really matter. When the pan is hot pour in the oil. As the oil begins to smoke add the garlic. Now quickly add the ginger. Don't let them burn. When they sizzle add the spring onions. Fry and stir; then add the chicken. Fry for a few seconds and then stir. Fry, then stir again. Keep cooking and moving the food round till the chicken starts to turn golden.

Add the green vegetables. Fry and stir for 2–3 minutes till the vegetables are cooked. Pour in the mixture of soy sauce, wine or sherry, salt and sesame oil. Stir-fry for 2 minutes more. Eat.

For 2, with rice – or not
•
225g/8oz boned chicken breast
100g/4oz broccoli or mange-tout
2 cloves of garlic
2.5cm/1 inch knob of fresh root ginger, peeled
1 tablespoon light soy sauce
1 tablespoon rice wine or dry sherry
1 egg white, lightly beaten
2 teaspoons cornflour
4 tablespoons groundnut oil
4 spring onions, shredded

For the sauce:
•
1 tablespoon light soy sauce
1 tablespoon rice wine or dry sherry
1 teaspoon sesame oil

▶ This is a basic stir-fried chicken with a thin sauce. For something more unctuous use a little thickener in the final sauce. Potato flour is traditional. Cornflour will do. Add 2 teaspoons cornflour dissolved in 2 tablespoons water to the sauce ingredients. Remove from the heat as soon as the sauce starts to thicken

▶ I cannot impress upon you enough the importance of having a hot pan when you stir-fry. Even if it does spit and pop

Thai Green Curry Paste

············

6 medium-hot green chilli peppers, about 5cm/2 inches long, seeded and chopped

2 stalks of lemon grass, chopped

2 tablespoons chopped coriander leaves (and its root if possible)

1 teaspoon ground cumin

2.5cm/1 inch knob of fresh root ginger, peeled and chopped (if you can get galangal, use it)

2 shallots, finely chopped

1 teaspoon coriander seeds

3 cloves of garlic

1 teaspoon black peppercorns

1 teaspoon chopped lime zest

1 tablespoon lime juice

I love green curries, especially the ones scented with basil or coriander, but have always avoided making them as I thought the green curry paste would be time consuming and the ingredients impossible to find. Wrong. It actually takes all of 10 minutes (and 9 of those is peeling the lime, and chopping the garlic, ginger and shallot) to make this lively, hot, versatile paste.

There is one, and only one, ingredient in this hot, fresh-tasting mix that you will not find in a decent supermarket: galangal. This knobbly, pinkish tuber looks like a cross between a ginger root and the flag irises in my garden. Its gingery, peppery, lemon flavour is hard to simulate, but Thai friends assure me it is not the end of the world if you miss it out. Their trick in desperate moments is to add ginger and a little lime juice instead. If you are passing, it is available in (or usually outside) oriental greengrocers, where it can also be bought dried. Occasionally I have seen it at branches of one of the major supermarkets.

Whizz to a paste in a blender, adding a little more lime juice if it sticks.

··

▶ *Now that you have made the paste you can use a little for either of the following recipes; store the remainder for up to a week in a screw-top jar in the fridge. Like pesto*

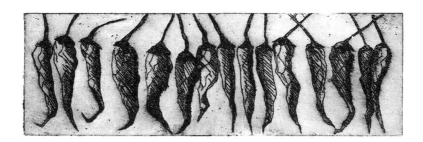

Quick Green Chicken Curry

....

Photograph between pages 192 and 193

The lime leaves are available in cute little packets from good supermarkets and in bunches from oriental grocers. They are essential here. I have found nothing else that will give the unique tart freshness they contribute. A beautiful, highly fragrant supper.

Cut the chicken into large bite-sized pieces. Gently bring the coconut milk to near boiling, but do not let it do so. In a shallow-sided pan, fry the chicken pieces in the oil till golden, about 2 minutes over a high heat. Stir the curry paste into the coconut milk, add salt and the lime leaves. Pour the warm, spiced coconut milk over the chicken and simmer, very gently, for 12 minutes. Scatter over the shredded basil leaves. Their peppery scent will rise immediately.

For 2, with rice
•
350g/12oz boned chicken breast
350ml/12fl oz coconut milk
1 tablespoon groundnut oil
2 tablespoons green curry paste
8 kaffir lime leaves
3 tablespoons basil leaves, shredded

Stir-fried Chicken with Basil

....

A idea ripped off from Keith Floyd. Who ripped it off from a street-stall cook in Thailand. I have tailored it very slightly to suit my own taste. Hey ho, another traditional dish lost to convenience and the timidity of the Western palate.

Heat the oil in a wok or frying-pan. Stir in the green curry paste. Throw in the chicken and stir-fry quickly over a high heat, stirring and tossing it in the oil and paste for 2–3 minutes. Add the coconut milk, sugar, fish sauce and chilli peppers. Cook for 5 minutes, stirring well. Just before serving, toss in the basil leaves. Pop a spoonful of coconut cream on top of each serving. Excellent with steamed rice.

For 3 (he says 4)
•
3 tablespoons vegetable oil
3 tablespoons green curry paste
450g/1lb boned chicken, thinly sliced
50ml/2fl oz coconut milk
2 tablespoons brown sugar
2 tablespoons fish sauce
2 tablespoons seeded and sliced mixed red and green chilli peppers
2 fistfuls of basil leaves
3 tablespoons coconut cream

Chow Mein

············

For 2

•

100g/4oz boned chicken breast

75g/3oz cooked or cured ham or sausage (this can be cold roast pork, prosciutto or even salami)

1 tablespoon light soy sauce

1 tablespoon rice wine or dry sherry

1 tablespoon sesame oil

250g/9oz dried egg noodles

1 tablespoon groundnut oil

2 cloves of garlic, finely sliced

a handful of French beans or mange-tout

4 spring onions, finely chopped

A standard dish on every Cantonese take-away menu – it means, literally, stir-fried noodles. In my experience it can be quite ghastly, and often the kitchen's way of getting shot of those embarrassing little bits hanging around in the fridge – at least that's how it seems. Properly made, though, chow mein is a perfectly respectable dish. Freshly cooked egg noodles, shredded chicken, a little ham or sausage lubricated with soy and rice wine (I use dry sherry), and made savoury with spring onion, garlic, soy and sesame oil. A welcome crunch comes from the addition of green beans, mange-tout or bean sprouts.

Cut the chicken breast diagonally into thin strips, but not so thin that it will dry out as it cooks. Cut the ham or sausage into similarly sized pieces. In a bowl combine the chicken with half the soy, wine or sherry and sesame oil. Let the chicken sit in the liquids, seasoned with salt and pepper, for 15 minutes.

Cook the noodles in boiling salted water. They should be tender 3–4 minutes after the water has returned to the boil. Drain the noodles, rinse them under running water to stop them cooking and set aside. Tossing them in a tiny drizzle of the groundnut oil will prevent them sticking together. Get the wok hot. Or the frying-pan – it really doesn't matter here. Pour in half of the remaining groundnut oil. When the oil is really hot, when you can see a little smoke rising from it, add the chicken and the shredded pork or sausage. Expect lots of spluttering. Cook over a high heat for 2 minutes, stirring continuously. Tip the cooked meat out on to a warm plate.

Reheat the wok, pour in any remaining groundnut oil and when it is hot add the garlic and green vegetables. As the garlic colours, start to stir the mixture round so that everything cooks easily. Add the drained noodles, cooked meats and fry and stir till hot through, about 1 minute, maybe 2. Pour in the remaining soy, sherry and sesame oil. Add the spring onions, fry and stir for a last 2–3 minutes, and eat while sizzling hot.

▶ **O**f course, the only set ingredients are the noodles, the flavourings and the liquids. The rest is as variable as your imagination. Though personally I wouldn't stray far from pork, chicken, ham, prawns, broccoli, mange-tout (despite the fact I am not really very fond of them), French beans, squid, scallops and bean sprouts

▶ **Y**es, of course you can use leftovers of cold meat and chicken. Just remember that chow mein is not Chinese for dustbin

Hoisin Chicken with Walnuts and Mushrooms

A doddle.

Cut the chicken breast into 2.5cm/1 inch cubes. Put into a bowl with the wine or sherry, cornflour, egg white and a little salt and pepper. Set aside for 15 minutes while you make the salad, cook the rice or whatever.

Set a wok over high heat. When it is really hot pour in the oil. When the oil is just starting to smoke add the garlic and fry till golden nut brown. But stop before it turns dark brown, when it will be bitter. Add the spring onions. Fry for 30 seconds and then add the chicken. Cook for 2 minutes. Lift out with a scoop or draining spoon and set aside. Add the mushrooms. Fry till tender and cooked right through – about 4–5 minutes – moving all the ingredients around with chopsticks or a scoop. Toss in the walnut pieces; if they colour a little it is all to the good.

Add the hoisin sauce, stir, and then return the chicken, with the bits of garlic and spring onion stuck to it, to the wok. Toss the chicken, mushrooms and walnuts in the sauce. When all is coated and sizzling, turn out on to warm plates or bowls.

For 2

•

450g/1lb boned chicken breasts

1 tablespoon rice wine or dry sherry

2 teaspoons cornflour

1 egg white, lightly beaten

4 tablespoons groundnut oil

3 cloves of garlic, sliced

4 spring onions, chopped

175g/6oz chestnut or button mushrooms, sliced

4 tablespoons walnut pieces

3 tablespoons hoisin sauce

Chinese Noodles with Chicken and Mushrooms

....

Photograph opposite page 64

Enough for 2 as a main dish, or 4 if you are serving another dish alongside.

•

225g/8oz dried egg noodles

1 red onion

1 tablespoon groundnut oil

4cm/1½ inch knob of fresh root ginger, peeled

2 cloves of garlic

350g/12oz boned chicken breast, cut into 2.5cm/1 inch strips

225g/8oz large brown mushrooms

2 tablespoons dark soy sauce

2 tablespoons rice wine or dry sherry

2 teaspoons cornflour dissolved in 2 tablespoons cold water

coriander leaves

Comforting, slightly doughy, Chinese noodles are a useful cupboard standby and a substantial base when you want to make a packet of mushrooms and a chicken breast into supper for two.

Cook the noodles in boiling salted water for 4 minutes. Drain and run cold water through them to stop them cooking. Peel and slice the onion into thin rings. Heat the oil in a wok or frying-pan; when it is hot add the onion rings, and stir till they start to soften. The heat should be quite high. Though not so high that you cannot control the cooking. Add the ginger and garlic. Continue frying and stirring till the garlic colours – it should be golden brown rather than the usual pale gold. Throw in the chicken, which should splutter a little if the oil is hot enough. Stir the mixture only when the chicken is gold on one side; leave to cook and then stir again.

Meanwhile, slice the mushrooms and add them. Continue cooking till the mushrooms are tender, about 4 minutes, adding more oil if they soak it all up. When all is tender and sizzling sprinkle over the soy sauce and wine or sherry. You will get a cloud of steam. Stir and add the cornflour mixture. Stir quickly, and then, as the mixture starts to thicken, drop the drained noodles into the pan. Toss the mixture round for a few seconds and then scoop out on to warm plates or bowls. Scatter over a few coriander leaves and eat while all is hot.

Grilled Chicken

....

I have already said (in *Real Fast Food*) that there is little I would rather eat than a piece of chicken that has been grilled over an open fire. It would be a leg, not a breast, boned and flattened. It would have been brushed with a little olive oil, seasoned with coarsely ground pepper and grilled over embers, its fleshy juice and its skin slightly charred. The only addition would be half a lemon on the side of my plate, and a bowl of green leaves to mop up the savoury, lemony juices and flecks of black from the chicken skin.

I still stand very firmly by that, and would add that I have had much success cooking said chicken on my ridged cast-iron grill pan that sits on the hob (twenty quid and worth every penny).

A Few Notes on the Perfect Grilled Chicken

• Choose a free-range bird – it has had a happier life and will taste better
• Legs always eat better than breasts when grilled. They stay moist while other cuts tend to dry out
• Marinate if you have time. Half an hour is pretty much the minimum, though a thicker marinade will form a crust round the chicken. But nothing will permeate in 10 minutes
• A boned leg gives the juiciest grill. Cut the tendons round the thin end of the leg and make a cut up the inside leg right through to the bone. Beaver away with your knife at the knuckle in the middle, prising and cutting the flesh from the bone. It is easy to find the bone at the fat (thigh) end. Just separate the flesh from the bone with your knife. You should be left with a fairly rectangular piece of chicken and a relatively clean bone. There may be a slight tear in the middle, but no matter. Cut away the toughest of the long white tendons. Rub with oil and season and you are ready for grilling
• Get the grill hot. A cast-iron pan works better than an overhead grill. If you have a charcoal grill, cherish it. Oil the food, not the grill. When the pan is seriously hot slam the chicken down, skin side first, then press the meat

down on to the grill with a spatula. Turn it over and lower the heat to cook it through

• Expect a boned leg to take about 10 minutes to cook through, turning once

• Season with pepper before and during cooking, salt afterwards. At least that's the way I do it. It just seems to taste better

I offer a few ideas in the way of embellishment for when you tire of such plain and simple fare.

Grilled Chicken in a Greek Marinade

Soak the boned chicken leg or breast in a marinade of 175ml/6fl oz olive oil, the juice of a lemon, the juice from a small grated onion, 2 teaspoons dried oregano and a generous grinding of black pepper, for as long as you can up to 12 hours. (Any longer and it will start to go woolly.) Grill till slightly charred and tender, and then sprinkle with sea salt, crushed a little between the fingers.

With an Egyptian Spice Mix

A Middle Eastern classic seasoning, from Claudia Roden's recipe. Scaled down but still too much. It will keep, in a tin. Toast the following ingredients separately in a frying-pan over a gentle heat till fragrant, a mere 3–4 minutes, maybe less, maybe more, depending on your interpretation of the word gentle and the individual spices: 75g/3oz sesame seeds, 25g/1oz coriander seeds, 25g/1oz hazelnuts, 25g/1oz ground cumin, generous amounts of salt and black pepper. Crush the seeds, nuts, and seasonings to a coarse powder. A short burst in the coffee grinder will do it, or a while longer in the pestle and mortar. When grilled, dip each forkful of hot chicken first into a fruity olive oil and then into the seasoning.

With Coriander Aïoli

An idea I picked up in Latin America, but made the cheat's way. Whizz a chopped, small green chilli pepper and a large clove of garlic with 150ml/5fl oz of good-quality shop-bought mayonnaise. Whizz in a handful of chopped coriander and a squeeze of lemon. Scoop into a bowl and drizzle over a tablespoon of very good olive oil. Spread it over the hot grilled chicken as you eat.

Mix equal quantities of salt and ground pepper with twice the total amount of dried mint. Sprinkle it over the chicken after grilling.

Toast a small baguette, split in half, lightly on the cut sides. Slather with butter into which you have stirred both crushed garlic and chopped parsley, and then add the chicken, straight from the grill. Squeeze over the juice from half a lemon, and press the other half on top. The garlic butter and the chicken juices will probably run down your chin, if not your sleeve.

With Middle Eastern Seasoning

In a Hot Sandwich with Garlic Butter

Crisp Spiced Grilled Chicken

....

Photograph opposite page 192

A Middle Eastern way to perk up a chicken piece.

In a small bowl make a paste with the olive oil, cumin, coriander, ground pepper, garlic (crushed to a paste with a little salt), pepper, parsley and lemon. Rub the paste over the chicken pieces, which can be the brown or white meat, and set aside for as long as you can. Fifteen minutes is long enough.

Meanwhile, get the grill really hot. The best results come from using a ridged cast-iron grill pan, one that sits on the hob. Place the chicken pieces on the grill, cook quickly to crisp the skin, but take care not to burn the spices, and then turn down the heat and cook until tender all the way through. About 12 minutes, turning once. Scatter with coriander, sprinkle over a little salt and serve with slices of lime and crusty bread.

For 2

•

3 tablespoons olive oil

2 teaspoons ground cumin

1 tablespoon ground coriander

½ teaspoon ground pepper

3 cloves of garlic

1 hot red chilli pepper, chopped

2 tablespoons chopped parsley

juice of ½ lemon

4 boned chicken pieces

coriander leaves

slices of lime, to serve

▶ *Little meat is grilled in the Middle East without having first been marinated. I wish I was the sort of person who could get himself organized enough to soak his chicken pieces in olive oil, cumin, coriander and garlic before I go out for the day, but I really cannot face a clove of garlic in the morning. I get round this affliction by anointing my chicken with a thicker version of the same when I come home. A marinade mixture that is more like a savoury paste. It has almost the same effect, but with the advantage of not making the meat wet and difficult to brown. Some marinated meat is infuriatingly difficult to get a golden, succulent coat to, it just sulks and stews*

Coconut and Coriander Chicken

For 2

•

1 teaspoon cumin seeds

1 teaspoon mustard seeds

1 teaspoon coriander seeds

1 teaspoon ground turmeric

1 small, hot green chilli pepper, seeded and chopped

2.5cm/1 inch knob of fresh root ginger, peeled and grated

2 cloves of garlic, crushed

100ml/4fl oz double cream

4 chicken pieces on the bone, thighs, drumsticks, or breasts

2 tablespoons groundnut oil

1 medium onion, chopped

225ml/8fl oz coconut milk

chopped coriander leaves

An attempt to repeat a chicken dish I ate at a beach hut in Colva, on the west coast of India. My notes, which made sense at the time, are rather vague about how much chilli actually went in. I have erred on the timid side. Chilli bores can happily double the quantity.

Put the cumin, mustard and coriander seeds into a dry frying-pan over a low to medium heat. Cook for a minute or two till their fragrance rises and the mustard seeds start to pop. Add the turmeric. Tip into a spice mill or a coffee grinder and whizz to powder, or grind for 3–4 minutes using a pestle and mortar.

Mix with the chopped chilli, grated ginger, crushed garlic and the cream. Place the chicken in a shallow dish and scoop the spice paste over them.

Heat the oil in a shallow pan and cook the onion until soft and golden, about 5–6 minutes, then add the chicken and paste from the marinade. As the chicken colours pour in the coconut milk and season with salt and pepper. Simmer (do not boil) for 15–20 minutes till the chicken is cooked through. Sprinkle over the coriander leaves and serve.

Chicken with Garlic, Cider and Cream

....

A voluptuous, ivory-coloured sauce that illustrates how sweet and mellow garlic can become when it is blanched in boiling water before being cooked. Accompany with French beans, properly cooked, not just dunked into boiling water, or continue the pale and interesting theme with bitter chicory, split lengthways, buttered and grilled till tender.

Drop the garlic cloves into a small, deep pan of boiling water. Blanch them for 4 minutes, by which time they will be paler in colour and have softened a little. Scoop them out with a draining spoon and remove the cloves from their skins. They should pop out satisfyingly when squeezed between your fingers.

Heat the oil in a shallow pan and melt the butter in it. When they start to sizzle lightly, fry the chicken breasts, skin side down first, till golden on both sides. A matter of 2–3 minutes. Turn down the heat, as low as it will go, add the garlic and a bay leaf if there is one around, and cover the pan with a lid. Cook gently till the chicken is cooked right through and the cloves are very soft, about 15–20 minutes. The butter and oil should be a rich golden colour; do not let them brown.

Lift out the chicken and set aside. Turn up the heat, pour in the cider and bring to the boil. Mash the garlic into the bubbling cider with a wooden spatula, scraping the tasty, crusty bits that have caught on the pan into the liquid. When the cider has almost evaporated and you have a sweet-smelling golden slush, pour in most of the cream, add a little salt and pepper from the mill, then taste, adding more cream if you wish. Return the chicken to the pan. Let the sauce bubble for 2–3 minutes, and then serve.

For 2
•

8 fat cloves of garlic (I know that sounds a lot, but trust me)

50ml/2fl oz olive oil

25g/1oz butter

2 large chicken breasts, skin on and small bone attached

a bay leaf, if you have one

100ml/4fl oz dry cider

75–100ml/3–4fl oz cream, single or double

Creamy Curry-powder Chicken

....

For 2, with rice

•

4 chicken pieces on the bone

50g/2oz butter

1 tablespoon groundnut oil

1 large onion, chopped

2 plump cloves of garlic, finely sliced

2 tablespoons curry powder, a decent brand, and from a newly opened tin

2 dessert apples, cored and diced

300ml/½ pint good chicken stock

100ml/4fl oz double cream

There are some horrible mixtures sold in the name of curry powder, but there are also some fragrant and well-balanced ones. I shall not name names because today's good brand is tomorrow's survivor on past glories, so I leave you to find one you trust.

Season the chicken with salt and pepper. Heat together the butter and oil in a shallow pan and cook the chicken till the skin is golden, about 4 minutes on each side. Add the chopped onion and the garlic, and cook till soft and golden. Sprinkle over the curry powder, add the apple and cook for 2 minutes. Pour in the chicken stock and simmer for 15 minutes.

When the juices have reduced and the chicken is tender and cooked right through, pour in the cream. Bring to the boil and serve, adding salt and pepper if necessary.

A Quick and Creamy Chicken Curry
············

I look for fragrance rather than heat in a curry. I am more interested in mellow, warm spicing than mind-blowing heat, and prefer my curries creamy rather than dry. This quick, no-doubt unauthentic version is rich with mild spices, cumin, ginger and cardamon, and is finished with yoghurt, cream and coriander leaves. Rice would be nice, or the dal on page 236.

Lightly brown the chicken in half the oil in a deep-sided pan over a high heat. Remove the chicken. Cook the onion, garlic, ginger and chilli in the remaining oil. Remove the black seeds from the cardamon pods and crush them, either using a pestle and mortar or in a small bowl with the end of a rolling-pin. When the onion is soft add the cardamom, cumin and turmeric and fry over a medium heat.

Return the chicken to the pan, pour in the stock and bring to the boil. Season with salt and pepper, cover and simmer till the chicken is cooked; about 20 minutes, depending on the cuts of chicken. When the meat is tender, turn the heat right down and stir in the yoghurt and the cream. Warm through gently over a low heat, then stir in the lemon juice and coriander, and serve.

For 2
•

6 chicken pieces, breasts and legs, on the bone
2 tablespoons groundnut oil
I medium onion, chopped
4 cloves of garlic, thinly sliced
4cm/1½ inch knob of fresh root ginger, peeled and grated
I medium-sized, medium-hot red chilli pepper, seeded and chopped
8 green cardamom pods
I teaspoon ground cumin
I tablespoon ground turmeric
200ml/7fl oz good chicken stock
100ml/4fl oz yoghurt
75ml/3fl oz double cream
I tablespoon lemon juice
I tablespoon chopped coriander leaves

Quick Korma

....

For 2, generously

•

50g/2oz butter

2 medium onions, sliced

3 large cloves of garlic, thinly sliced

4cm/1½ inch knob of fresh root ginger, peeled and grated

1 teaspoon ground cumin

½ teaspoon ground cardamom seeds from 6 green cardamom pods lightly crushed

½ teaspoon ground turmeric

½ teaspoon chilli powder

50g/2oz shelled cashews or almonds

2 bay leaves

2 large, boned chicken breasts

150ml/5fl oz yoghurt

150ml/5fl oz double cream

2 tablespoons chopped coriander leaves

A contradiction in terms if ever there was one. Korma is a form of slow cooking where the flavour of the spices is gradually drawn out and the meat slowly stews into melting tenderness. Yet speeded up it is actually not so bad, except that you only have 30 minutes, or just over, to inhale the magical fragrance, instead of the traditional 2 hours. Some will find my version pure heresy. I am only making something for supper, you know – not entertaining a Moghul emperor.

Melt the butter in a deep, heavy-bottomed casserole, add the onions, garlic and ginger, and cook for about 5 minutes till golden. It is essential not to burn the butter; add a little oil if it is browning. Add the spices, nuts and bay leaves, stir, and cook for 3 minutes, stirring almost continuously.

Cut the chicken into large bite-sized pieces. Add to the casserole and when it has coloured a little pour in 225ml/8fl oz boiling water. Season with salt and pepper and leave to simmer on a reasonably high heat till the chicken is tender, about 15 minutes. Mix the yoghurt and cream and stir into the chicken and spice mixture. Simmer slowly, almost imperceptibly, for 4–5 minutes. If it boils it will curdle. I promise. Scatter over the coriander and serve with pilaf or bread to soak up the nutty, creamy juices.

....

▶ *Korma is the Indian term for braising. The meat is gently cooked with onions and spices, and then finished with yoghurt and cream. The gentle spices, ginger, cumin, mace, cinnamon and cardamom, are most often used, while the small amount of chilli is tempered by the dairy products. Tradition decrees such dishes be served with a fragrant saffron pilaf*

Chicken with Lemon and Olives

....

Chicken simmered slowly with spices, onions, lemons and olives is an ancient Moroccan dish. I first came across it in a restaurant in Marrakesh, hidden down an alleyway. A rather dubious alleyway, now I come to think of it. This is my version, bastardized for the sake of speed. Mine lacks the intensity of flavour you can only achieve by marinating the chicken overnight (in a slightly lighter mixture), from simmering slowly for a couple of hours, and using preserved lemons. But I think my versions wins on texture (in traditional versions the chicken falls apart) and perhaps tastes somewhat more lively. A sprinkling of parsley wouldn't go amiss.

Crush the garlic cloves to a paste with a little salt. Mix with the paprika, cumin, black pepper and half the olive oil. Toss with the chicken and leave as long as you can.

Heat the remaining olive oil in a shallow casserole. Add the chicken pieces and cook on all sides till golden. Lift the chicken out with a draining spoon and add the onion, with a little more oil if it is getting low. Cook, stirring from time to time, till golden, and then add the saffron, the turmeric and the olives. Cook over a medium heat for 2 minutes and then return the chicken to the pan. Pour over the juice of a lemon and 225ml/8fl oz cold water. Slice the second lemon and add to the pan. Bring to the boil, cover with a lid and then simmer till the chicken is cooked, about 15 minutes, basting regularly.

You need about 5 tablespoons of spicy sludge per person; if too much liquid remains, boil hard to reduce it slightly. (You may well find you do not need to.) Check the seasoning, adding salt if necessary, depending on how salty the olives are. Serve the chicken with the sauce spooned over. And with rice pilaf if you wish.

For 2

•

2 plump cloves of garlic, peeled

2 teaspoons paprika

2 teaspoons ground cumin

½ teaspoon ground black pepper

4 tablespoons olive oil

4 butcher's chicken thighs, or 6 supermarket ones, on the bone

I medium onion, finely chopped

I teaspoon saffron threads

2 teaspoons ground turmeric

100g/4oz green olives, stoned

2 large lemons

30-MINUTE STORE-CUPBOARD IDEAS

Lemon Chicken

....

For 2

•

6 chicken pieces, on the bone

juice of 2 large lemons

2 cloves of garlic, crushed to a paste with 1 teaspoon salt

2.5cm/1 inch knob of fresh root ginger, peeled and grated

1 tablespoon groundnut oil

oil for frying

In Indonesia they make a pretty quick fried chicken where the bird is soaked in tamarind juice, garlic, oil and ginger, and then fried. Having arrived at a hotel room at dead of night and with a thirst that could kill, to find the only offering was a forlorn, tepid tetrapack of brown, sour tamarind juice, I have less enthusiasm for it than perhaps I should. I now use their recipe, but with lemon juice instead. A good way to cheer up a supermarket tray of chicken thighs.

Place the chicken in a shallow dish. Mash together the other ingredients and rub into the chicken. Leave for 15 minutes. Heat a half inch or so of groundnut oil in a shallow pan, and then dust the chicken pieces with flour and fry till golden. Turn down the heat, cover with a lid and cook for 7–10 minutes till cooked through. Sprinkle with salt; eat the hot chicken with your fingers.

Mustard and Vinegar Chicken

....

For 2

•

2 boned chicken legs or breasts, batted out if thick

3 tablespoons red-wine vinegar

4 tablespoons Dijon mustard

4 tablespoons olive oil

chopped parsley

Simple, French and utterly delicious.

Place the chicken joints in a shallow dish. Mix the vinegar, mustard and oil, and spread them all over the chicken. Cook under a preheated grill, about 15–20cm/6–8 inches from the heat source, for 8–10 minutes. Turn the chicken over, baste with the somewhat curdled cooking juices, and grill for a further 8 minutes until it has coloured nicely. The juices should run clear when the meat is pierced with a skewer. Scatter over the parsley and eat with bread and a salad.

Parmesan Chicken

....

Crisp, golden chicken with a tart little sauce of capers, anchovies and mustard. Some broccoli might be nice with it, for a change.

Get the grill hot. An overhead one will be most successful for this. With a heavy implement such as a rolling-pin, or with your fist, bat out the chicken breasts so they are no more than 1cm/½ inch thick.

Mix together the Parmesan, breadcrumbs and parsley and tip on to a plate. Dip the breasts into the beaten egg, which you have seasoned with salt and pepper, and then press them down into the cheese and parsley crumbs. Coat both sides of each piece of chicken. Drizzle with a little olive oil, enough to wet the crumbs fully. Place under the preheated grill, about 15–20cm/6–8 inches from the heat, and cook both sides till crisp, about 6 minutes for the first and 4 for the second. Add a little more oil if the underside looks dry.

Meanwhile, make the sauce. Chop together the anchovies and capers, and mix with the other ingredients, beating the oil in as if you were making mayonnaise. You should end up with a barely amalgamated, very piquant dressing. Spoon it over the chicken and serve.

For 2

•

2 large, boned chicken breasts

scant 50g/2oz grated Parmesan cheese

50g/2oz fine, fresh white breadcrumbs

1 tablespoon chopped parsley

1 egg, beaten

olive oil

For the sauce:

4 anchovy fillets, rinsed

1 tablespoon capers, rinsed

2 tablespoons lemon juice

1 tablespoon chopped parsley

2 teaspoons Dijon mustard

5 tablespoons extra virgin olive oil

coarsely ground black pepper

....

▶ If you have a shallow grill, with less than 15–20cm/6–8 inches underneath the heat source, you would do better to pan-fry the crumbed chicken in olive oil

SOME 10-MINUTE STORE-CUPBOARD IDEAS

With Honey and Soy

Slice a couple of boned chicken breasts into strips about as wide as your finger. Toss with 1 tablespoon light soy sauce, the juice of a lime and 1 tablespoon runny honey. Get a wok hot, heat a tablespoon of groundnut oil in it until just smoking and then fry a thinly sliced garlic clove in it. As it starts to turn golden brown (not gold or brown), add the chicken. Fry for 4 minutes, stirring constantly over fierce heat. When golden, pour in the juices and allow all to evaporate. Sprinkle with chopped chives and serve. Particularly good stuffed into a soft floury bap. For 2.

With Orange and Mint

Squeeze 2 juicy oranges and half a large lemon. Mix the juices. Rub a dozen chicken wings with salt and pepper. Brush them with olive oil and cook them in a little butter for 4 minutes till golden, turning once. Pour in the orange and lemon juice – it will sizzle – then boil hard for 2 minutes. Stir a good knob of butter into the juices, scraping up any tasty bits that may be stuck to the pan. Toss in a couple of tablespoons of chopped mint, grind over some black pepper and serve. For 2.

With Spices and Butter

In a small bowl mix 1 tablespoon paprika, 1 tablespoon garam masala, 1 teaspoon ground black peppercorns, 2 cloves of garlic, crushed to a paste, 1 tablespoon lemon juice and 50g/2oz softened butter. Spread generously over a dozen chicken wings and grill them under a medium heat for 4–5 minutes till golden, turning once and basting with the spiced butter. For 2.

AND A NEW WAY WITH TURKEY

Turkey Escalope with Prosciutto and Lemon

....

Photograph between pages 192 and 193

Saltimbocca, the Italian escalope of veal cooked with prosciutto and sage, was the inspiration for this. I cannot claim to be a fan of sage, or veal for that matter, and find the substitution of turkey for the veal and a lemon slice for the sage something of an improvement on the original. You will need a cocktail stick or two to hold the parcels together.

Bat out the steaks with your fist to a thickness of about 5mm/¼ inch. Place a slice of prosciutto on each, folding it over to fit. Put a slice of lemon on each escalope and secure the lemon and prosciutto to the escalope with a cocktail stick. Dust with a little flour on both sides.

Heat the oil in a shallow pan over a high flame. Place the escalopes in the oil and fry for about 2 minutes on each side. When they are golden brown, tip off the oil and place the pan back on the heat. Pour in the wine – the pan will sizzle – then let the liquid almost evaporate.

Lift the escalopes on to warm plates, drop the butter into the pan, still over the heat, and swoosh it round. When the butter and remaining juices have mingled into a rough sauce pour them over the escalopes and scatter over the parsley.

For 3
•
6 turkey breast steaks (they are sold as such at most supermarkets) about 450g/1lb in weight

6 slices of prosciutto

6 slices of lemon

a little flour

2 tablespoons olive oil

100ml/4fl oz dry white wine

50g/2oz butter

chopped flat-leaf parsley

GAME

You may never have thought of game as a fast food. Well, it is. At least some of it is. Partridge, crisply roasted in a hot oven, spiced with juniper and bay, will be ready in 20 minutes or so, quail, the tiniest of the family, can be roasted or grilled in even less time, and pigeon will emerge succulent and tender from the grill in 10.

In season, most supermarkets stock a fair number of game birds, plucked, cleaned and ready for the oven. The flavour will vary from mild to positively piquant, though in my experience the birds from the supermarket tend to be milder than those from the fishmonger. Robust herbs, thyme, rosemary and bay, are the ones you want for game – the fragile varieties cannot compete with game's rich flavours. Best of all, though, are the salty, savoury bones, just the right size to pick up and suck.

Roast Partridge with Mushrooms and Bacon

....

2 partridge, ready for the oven, or 4 if small

75g/3oz butter

100g/4oz mushrooms, any variety

thyme, bay leaves

8 rashers of unsmoked streaky bacon

I am particularly fond of partridge. Chubby little birds, one apiece, make a splendid supper, and will roast to perfection in 20 minutes.

Preheat the oven to 220°C/425°F (gas mark 7). Place the birds in a roasting pan, but not too close together. Stuff a knob of butter about the size of a walnut into each bird. Add the mushrooms to the pan – you had better halve or quarter them if they are large – and season each bird with salt and pepper.

Add a few herbs to the partridge, 3–4 sprigs of thyme and a couple of bay leaves should be enough, and then dot the rest of the butter over the birds. Lay four of the bacon rashers over the birds. Roll up the other four and put them in the pan. Roast in the preheated oven for 20 minutes.

Baste the birds and the mushrooms with the pan juices at least once during cooking. Remove the bacon from the birds' breasts (it is perfectly tasty, so you can add it to the others) and return them to the oven for 5 minutes. Serve with the pan juices (there won't be many but what there is will be delicious), mushrooms and bacon. A dollop of redcurrant jelly and some large, thick potato crisps, a leafy salad and some bread to soak up the juices is all the accompaniment you need.

▶ *Partridge are in season from 1 September to 1 February. Fishmongers and supermarkets will have some in stock at least until January, though supplies tend to become a bit thin later in the season. Go for the English rather than the French, in other words, grey legs rather than red – although the red is larger than the grey partridge, the flavour is less interesting, though only marginally so. Generally sold wrapped in bacon and tied with string, they are neat little things, though I tend to remove the bacon, leaving the string intact, and butter the bird before replacing with my own rashers. With a good strong cook's knife they are easy to cut in half for sautéeing*

Sautéed Partridge with Plums

For 2
•
2 young partridge, ready for the oven, or 4 if very small
50g/2oz butter
a few drops of oil
a sprinkling of plain flour
150ml/5fl oz dry white wine
225g/8oz small ripe plums
225ml/8fl oz double cream

I shall claim no credit for this super idea. It is, in fact, a close adaptation of Nicola Cox's Partridge with Little Plums, from her book *Game Cookery*. I also go along with her suggested accompaniment of bulgur wheat pilaf, a recipe for which is on page 208 of this book – and there are several more in *Real Fast Food*.

Halve the partridge down the length of their bodies with a large heavy cook's knife. Season the pieces with salt and pepper. Heat the butter in a large sauté pan with a few drops of oil to stop the butter burning. Put the halves of partridge into the pan and cook over a medium heat until golden on both sides. Scatter a little flour over them and cook for a minute again on each side.

Add the wine, scraping at the base of the pan to loosen any sediment into the sauce. Cover with a lid and simmer gently for 15 minutes. Add the plums, stoned if you can be bothered, and cook for a further 5 minutes till they have softened. (If by chance you are using unripe fruit, then add even earlier.) Scoop the birds out on to a warm dish. Turn up the heat, pour in the cream and stir gently till thoroughly warm; taste and season, and then return the birds to the pan. Serve hot.

10-Minute Pigeon
....

Or 15-minute pigeon if rare game is not your thing. Most major food stores sell pigeon and when it's young it can be very good – piquant and succulent, particularly if you pick the legs up to eat them. Disaster stories with pigeons are legion, but most involve slow cooking. I now prefer to flash-roast the birds, cut into portions, in a very hot oven.

Cut each of the pigeons into 4 pieces, 2 breasts and 2 small legs. Put the pieces into a flameproof glass, stainless steel or china dish with the wine, oil, herbs, garlic and peppercorns. Set aside for as long as you can – an hour will just suffice, though overnight would be better in terms of flavour. If the worst comes to the worst, 15 minutes will do.

Heat the oven to 240°C/475°F (gas mark 9). Place the breasts on the top shelf of the hot oven and cook for 5 minutes, 6 if the breasts are large. Add the legs and the marinade and cook all for a further 6 minutes or until the birds are cooked to your liking.

Remove the birds to a warm plate to rest – the switched-off oven will do – put the roasting pan over the heat and get the cooking juices really hot; stir in the balsamic vinegar, taste for seasoning and add a little salt and pepper if you wish.

Serve the roast meat, generously sprinkled with coarse salt, with the pan juices and lots of bread.

• cabbage, stir-fried with a little soy, would be a toothsome addition to a plate of pigeon
• the Pan-fried Mushrooms on page 57

For 2
•
2 wood pigeon, prepared
I wineglass of red wine
2 tablespoons olive or nut oil
thyme, a couple of sprigs
I bay leaf
I small clove of garlic, crushed
I teaspoon black peppercorns, roughly crushed
2 teaspoons balsamic vinegar

Partners for pigeon

Grilled Quail

....

For 2

•

4 quail
olive oil
a sprig or two of thyme
lemon, to serve

Tiny, moist little birds with the sweetest flesh imaginable. Most are farmed nowadays, and come neatly packed in twos or fours. Small enough to cook in little more than the time it takes to grill a fish finger, you really need two per person. To be eaten with your hands, hot from the oven, rather than knife and fork. You will need bread to mop up the meagre, but delectably savoury juices.

Heat the grill, rub each quail with a generous amount of olive oil, and then scatter the thyme leaves over them. Place under the preheated hot grill, a good 15cm/6 inches away from the heat.

Cook for 5 minutes on each side, then turn breast up and cook for 2–3 minutes till golden brown. If they show any sign of drying, then anoint them further with olive oil. Remove them from the grill, season with salt and a little coarsely ground black pepper. Squeeze a little lemon juice over the meat as you eat.

Quail accompaniments

• Bread sauce would be nice, but it's a bit of a fiddle for a quick supper; I often just serve some good white bread with my quail
• A blob of wobbly redcurrant or rowan jelly. The softer the better; French brands tend to be softer set and less sweet than English ones
• A salad of spinach leaves and grapes would be my choice; use a simple dressing of walnut oil and lemon juice

Lamb, Pork and Other Meats

There is little that can approach the succulence of grilled, roast or sautéed meat, though I admit it is not the first thing that springs to mind when I am contemplating supper. Over the last few years I have taken to thinking about vegetables, chicken, game and fish before considering meat.

As the quantity of red meat I eat declines, the fussier I become about what I buy and how I cook it. I am lucky in having a butcher who sells meat from named farms, all reared and slaughtered humanely by farmers who care about both livestock and the meat itself.

Having chosen my meat with care, making sure that it is labelled free range at the very least, I am not going simply to bung it under the grill and hope for the best. There are thousands of ideas used throughout the world for a quick meat supper. There are sizzling, spice-laden kebabs from Morocco, creamy pork and mustard sautés from France and, of course, garlic and soy stir-fries from China. And I can assure you that you can make a perfectly fine curry in 30 minutes.

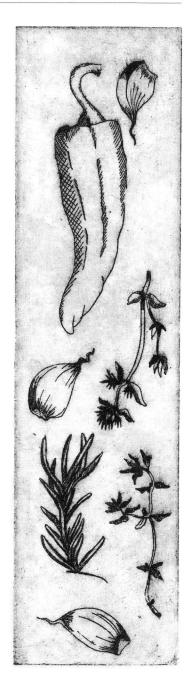

LAMB

Not for me the dinky noisettes of lamb with a puddle of sticky sauce made from reduced stock and garnished with fanned, lightly cooked vegetables and a couple of asparagus spears. Lamb, more than any other meat, demands to be eaten in robust fashion. A chop, grilled till its fat crisps and its bones turn brittle, rich, juicy pink inside, and preferably held in the hand, is the way to eat this naturally free-range meat.

It is flattered by both the wild herbs of Provence and the potent spices of the Middle East. No matter how I try, I cannot share this country's unique love of mint sauce as an accompaniment to a traditional roast. Cumin, coriander and cinnamon, rosemary, thyme and bay, garlic, lemon and olives all have something to offer lamb. Mustard, a mild French one, is magic with lamb, as are the piquant lime pickle of India and the salty preserved lemons of Morocco. Fruit, with the possible exception of tart, dried apricots, mango and fresh redcurrants, is not a marriage made in heaven.

I am convinced that grilling and roasting are the best methods of exploiting lamb's unique succulence, and I tend to lose interest when lamb meets liquid. Stewing either in the French manner with tomatoes and onions or in the Indian way with yoghurt and spices is more suitable for other meats, by which I really mean chicken and pork. At the risk of sounding provincial, I find the smell of stewing lamb, even with fragrant spices, not deeply appetizing. I blame my stepmother, who used to boil breasts of lamb for the dogs, filling the house with a vile smell for hours on end. (She would then throw the fatty, grey carcasses on to the lawn, turning the garden into a scene from *The Hound of the Baskervilles*.)

As something of a peace-offering for those who like Indian spices with lamb, I offer a fast version of a traditional dry curry, thick with garam masala, garlic and tomatoes. Though I will admit that this is not one of the more 'ethnic' sections of the book.

Colour is not always as sound a guide as I was led to believe. The old legend of pale pink lamb with white fat being from the youngest animal is true, but many of the more unusual breeds are blessed with dark meat, almost maroon in colour. Whatever, the fat will be creamy white, brittle and waxy to the touch.

Buying Lamb

The quick cook will have little or no interest, on weekdays at least, in the legs, loins and shoulders so perfect for large weekend gatherings. Cutlets, chops cut from the loin and cubed leg or shoulder offer possibilities, as does the delicious chump chop and the best end of neck, known also as the *carré*.

Choosing the Right Cut

These rather expensive lean rounds of meat are cut from the boned loin. They cook quickly, and have no waste on them, but I prefer to cook meat on the bone, and find noisettes a bit 'dinner-partyish'. If you know what I mean.

Noisettes

This expression covers a multitude of cuts, including plump chump chops cut from the back end and the more elegant cutlets from further up the animal, at the base of the neck, where it joins the saddle. Chops are the quintessential grilling cut. Their bones cook sweet and tasty, and to miss picking them up and gnawing at them for the sake of etiquette is a shameful waste.

Chops

In Middle Eastern cultures this is the food that is threaded on to skewers and grilled over hot coals as the kebab. A much maligned term if ever there was one. Both the leg and shoulder meat are strong enough in flavour to take a serious dose of spice.

Cubed Shoulder or Leg

Also known as a rack. A collection of tender, quick-cooking cutlets, sold in one piece. They make a sublime, tender roast and their layer of fat keeps them moist as they cook. A pair of them, bent round and tied back to back, make that silly dish known as Guard of Honour. Contorted to look like a crown, it is a well-known dinner-party trick in certain circles, complete with ridiculous paper cutlet frills to cover the naked bones. An affected gesture which, like Beef Wellington, is best forgotten.

Best End of Neck

A Few Good Things to Eat with Lamb

....

• A rice pilaf, similar to the one on page 215, scented with cinnamon, cayenne and black pepper, and spiked with almonds and raisins
• Thinly sliced potatoes, simmered till tender in a little water with a crumbled stock cube
• Long green beans, the rounded sort they call the Kenya bean, cooked till slightly limp rather than the crisp norm. There is something about these particular beans that renders them quite tasteless unless cooked within an inch of their lives
• Tiny roast potatoes made from new potatoes cut in half and cooked in butter and oil in a hot oven. A scattering of garlic and rosemary spikes will not go amiss
• A thin gravy made from the pan juices
• Courgettes, sliced as thin as pound coins, steamed for 4 minutes and then sprinkled with raisins and toasted pine nuts
• Toasted pitta bread, the doughier the better. (Wrap the warm bread in a tea towel to discourage them from turning crisp)

30-Minute Roast Lamb

....

For 2

•

2 cloves of garlic

3 tablespoons herbes de Provence

juice of ½ lemon

1 tablespoon olive oil

1 prepared rack of lamb, with about 6 bones in it

A rack of lamb, with its sweet nuggets of flesh and its long, thin bones for gnawing on, is far from the extravagant gesture it once was. Keenly priced and neatly packaged, a six-boned rack of lamb is perfect for two for a Sunday roast, and most supermarkets and many butchers have them there for the asking.

Crush the garlic cloves and mix them with the herbs, lemon and oil, a little salt and generous amount of freshly ground pepper.

Spread this mixture over the lamb, both the fat and the exposed meat. Roast for 20–25 minutes in a preheated hot oven, 200°C/400°F (gas mark 6), which will give you a reasonably pink, though far from rare, roast. Leave to rest for 5 minutes before cutting into chops with a heavy, sharp knife.

• a green salad made with tender, floppy leaves such as *mâche*, chervil, oak-leaf lettuce, to mop up the juices on your plate
• green beans and new potatoes, tossed with olive oil and coarsely chopped parsley

To accompany

▶ *If you fancy a little thin gravy with your lamb, remove the joint from the pan and set in a warm place, put the roasting tin on the gas and pour in a small glass of dry white wine. Scrape away at the bottom of the tin with a spatula to dislodge the herbs and meagre, though delectable, sediment into the gravy. Reduce over a high heat until little more than 3–4 tablespoons are left. Season with salt and pepper and serve, very hot, with the lamb*

Roast Lamb with Mustard and Thyme

Mustard is probably not a first choice for eating with lamb, and I would be the first to agree that a hot English mustard is not right for the job here. But one of the gentler, more aromatic French mustards is a most suitable partner to such sweet and tender meat.

Mix together the mustards, thyme, 4 tablespoons of the olive oil and the crumbs and season with salt and pepper. Spread this all over the meat, both exposed flesh and fat. Pour over 2 tablespoons olive oil.

Roast in a preheated hot oven, 230°C/450°F (gas mark 8), for 25 minutes, until the outside is crisp and the inside is pink. Serve with a salad of green leaves, dressed with lemon juice and olive oil.

For 2
•
2 tablespoons smooth Dijon mustard

2 tablespoons grainy mustard

1 tablespoon chopped thyme

6 tablespoons olive oil

6 tablespoons fresh white breadcrumbs

1 prepared rack of lamb, with about 6 bones in it

Lamb Chops with Onions, Mustard and Chick-pea Purée

....

For 2

•

1 large or 2 medium onions, peeled

1 tablespoon olive oil

1 × 400g/14oz tin chick-peas, drained and rinsed

a sprig of thyme

2 cloves of garlic, peeled and left whole

4 small or 2 large lamb chump chops

50g/2oz butter

3 tablespoons Greek-style yoghurt

6 tablespoons red wine

2 tablespoons grainy Dijon mustard

2 tablespoons chopped parsley

A robust way to eat grilled lamb with red wine, caramelized onions and mustard, with a chick-pea mash to drizzle the mustardy gravy over.

Cut the onions into segments from stalk to root, to give 8–10 wedges of onion. Separate the layers and cook with the oil over a medium heat in a shallow pan. Empty the chick-peas into a pan and cover them with water. Throw in the thyme and garlic. Salt, and simmer for 15 minutes.

When the onions are soft, translucent and starting to brown at the edges push them to one side of the pan and turn up the heat. Place the chops in the pan and cook on both sides till the fat is golden and crisp, the meat browned and the insides pink and juicy. Probably about 4 minutes on each side. Meanwhile, drain the chick-peas, remove the thyme, and mash with a potato masher. Stir in the butter and yoghurt. Season with pepper. Lift the onions, which should be soft with slightly crisp edges by now, and the lamb on to warm plates.

If there is more than a film of fat in the pan, pour it away. Pour in the red wine, scrape any crusty bits from the pan with a wooden spatula, and set over a high heat till half of the wine has evaporated, a matter of a minute or two. Stir in the mustard and most of the parsley. Season with salt and pepper, and simmer for a minute or so till thoroughly hot. Spoon the sauce over the chops and onions. Scatter over the remaining parsley.

Grilled Lamb with Onions and Spices

....

Photograph opposite page 97

I cannot resist the salty, spicy hunks of lamb sold in the streets in Morocco. Hot from the grill, with enough grated onion and red spices to make your lips tingle, they are one of the most delectable examples of street food. Shame on our vile hamburgers in flabby buns.

I cannot quite conjure up the lively spicing and lip-smacking succulence of that Moroccan street lamb at home, but I have come pretty close to it. The trick is to spice the hot meal *after* it leaves the grill. A dollop of hummus and a slipper of pitta bread is my unorthodox accompaniment.

Place the cubed lamb in a dish with the onion, oil and a good grinding of salt and pepper, and set aside for at least 15 minutes, longer if you can. Toast the cumin seeds in a shallow pan over a medium heat and then grind to a powder.

Heat the grill. I use a ridged grill pan over a gas hob, but an overhead grill will do at a push. Remove the meat from the marinade and place on the hot grill pan or under the heated grill. Cook till lightly charred on each side, turning where necessary. Probably about 4 minutes on each side. Warm the pitta bread. Spread lavishly with chutney or lime pickle.

Dust the cooked lamb with the ground paprika and the toasted ground cumin. Season generously with salt. Stuff into the pickle-filled pittas.

For 2

•

450g/1lb cubed lamb (a little fat is all to the good)

1 small onion, very finely chopped or grated

2 tablespoons olive oil

1 tablespoon cumin seeds

paprika

pitta bread and spicy chutney or lime pickle, to serve

The Kebab

....

The Persian kabâb, Greek souvlakia, Turkish kebabi, the seekh kebab of India are all evidence of the magic that occurs when tender lamb is cooked over hot coals. No other cooking method can quite achieve the sublime succulence of slightly charred lamb fat and juicy pink meat. Whether the meat is seasoned with the robust oregano and garlic of Greece or the mouth-puckering hot red pepper and onion of the Moroccan version, it must be the most fragrant of feasts. And is well within the reach of the 30-minute cook.

Of course, cooking over glowing charcoal embers is not realistic other than in the garden during one of our short summers. And that is only when you have spent an hour getting the barbecue (horrid word that) to the right temperature. Most of us must make do with a domestic grill. An overhead one at that. If you have a ridged cast-iron grill pan for cooking on the hob at least you will get something that looks the part. With the bonus that the moisture will run off, the ridges keeping the meat away from the liquid that encourages the meat to stew rather than grill.

If your only experience of kebabs is from one of those grey, fatty lumps of dog-food that rotates on a vertical spit in the local take-away, I urge you to forget it ever happened, and try one of the recipes that follow. Even without a charcoal brazier and the scent of thyme under foot, they are in a different world. You will need some sort of bread to hold the hot meat in, pitta or some such thing.

You will notice a lack of kebabs with tomatoes and peppers threaded on to skewers in this section. This is because I have never quite understood the point of such a presentation. The peppers never achieve any succulence in the few minutes it takes to cook the lamb while the tomatoes just turn to a slush.

Souvlakia

....

I virtually lived off these spicy parcels, bought for the equivalent of a few pence, and wrapped in thin, slightly greasy pitta, when I used to spend a month each summer in Greece. They were copiously spiced with onion and hot pepper, with a slick of thin sour yoghurt to drip through the fingers, rendering them deliciously lickable.

Put the lamb into a deep bowl. Whizz the onion to a mush in a food processor or blender with the oil, garlic, cumin, cayenne and a good grinding of black pepper. Scoop the spicy slush over the lamb cubes. Toss them around a bit. Set aside for as much time as you have. An hour is ideal, though 15 minutes is better than nothing.

Heat the grill. It should be very hot so that the outside of the lamb crisps nicely before the inside is more than pink. Shake any excess marinade from the cubes, then grill till slightly charred but still juicy inside – you will have to test one to see, but it will take about 4–6 minutes on a hot grill tossing them about from time to time to get all sides cooked.

Sprinkle with salt, stuff them into a pitta bread, or not, and drizzle yoghurt over them. Sprinkle the top with chopped raw onion and a dusting of hot cayenne.

For 2

•

350g/12oz cubed lamb

1 medium onion, peeled

50ml/2fl oz olive oil

4 cloves of garlic, peeled

1 teaspoon ground cumin

1 teaspoon cayenne pepper

4 pitta breads

4 tablespoons yoghurt

a little chopped raw onion and a sprinkling of cayenne pepper, to serve

Turkish Lamb Kebabs

....

For 2

•

350g/12oz cubed lamb
juice of 1 lemon
2 tablespoons olive oil
1 tablespoon dried oregano (it is actually better than fresh for this)

I never tire of the lemon as a flavouring for meat or fish, particularly that which has been grilled till faintly crisp outside while retaining succulence within. The Turks and the Greeks have made much of the lemon in their cooking, using it both as marinade and dressing. These kebabs rely on nothing but lemon, pepper and the oregano which grows all over the mountainsides. The ones that the locals haven't built a nightclub on.

Season the lamb with the lemon juice and oregano, and coarsely ground black pepper. Grill, on skewers if you can be bothered, till the outside of each cube of lamb chars slightly at the edges. The inside should remain pink. Assuming that you are not cooking this over the coals of a barbecue, the best results come from using a ridged grill pan over a fierce gas jet, making sure the pan is really hot before you brush on some olive oil and add the meat. Toss the meat around a bit as it browns. Crumble over some flakes of sea salt as soon as it is done to your liking, and eat with a salad of some sort, green leaves or sliced tomatoes drizzled with olive oil.

....

▶ *Sometimes, but not always by any means, kebabs are left to marinate overnight. A traditional Turkish marinade is nothing more than onion juice, to which a bay leaf and some black pepper is added, and perhaps a spoonful of olive oil. Easy enough if you are the lucky sort whose eyes are unaffected by grating onions. I can honestly say that I have found the rubbing of an onion against a grater too painful an experience ever to repeat*

▶ *Add garlic, cayenne pepper, ground cinnamon and cumin to the marinade at will. Leave for a couple of hours before grilling*

Deep-fried Lamb with Cream and Chillies

....

Indian spicing, crisp deep-frying, with ripe mango as a relish provide a succulent mouthful. Last time I made these I accompanied them with an English-style new potato salad sprinkled with chives and pepper, made with thick yoghurt rather than mayonnaise.

Put the lamb cubes into a glass or china bowl. Smash the garlic to a pulp with the flat blade of a knife and a little salt, or in a pestle and mortar. Grate the ginger finely and add it with the garlic, chilli powder and cream to the lamb. Allow to sit for as long as you can, up to an hour, though if 20 minutes is all you have then that will do.

Meanwhile, peel and slice the mango and whizz in the processor or blender to a fine slush, or at least until finely chopped. Stir in the coriander leaves. Put the egg into a bowl and the crumbs on to a plate. Heat about 5cm/ 2 inches of oil in a deep pan (a wok will do) until hot enough to turn a little cube of bread golden very quickly, about 190°C/375°F if you have such a thing as a cooking thermometer. (I have to admit to buying one recently and have found it worthwhile.)

Drop the lamb cubes first into the egg and then into the crumbs, pressing down gently on all sides to encourage the crumbs to stick. Deep-fry the crumbed lamb in the hot fat till crisp and golden, taking care not to overcook. Serve hot, with a dish of the mango and coriander as relish on the side.

For 2

•

350g/12oz cubed lamb
4 cloves of garlic, peeled
5cm/2 inch knob of fresh root ginger, peeled
1 teaspoon chilli powder
4 tablespoons double cream
1 very ripe mango
1 tablespoon coriander leaves
1 egg, beaten
2 handfuls of dry breadcrumbs
groundnut oil for frying

A Quick Lamb Curry

....

For 2

•

25g/1oz butter

1 tablespoon groundnut oil

450g/1lb cubed lamb

1 medium onion, chopped

3 cloves of garlic, crushed

1 cinnamon stick, broken in two

6 green cardamom pods, crushed open

1 teaspoon ground cumin

1 teaspoon ground ginger

1 tablespoon garam masala

1 teaspoon chilli powder

A dry curry, delectably spicy and aromatic rather than blisteringly hot. To be scooped from your plate with any of the Indian breads on sale at the supermarket, warm from the grill or oven.

Melt the butter in a deep-sided frying-pan and add the oil; when it starts to sizzle fry the lamb till just coloured on each side. Remove with a draining spoon. Add the onion and fry till golden, scraping up any residue from the lamb at the same time. Add the garlic and fry for a minute more.

Now add the whole spices. Cook for 2 minutes or until the cardamom pods have coloured a little and then add the ground spices. Cook until their fragrance starts to rise, but make sure they do not burn. Return the lamb to the pan. Pour in 225ml/8fl oz water – you can use meat or vegetable stock if you have some knocking around – and stir thoroughly. Turn the heat to medium and simmer gently till the sauce has thickened, about 10–15 minutes.

Lamb Hash

....

The American 'hash', where meat and potatoes are cooked to a crisp in a shallow pan, works as well with lamb as with the more orthodox corned beef. You will need about 225g/8oz cooked lamb, preferably from a slightly underdone roast. Chop it finely or shred it if that is more suitable to the cut. Fry a large chopped onion in 4 tablespoons dripping or butter till golden, about 5 minutes. Stir in a tablespoon of plain flour. Add about 225g/8oz chopped cooked potatoes and the lamb. Season with salt and pepper – be generous, we are talking about leftovers here – and pour over 225ml/8fl oz stock (a weakly reconstituted cube is a possibility here), cover and simmer for 15 minutes until a crust forms on the bottom, stir it in, and then simmer again. The hash is ready when the bottom is crisp and there is a little liquid left. A deeply savoury dish.

Lamb in Spiced Gravy

....

An Indian spiced cream sauce for leftover lamb. Cut slices of cold roast lamb, as thin as you wish, but no thicker than pound coins. You should aim for about 350g/12oz. Fry a finely chopped onion in a little butter till golden in a casserole, for about 5 minutes, then add some sliced garlic – 2 big cloves will probably be enough. Stir in ½ teaspoon cayenne pepper, 1 tablespoon ground coriander and a small tin of chopped tomatoes and their juice and 225ml/8fl oz stock or, at a push, water. Simmer for 10 minutes. Stir in 100ml/4fl oz soured cream, a teaspoon of garam masala and add the sliced meat. Spoon the sauce over the meat and simmer for 10 minutes.

A Few Other Quick Ideas with Lamb

Tarragon Lamb

Tarragon, the long, thin-leaved aniseed herb, has a certain charm with lamb. A typically French dish, luxurious in its ingredients yet simple enough to reproduce at home, Noisettes d'Agneau à l'Estragon is a quick classic. Sauté 4 noisettes of lamb about 2.5cm/1 inch thick, in a couple of tablespoons of olive oil for 3 minutes on each side. Remove the lamb to a covered, warm plate. Drain off the oil and add a scant 50g/2oz butter. Pour in 4 tablespoons Madeira, a couple of tablespoons of chopped tarragon leaves and 3 tablespoons crème fraîche or double cream. Boil for a minute or two to reduce and concentrate its flavours, and then spoon the sauce over the lamb. A wonderful dish, rich with cream and deep aniseed notes, best eaten with a side dish of wide noodles.

Crumbed Lamb Steaks

Dip some of those boneless lamb steaks, which you have first batted out a little thinner with your fist, in a little flour, beaten egg and then an equal mixture of fresh white breadcrumbs and grated Parmesan cheese. Fry till golden and butter and serve with lemon.

Balsamic Lamb Steaks

Fry 2 lamb steaks in a little butter; 3 minutes on the first side and 2 on the second will do if the heat is high enough and the butter sizzling. Sprinkle a few drops of balsamic vinegar in the pan, salt and pepper the lamb, and serve immediately.

Lamb Chops with Bacon

Salty, smoked bacon is surprisingly good with lamb. Cut up some thick rashers into dice the size of dolly mixtures. Fry them till their fat is golden and then add a little olive oil and sauté your lamb cutlets, chops or steak as usual. Scrape up the golden-brown residue from the pan with a small glass of dry white wine, seasoned with a little salt and some pepper, and then boil it hard for a minute before serving the lamb.

It's worth reminding you of how delicious lamb chops are with fried potatoes. The quickest way is to slice up some of the cold potatoes in the fridge and fry them in olive oil till golden with a little dried thyme and a handful of stoned olives. The potatoes will crumble but no matter. Serve them with grilled chops.

And with Potatoes

You are cooking lamb chops, cutlets or leg steaks in a pan with a little oil or butter, or both. A traditional sauté. When the lamb is almost ready add any of the following:

And a Few Things to Throw in the Pan

- a spoonful of rinsed capers
- a handful of chopped parsley and finely chopped garlic
- a couple of sun-dried tomatoes, sliced into strips
- a few olives, green or black
- a little lemon juice
- two big dollops of the cold gravy from the fridge
- a few shakes of mushroom ketchup

Monday Supper

....

For 1

•

1 heaped tablespoon dripping or fat from the meat, plus the odd sprig of thyme, bay leaf, garlic clove, etc. from the pan

2 big handfuls of leftover pork, chicken, goose, lamb, beef, whatever, off the bone and cut into shreds or cubes, or generally hacked about a bit

2 double handfuls of crisp fresh green cabbage, not leftovers, roughly shredded

a few glugs of red wine

a wineglassful of gravy

I hate those 'good ideas' for using leftovers. Specially the ones where everything is minced and then stuffed into some poor unsuspecting pepper. It's always peppers. Everybody knows that you found the ingredients lurking in the back of the fridge anyway. People write whole books about the subject. The thing that really annoys me is the way these imaginative, frugal cooks manage to miss the whole point. It's the crunchy bits round the pan, the dripping, the garlic and herbs you cooked with the roast, and all the luscious, crusty, gooey bits that are the things worth recycling. Not the Brussels sprouts.

Melt the dripping, or oil if you have none (what did you do with it?) in a wok or large frying-pan. Get it really hot. Throw in the meat, cook for 2 minutes and then add the cabbage, which must be crisp and fresh and dark green. You can use leftover cabbage but I think you may be disappointed by its texture. Fry the cabbage and meat till the greens are vivid and then throw in the wine – 3–4 tablespoons will probably be enough. Boil hard till almost evaporated, about 2 minutes, maybe less, then add the gravy. Season with salt and pepper. Be generous. When all is hot – it must be really hot if it is to be good – scoop on to a warm plate and drink the rest of the wine.

....

▶ *The best version of this I have ever eaten was when I had some leftover* confit *of goose brought back from France and half a cabbage. Possibly the best thing I have ever eaten*

PORK

Pork is the backbone of much of the world's quick meat cookery, either in the form of sausages, bacon and rissoles, or as cured meats such as prosciutto and salami used for snacking on. In China, and to a lesser extent in Thailand, pork features heavily in fast family meals such as the ubiquitous but highly enjoyable stir-fry.

It is hard to talk of Chinese food without some reference to the meat of the pig. It is well known that Chinese cooks use every part of the pig bar the squeak. Pity, really, I like the thought of Stir-fried Pig's Squeak. Because pork carries so much in the way of flavour, unlike that other staple of Chinese diet tofu (you won't find much of that in this book), you can get away with just a few other ingredients to make a very good dish indeed. A simple stir-fry needs very little that isn't in the cupboard anyway.

Frankly, there is not much to it, a quick shake in a blisteringly hot wok with spring onion, garlic and ginger, a sprinkling of soy and you have a supremely palatable, if slightly crude, supper. A little more thought, and a few green vegetables, and the result can be really worth while.

Buying Pork

I am lucky in that my local butcher sells only traditionally reared 'free-range' pork. Not everyone is so lucky. Most large chain stores offer a similarly reared pork, though the cuts will be limited and you will, of course, be expected to pay a premium. But it is worth it. For the flavour, yes, but even more so for the knowledge that the animal has had a decent life and a natural diet. I am convinced the meat from happy pigs tastes better. I am prepared to pay more for it and suggest that others should be too. I eat meat less than ever now, and demand that when I do, it should be really good.

Look out for labels that say the pork has been traditionally reared. Some smaller, high-quality butchers may even name which farm the meat comes from. Remember that most pork not labelled 'free range' or 'conservation grade' or without the Soil Association logo has almost certainly been intensively reared, for which read 'unhappy pigs'. Pigs need a varied diet, access to daylight, fresh air and shelter, and somewhere interesting to root and snuffle.

Choosing the Right Cut

Many cuts of pork are suited to long cooking, either roasted or braised with stock or wine, or as a pot roast with herbs and vegetables. These include the leg, whole loin and delicious extremities such as trotters and hocks. Fortunately, there are several smaller cuts of interest to the 30-minute cook:

Belly

A favourite cut of mine with plenty of fat, the outside of which crisps nicely. Its moistness makes it a good cut for quick cooking, particularly stir-fries. Especially good if the fat is allowed to turn a rich golden colour.

Chops

Chump or Loin. Chumps come from the back of the animal, loins from the middle. Ideal for grilling, they offer a substantial piece of meat, though they can sometimes be expensive and are often too large. The bones are particularly delicious to gnaw on. Try them grilled with crushed rosemary and slices of garlic.

Shoulder

Cut into large cubes, this must be one of the most useful cuts to those who have little time on their hands. Useful in a stir-fry or for grilling, threaded on to skewers if you want, the cut is tender, reasonably priced and stocked by most butchers and all major chain stores. Marinate if you have time in red wine, olive oil and squashed juniper berries.

Spare Ribs

Great to eat but not really on for the quick cook unless you are a dab hand with the cleaver or can talk your butcher into chopping them up into bite-sized pieces for stir-frying (which would be delicious).

Tenderloin

Weighing about 1lb (okay, 450g), this tender cut from the rear of the loin is good for roasting. It is rather lean, so needs cooking carefully if it is not to dry out, but it is particularly useful sliced into rounds, when it can be sautéed in minutes. Try it pan-fried with mushrooms, stirring in a little Marsala at the end.

A Few Good Things to Eat with Pork

....

Friends of the pig include robust herbs such as sage, rosemary and thyme, spices such as ginger, juniper and coriander, and aromatics like bay, shallots and orange zest. Honey, lemons and pickles make fine partners for this meat too. Fruit, particularly pears, apples, prunes, plums and sharp oranges, work well, cutting its sometimes overwhelming richness. And what can be finer than a plate of cold roast pork, pickled cabbage and walnuts, and some cold crackling to chew?

Stir-fried Pork with Winter Greens

....

For 2

•

350g/12oz boneless pork, shoulder or leg

2 tablespoons rice wine or dry sherry

1 teaspoon sesame oil

1 tablespoon light soy sauce

1 teaspoon cornflour

½ small firm Savoy cabbage

2 tablespoons groundnut oil

3 spring onions, chopped

A straightforward stir-fry, as easy a supper as is possible to get. Use any cut of pork, but one with a bit of fat on it would be good with the cabbage.

Cut the pork into cubes or strips about 1cm/½ inch diameter. Toss the pork with the wine or sherry, sesame oil, soy and cornflour. Don't worry too much about the lumps. Set aside for 15 minutes. Meanwhile, shred the cabbage quite finely.

Heat a wok or large, deep-sided frying-pan until it is really very hot. And I mean hot. Add the groundnut oil and gently swoosh it about a bit. Just as it starts to smoke, which will be a matter of seconds, add the pork, but not its marinating juices (there won't be many). Cook quickly, stirring around with a couple of chopsticks or some of the Chinese cooking implements if you have them (I am not quite sure what does what), for a couple of minutes till brown around the edges. The pork must brown slightly if it is to be good.

Add the spring onions, a good grinding of pepper and some salt (remember the salty soy sauce, though), then add the shredded cabbage. Cook, stirring and frying, for 4–5 minutes till the pork is cooked through and the cabbage is bright green and just starting to wilt. Tip in any marinating juices from the pork, bubble once or twice and eat while hot. Pass the soy sauce at the table.

▶ *A recipe such as this is really just a starting-point. Chop and change to your heart's content. Savoy cabbage has a deep strong flavour that works well with the soy, but a crisp white cabbage is a possibility instead, or better still some of the tender Chinese greens such as fleshy, oval-leafed pak choi. Add them a little later, though, as their tenderness means that they cook quicker than cabbage*

▶ *I have been known to add celery to this recipe, cut in strips and thrown in shortly after the onions. Broccoli too*

Pork Steaks with Mustard Sauce

....

A unctuous but thankfully piquant sauce spiked with French mustard and brought down to earth with lots of chopped parsley. Put some potatoes, nice floury old ones rather than new, on to boil before you start to cook the pork. Salad, a spiky green one, with frisée and chicory, would be a clever way to mop up the creamy, mustardy sauce from your plate.

Melt the butter in a sauté pan over a medium heat. Add the oil and when it starts to foam pop in the garlic. Cook for a minute or two until soft and then add the pork steaks. Sauté over a medium heat on both sides till golden and just cooked, about 7 minutes. Whip out the garlic clove, lift the pork out on to warm plates and then pour away all but 1 tablespoon of the cooking oil and butter. Throw in the chopped parsley and the cream, add the mustard and bring slowly to the boil, stirring in any juices from the pan. Simmer gently for 3–4 minutes. Taste, season with salt and pepper, and spoon over the pork.

For 2
•
25g/1oz butter
1 tablespoon olive oil
1 large clove of garlic, squashed flat
2 large pork leg steaks
2 tablespoons chopped parsley
225ml/8fl oz double cream
3 tablespoons Dijon mustard

▶ *A squeeze of lemon juice, added at the very end, will lift the sauce a little, though it is by no means essential. Especially if you have taken my advice about the frisée salad*

▶ *Sometimes I use a smooth tarragon-flavoured Dijon mustard. Other times, a grainy coarse one*

Pork Chops with Tarragon and White Wine

....

For 2

•

a large knob of butter

1 tablespoon groundnut oil

2 large or 4 small pork chops

2 tablespoons tarragon leaves

100ml/4fl oz white wine – not too dry

another large knob of butter

Aniseed notes are rather good with pork. This classic French way with pork is very much the sort of thing I hope to be offered on a plain white plate on a plain white paper cloth in a roadside café. But rarely am.

Put the butter, a lump about the size of a whole walnut in its shell, into a frying-pan with the oil. You can use olive oil if that is what you have. As soon as it is hot, but before it starts to smoke, add the chops. Cook them over a moderate heat until both the meat and the edges of the fat have browned on each side, which should take about 5 minutes on the first side and 3–4 on the other. I don't know why it takes less time to cook the second side, I only know that it does.

Pour out any excess fat from the pan, season the chops with salt and ground black pepper, and scatter over the tarragon leaves. You can chop them if you like but there is little point. Pour in the wine and simmer, covered with a lid, for a couple of minutes more, turning once. Remove the chops to a warm place, turn up the heat under the pan and boil until the liquid has reduced to a little more than a couple of tablespoonfuls; then add the second knob of butter, a little smaller than the first. Swish round the pan till it sizzles, and pour over the chops.

....

▶ *A plate of green veggies, dark green ruffle-leaved Savoy cabbage or green beans cooked till slightly floppy, would be my choice of accompaniment here*

Escalope of Pork with Asparagus and Cheese

....

I have a soft spot for tinned asparagus. It compares unfavourably with fresh in terms of texture, colour and subtlety of flavour, and nowadays even price, but I like the tinned stuff for what it is. You can, of course, use fresh asparagus here in this Italian recipe and will probably end up with an altogether finer result, but as I said, I have a soft spot for tinned. Simple potatoes, perhaps just boiled new ones, would be a suitable accompaniment.

Bat out the pork chops till they are really quite thin, about ¼ inch, or 5mm if you have gone metric, using a cutlet bat, rolling-pin or, gently, your fist. Dip both sides in a little flour. Drain the asparagus or, if you are using fresh, cook till tender in simmering water. Heat the oil and butter in a sauté pan or frying-pan. When the mixture foams and bubbles add the batted-out pork chops.

Fry for a minute or two on each side, until they are golden brown, and then transfer to a baking sheet. Heat the grill. Lay the asparagus spears over the pork, about 10 thin spears on each. Cover with the cheese, either grated or sliced, whichever is easier, and place under the grill.

Cook until the cheese starts to melt, but stop before it colours, when the heat may toughen the cheese or over-cook the meat. While they are cooking (they will only take 3–4 minutes or so) pour off the oil from the frying-pan. Set it over a high heat and pour in the Marsala and any juices that have collected on the plate. Bring to the boil, scrape at the crusty bits on the bottom of the pan, if there are any, and allow to bubble away for a minute.

Pour the glistening pan juices over the grilled pork as you serve it.

For 2
•
2 boneless loin pork chops
a little plain flour
175g/6oz asparagus
1 tablespoon olive oil
a large knob of butter
100g/4oz Fontina, Gruyère or Cheddar cheese
4 tablespoons Marsala

Pork Steaks with Gruyère and Marsala

....

For 2

•

100g/4oz smoked streaky bacon

1 shallot, finely chopped

4 medium flat brown mushrooms, finely diced

a little olive oil or butter

2 boneless loin pork chops

6 tablespoons Marsala

100g/4oz Gruyère cheese, diced small

3 tablespoons chopped parsley

Rich, piquant and succulent in the extreme.

Cut the bacon into short strips and put into a wide, shallow pan. If you are using a sauté or frying-pan make sure that the handle is ovenproof. Fry over a medium heat until the fat runs and the bacon turns golden at the edges. Add the shallot and cook over a medium heat until translucent. Add the mushrooms and a drizzle of oil or a knob of butter if there isn't enough fat left from the bacon. Cook until the mushrooms are tender.

Meanwhile, bat out the pork chops a little with an oiled rolling-pin or similar implement. Your fist will do. Turn up the heat a little and then add half the Marsala. It will sizzle and spit. With a wooden spatula, scrape up the sediment in the pan and stir into the mixture. Remove from the heat and spoon the mushrooms, bacon and shallot into a small bowl. Add the cheese and half the parsley, season lightly and mix gently. Set aside and get the grill hot.

Place the pan back over the heat – it should still have some of the cooking juices left in it – if not, add a tablespoon of oil. Get the pan hot, then add the pork. Cook for 2 minutes – no longer or they will toughen – and then turn and cook the other sides. They should be juicy and golden brown. Whatever you do, don't let them dry out.

Turn off the heat and divide the mushroom and cheese mixture between the pork slices, spooning it carefully on top of each. Place the pan under the grill for about 2 minutes, maybe less, until the cheese is bubbling and the mixture sizzling. Lift out the pork slices and put them on warm plates. Place the pan back on the heat (remember that the handle may be very hot) and leave for a few seconds until it sizzles. Pour in the remaining Marsala and boil for a few seconds, stirring to collect any crusty bits from the pan. Pour the mixture over or around the pork. Sprinkle over the rest of the parsley.

SAUSAGES

All the world loves a sausage. Unless, of course, your religion forbids it. Finely minced meat, generally pork, seasoned with pepper, parsley and perhaps a little sage or oregano is what most of us think of as a sausage. I can't remember who described a sausage as a 'faggot in tights', but they deserve an Oscar for it. There is something so appealing about a glistening hot sausage that it is invariably cited as the hardest thing new vegetarians find to give up. I may well end my days as a vegetarian who eats sausages.

It is easier now to buy a sausage that appeals to you than it has been for years. There is something of a renaissance for such hearty fare, with butchers expanding into herb, garlic and spicy types, supermarkets on the lookout for old-fashioned butchers' recipes and grocers stocking spicy Spanish chorizo and garlicky French Toulouse. There are even a number of specialist sausage shops opening up.

All this is good news to those who find a golden brown and black-tinged sausage sizzling in its pan one of the most irresistible foods in the world. There are still horrid sausages around, though, and it really is a question of trying them all and finding one you like. I have found that butchers' own sausages are generally the best, plump, peppery and moist. There is nothing worse than a dry sausage. You can do a great deal worse than trying your local butcher first, or the supermarkets' premium brands. And remember, there is nothing sadder than a skinless sausage.

Cooking sausages

Cooking a sausage demands, if not skill, a certain amount of thought. For the most detailed discussion of cooking a sausage I should refer you to *The Sausage Directory*, edited by Matthew Fort. He suggests a frying time of 40 minutes over a low heat. I am not sure I have the patience to wait the best part of an hour for a sausage; 20–25 minutes is as long as I can hold off for. In my book, a sausage will be ready after 20 minutes' cooking over a low to medium flame. If you have not pricked it, so that its juices are still inside instead of evaporated in the pan, it will be moist. If you chose it well then its flavour will be fine, and if the heat wasn't too high then it will not have split. But I do agree with Mr Fort on the method of cooking. Frying, in a pan 'gleaming genially with layers of accumulated grease that have fused into a naturally non-stick surface', is by far the best method for cooking whole sausages.

Pork, Prosciutto and Sausage Kebabs

....

For 2

•

350g/12oz pork fillet, cut into large cubes (4cm/1½ inches)

175g/6oz piece of bacon or prosciutto, cut into 2.5cm/1 inch cubes

4 large herby pork sausages, cut into 2.5cm/1 inch lengths

cubes of white bread, the same number as pork cubes

olive oil

a little chopped marjoram, sage and/or thyme

A trio of pork products on a stick. I first met the matching of fresh and cured pork in this way in a restaurant in Florence (although it is actually a Roman dish). It was a busy Saturday night and, knowing about as much Italian as I do Mandarin, I saved the harassed waitress a few minutes, and me some embarrassment, by simply pointing at what the people at the neighbouring table were eating. This is what I had.

Thread the cubes of pork, bacon and sausage on to long skewers with cubes of bread. Any arrangement will do. You can stick the odd bay leaf in too, though I am not sure it will achieve much in this instance. Brush with olive oil and sprinkle with the chopped herbs.

Cook under, or over, a preheated hot grill – a good 10cm/4 inches away from the heat, and turning from time to time – until firm and sizzling. About 15 minutes. They will smell wonderfully savoury and herby. Season with a little salt and pepper and serve with salad.

Opposite Crisp Spiced Grilled Chicken (page 151)
Over, left Turkey Escalope with Prosciutto and Lemon (page 161); *right* Quick Green Chicken Curry (page 145)

Sausage with Lentils

....

Sausage and lentils is one of the most satisfying dishes imaginable. Tinned lentils are a possibility, though somewhat pointless here as small green or brown lentils do actually cook in less than 30 minutes. Just.

Rinse the lentils in a sieve in running cold water. Cut the pancetta or bacon into small cubes and fry in a deep pan till the fat runs. If it fails to, in other words if your bacon was too lean, then add a tablespoon of oil. Fry the onion in the fat for 4–5 minutes till it starts to soften and then add the mushrooms and the garlic. Stir, cover with a lid and cook for 5 minutes.

Add the lentils and enough boiling water to cover them by an inch or so (about 600ml/1 pint). Cook over a moderate heat for 20 minutes, then test for doneness. They will probably need another 5 minutes. Season with salt and black pepper, and stir in the parsley. Meanwhile, fry the sausages till they are done to your liking. I suggest at least 20 minutes over a moderate heat with a bit of fat. When the sausages are brown and tender, turn up the heat under the lentils to evaporate most, but not all, of the liquid, while you slice the sausage. Serve them on hot plates on a bed of the lentil and mushroom mixture.

For 2

•

100g/4oz small brown or green lentils, such as those from Le Puy

75g/3oz pancetta or smoked bacon

1 small onion, finely chopped

100g/4oz brown mushrooms, chopped

1 large clove of garlic, sliced

2 tablespoons chopped parsley

4 plump pork sausages, spicy Italian ones or best butcher's

....

▶ *Italian grocers, and some supermarkets, sell spicy Italian sausages. Even the one they call mild is spicier than ours. Don't eschew the type sold in vacuum packs, they are surprisingly good, and usually very juicy. Unopened, they will last for a couple of weeks in the fridge, though check the sell-by date. I find them a little too garlicky as a breakfast sausage*

Flash-fried Moroccan Chicken (page 142)

Broad Beans and Black Pudding

....

For 2, as a light supper

•

350g/12oz black pudding

225g/8oz smoked ham, in one piece

4 spring onions, chopped

450g/1lb shelled broad beans (they *can* be frozen)

1 small glass of dry white wine

2 sprigs of mint

The Spanish, some of the most enthusiastic pork eaters in the world, often include a dish of skinned broad beans tossed with ham in a selection of tapas. Black pudding is a popular alternative, and one I prefer.

Cut the black pudding into thick slices, about 2.5cm/ 1 inch wide. Cut each slice in half. Cut the smoked ham into cubes, no bigger than 2.5cm/1 inch. In a shallow pan, fry the black pudding and the ham with its fat until sizzling. If the ham does not produce enough fat, add a tablespoon of oil. Add the spring onions and fry till wilted.

Add the broad beans and toss in the fat, pour in the white wine and the mint. Simmer for 15 minutes, by which time the beans should be tender and much of the wine evaporated. Taste and season with salt and pepper.

Sausage Bubble and Squeak

....

a large knob of butter or dripping

half the weight of the potatoes and greens below of good-quality butcher's sausage

equal amounts of cold mashed potato and cooked greens (volume, not weight)

One of the more sensible options for the resurrection of leftovers. The point here goes far beyond frugality – the combination of mashed potatoes and cabbage is good chemistry indeed. I have added sausages to the classic recipe to make this more of a complete meal. A fried egg if you like such things, or cold cuts, is another idea. The quantities are deliberately vague – this is far from *haute cuisine*.

Melt the fat in a deep-sided frying-pan, slice the sausage into thick rounds and fry until light golden brown. Mix together the potato and greens and tip into the sausage pan. Squash the mixture down with a palette knife and cook till the bottom has browned and crisped in the butter.

If you wish, turn the whole thing over in the pan to brown the other side. I rarely bother, rather liking the contrast between crisp and soft.

▶ **B**ubble *and squeak gets its name from the way the cabbage tends to squeak in the pan. At least that is what I have been told. Kale, or spinach, cooked and chopped roughly, is as good, sometimes better than cabbage. As with all leftovers, generous seasoning is crucial. This can include a spring onion or two, chopped and fried with the fat. I once made it with bacon, which was a success, and with mushrooms, which wasn't*

Chorizo and Chick-peas

Chorizo, the rust-red, chewy, spicy sausage so beloved of the Spanish, is now available here in delis, food halls and the major chain stores. Spiced with paprika and garlic it has a robustness that will perk up lentils, haricot beans or, in this case, chick-peas. A warming, frugal and hospitable supper, best eaten with a glass of cold beer.

    Heat the oil in a deep pan and fry the onion in it till soft and golden; about 5–7 minutes, maybe a bit longer. Add the garlic and the chorizo sausage sliced into pieces a bit thicker than pound coins. Cook till the sausage sizzles and colours very slightly. Drain the chick-peas of their rather dubious-looking canning liquor and stir them into the onion and sausage. Add the tomato passata, or chopped tinned tomatoes and their juice if that is what you have, and chopped parsley, and cook over a medium heat for 5–6 minutes till the chick-peas are bubbling. A little salt and pepper would not go amiss.

For 2, as a light supper
•
1 tablespoon olive oil
1 small onion, finely chopped
1 clove of garlic, crushed
175g/6oz chorizo sausage
2 × 400g/14oz tins chick-peas
6 tablespoons tomato passata
2 tablespoons chopped parsley

Sausage and Bean Hotpot

....

Photograph between pages 64 and 65

Serves 3

•

6 fat tasty butcher's sausages

2 × 400g/14oz tins flageolet or lima beans, drained and rinsed

1 × 400g/14oz tin butter beans, drained and rinsed

1 × 540g/19oz jar tomato passata

2 teaspoons chilli paste such as *harissa* or 3 hot red chilli peppers

2 tablespoons grainy mustard

1 teaspoon made English mustard

3 tomatoes, halved

chopped flat-leaf parsley

The sausage and bean hotpot is known in many cultures. The Italians use cannellini beans and *zampone*, a sausage-meat-stuffed trotter, the French have their steaming cassoulet, full of haricots blancs and the coarse and garlicky *saucisse de Toulouse*. The Spaniards tuck into *fabada*, made with beans, pork and chorizo, the paprika sausage, while the Polish version contains *kielbasa*, a highly seasoned, sometimes smoked version. Britain has no national bean and sausage dish even though we eat beans in their millions and make some jolly fine sausages. We seem to prefer beans and chipolatas in tins. Here is a fast version that I offer as our version of the genre.

Fry the sausages, if necessary in a little oil, till golden, but not brown, on each side. Mix the remaining ingredients, apart from the parsley, and spoon into an ovenproof casserole. Add the sausages and bake in a preheated oven, 230°C/450°F (gas mark 8), for 20–25 minutes till everything is bubbling and lightly browned on top. Scatter over the parsley.

....

▶ I *have suggested flageolet or lima beans here as they survive the canning process rather better than some. Haricot beans are another possibility*

The Sausage Sandwich

....

Even at its most basic, the sausage sandwich is a thing of joy. The crux of the matter is, of course, the quality of the sausage. As always, your favourite is the best. A fat, juicy pork sausage, perhaps one with a few herbs (but absolutely no garlic), is probably better than some of the more fanciful ones. I think the bread should be white. And preferably of the worst kind. Oh, and it should be eaten while the sausage is really too hot to eat.

The Basic

Fry the sausage, or grill it if you prefer (I do not), till the skin is golden brown with a few black patches, and swollen to bursting. Slap it between two slices of bread and press down hard.

The Sausage and Onion

For 1

•

1 small onion, cut in rings
a knob of butter
2 fat, juicy pork sausages
2 slices of white bread
smooth French mustard

Fry the onion in the butter over a medium heat till it is soft, translucent and golden. Lift it out with a draining spoon and add the sausages to the pan. Cook until the skins are tight, gold, brown and black in whatever ratio you prefer. Return the onion to the pan for the last couple of minutes. Spread the bread with smooth, mild French mustard, scatter over the onions and place the sausages on top of one slice. Slap on the second piece. You will find that some of the onions will fall out as you eat it. And the butter will soak through the bread. At least I hope so.

The Spicy

Chilli sauces, smooth English mustard and even salty, tangy lime pickle have much to commend them as bedfellows in a sausage sandwich. Tabasco is another possibility. Worcestershire sauce adds a piquant richness.

Mix a tablespoon of tomato ketchup with a teaspoon of Worcestershire sauce, a little lime pickle, chilli sauce (Thai or American for preference), and a small blob of made English mustard. Taste and add whatever you think it needs. It may well be more tomato ketchup. Slather the sauce on to the bread, and then add the sausages.

Sausages Braised in White Wine

....

For 2

•

4–6 pork sausages depending on
their size

1 tablespoon olive oil

2 shallots, finely chopped

100ml/4fl oz good chicken stock

1 small wineglass of wine, red or
white

2 tablespoons grated Parmesan
cheese

a knob of butter

chopped parsley

An Italian idea based on a recipe in *La Vera Cuciniera Genovese*. Accompany with mashed potatoes or wide, buttered noodles.

Butter a heavy, heatproof dish. Place the sausages in the pan with the oil and set over a medium heat. Brown them on all sides very lightly. Scatter over the shallots and cook for a minute or so; then add all the other ingredients except the parsley.

Cover and simmer for 15 minutes till the sausages are tight and tender. Check from time to time that the liquid has not completely evaporated – there should be just enough left to make a bit of a sauce with. Lift out the sausages, drop in a large knob of cold butter (about as big as a walnut in its shell) and whisk or stir in the butter till the sauce thickens. Scatter over the parsley and serve hot.

....

▶ *The best version I made of this was one where I threw in last night's cooked and leftover green lentils (they had a bit of bacon and a few mushrooms in with them) just after I had made the sauce. Stirred for 3 minutes till warm, it was quite sublime. Even if it was another version of sausage and beans*

KIDNEYS

The only kidneys I cook are lamb's. Neat, chubby little lamb's kidneys are sweet, tender and cooked in minutes. To be good they must be very fresh. Occasionally they can be bitter, although less so nowadays. They should be skinned of their gossamer-like membrane and halved to reveal a little core of white fat. It is easy to cut it out with the point of a sharp knife. Left in, the kidney will curl into a ball as the tendons tighten.

Although the Chinese stir-fry kidneys with spring onions, ginger and peppers to good effect, it is really the Europeans who have the best recipes for these little morsels. Spanish recipes use sherry to mingle with the kidneys' cooking juices, while the French make much of mild mustard, red wine and cream. I have also eaten very good sautéed kidneys in Sweden with thyme and crushed juniper berries.

The worst sin you can commit with kidneys is to overcook them. A minute too long and they will turn into little rubber balls. Cooked too slowly, though, they turn pale, flaccid and uninteresting. Quick cooking, in a moist environment rather than naked on the grill, seems to bring out the best in them. As does a splash of Pernod or gin.

Stir-fried Lamb's Kidneys and Mushrooms

············

A straightforward stir-fry with mercifully little preparation. Serve with noodles or rice.

Make sure that the kidneys are thoroughly cleaned and their outer membrane has been removed. Rinse them well and dry them. Heat the groundnut oil in a wok or large frying-pan and when it is really hot add the chopped chilli. Stir-fry for a second or two and then add the garlic. As soon as it starts to sizzle, and before it has had time to colour, add the mushrooms.

Fry the mushrooms, stirring almost constantly until the mushrooms are golden brown, about 3–4 minutes. Add the kidneys to the pan and brown quickly for 1 minute. Pop in the remaining ingredients apart from the parsley and continue to cook for a further 2 minutes. Add the chopped parsley and serve while still sizzling hot.

For 2

•

350g/12oz lamb's kidneys, halved, cored and cleaned

1 tablespoon groundnut oil

1 medium, mild red chilli pepper

2 plump cloves of garlic, sliced

100g/4oz medium-cup mushrooms cut into quarters

1 tablespoon rice wine or medium-dry sherry

1 tablespoon light soy sauce

1 teaspoon sesame oil

2 tablespoons chopped parsley

LIVER

The world is divided into those who like liver and those who don't. I have a theory that those who do also like kidneys, gooseberries, rhubarb, mackerel and capers, those other love 'em or loathe 'em ingredients. Flash-fried liver with capers, steamed cabbage and gooseberry crumble must be one of my dream meals. For many it would be a nightmare.

Lamb's liver, which is far more subtle and tender than pig's, can be a joy to the quick cook. Thirty minutes? More like thirty seconds! Liver, when sliced thinly, cooks in the time it takes you to pour a glass of wine. It is good value for money, a storehouse of vitamins and minerals (if you care about such things), and is the most tender meat of all.

It has an affinity with any number of storecupboard ingredients: onions, shallots, red wine, sherry, wine or balsamic vinegars, oranges, bacon and lemons. Tart, peppery greens, such as watercress and rocket, do pan-fried liver any number of favours. Particularly when they are used to soak up its rich, dark juices from the pan.

Pan-fried Liver with Onions and Sherry Vinegar

....

Or wine, or balsamic vinegar, if you prefer. Toss a large salad of spicy rocket, curly frisée and peppery watercress before you start. There won't be the usual time to kill while the meal is cooking. A few tomatoes, grilled whole till their skins char, would be welcome too, or perhaps some buttered wide noodles.

Put the onions in a heavy-based pan with the oil and cook over a medium-to-low heat, covered with a lid, until they are soft and golden, and have caramelized in patches on the bottom of the pan. You can expect this to take 15 minutes or so.

Remove the onions from the pan with a draining spoon and set them aside on a plate or in a bowl. Turn up the heat under the pan. Fry the liver, adding a little oil if the pan is dry, for a minute or so on each side until it is golden. Remove and set it with the onions.

Pour off almost all of the oil. Add the sherry vinegar to the pan with 2 tablespoons water, scrape at the crusty bits in the pan with a wooden spatula and stir them into the vinegar. Add the butter, cut into chunks, and stir quickly, beating with a small whisk until it thickens. Season with salt and pepper, return the liver and onions to the pan for a minute or two, and then serve.

For 2

•

2 medium onions, sliced very thinly

3 tablespoons olive oil

275g/10oz lamb's liver, thinly sliced

2 tablespoons sherry vinegar

50g/2oz butter

Lamb's Liver with Mustard and Madeira Gravy

....

For 2

•

275g/10oz lamb's liver, thinly sliced

a little plain flour

50g/2oz butter

100ml/4fl oz Madeira

1 wineglass of red wine

2 teaspoons capers, rinsed

1 tablespoon grainy French mustard

Piquant flavours – here capers and mustard – perk up a piece of liver like nothing else. A 10-minute meal this one, except that I really think it is at its best with some buttery mashed potatoes or, even better, a mash of half potatoes and half parsnips, which will, of course, take you well into 30 minutes. Noodles, cooked in 10 minutes and tossed in softened butter and garlic, are a quicker option.

Coat the liver lightly in flour. Melt half the butter in a shallow pan and when it stops foaming add the liver. Cook over a medium heat for about 1 minute per side, a little longer if your liver isn't as thin as it might be. Lift out the liver to a warm plate and then pour in the Madeira and the red wine.

Reduce the liquid over a high heat till half of it has evaporated. Stir in the capers and the mustard, and a little black pepper and salt. Stir and leave to bubble for 2 minutes. Replace the liver, and any juices that may have run out. Cook for a minute longer and then serve.

CHICKEN LIVERS

I love a chicken liver. Golden brown and slightly cara-melized outside, pink and grainy within. One of my desert island dinners would include a plate of the sautéed livers, served on a bed of wispy, spiky frisée and soft baby spinach leaves, with the juices from the pan dribbling over them. They keep very well in the freezer, and with the application of a little hot butter, mustard, capers, anchovies and red wine, balsamic or sherry vinegar or perhaps a slug of port, they can be the most sublime of suppers in a mere 5 minutes.

A little pot of chicken livers, fresh or frozen, is one of the most useful things a 30-minute cook can find in the fridge. If I wasn't lucky enough to be blessed with a butcher who sells fresh ones, I would certainly keep a pack in the freezer. They will thaw out quick enough in a colander with a little cold water running through them. If I have time, then I make Paula Wolfert's magical livers from her book *The Cooking of South-west France*; it takes about 3 hours, but the sweetness of the onions cooked for 2 hours, and the chemistry between them and the garlic, vinegar and anchovy, makes this very special indeed. I include a humble, speeded-up version here.

Almost without exception they are best dumped on top of a salad of an imaginative mixture of leafy greens; rocket, *mâche*, baby spinach and chicory. The whole point of a chicken liver is lost if it is allowed to overcook. Somehow its joy is all but gone once its inside has turned from pink to brown.

A handful of good things to do with a pot of chicken livers. Rinse the livers in cold running water and then dry on kitchen paper. Pull away any sinews and cut off any green or bruised bits. For 2.

With Vinegar and Onions

Cook 2 medium onions, thinly sliced, in 25g/1oz butter and a tablespoon of olive oil, for 15 minutes till soft, golden and sticky. Add 4 anchovy fillets, rinsed and chopped, and cook for another 5 minutes. Toss 350g/12oz chicken livers in a little plain flour and then cook in a sauté or frying-pan with another 25g/1oz of butter for a minute or so on each side, till golden brown. Lift the livers out and into the onions. Add 50ml/2fl oz red wine vinegar to the pan and swirl it round. Add a knob of cold butter and stir for a minute till the sauce is glossy. Season with salt and black pepper, and then stir into the onions and chicken livers. A scattering of parsley would not go amiss. Serve with toasted French bread and a salad. For 2.

Moroccan Chicken Liver Brochettes

Put 2 teaspoons paprika, 1 of salt, 1 of ground cumin and a good pinch of chilli powder in a small plastic bag. Add 350g/12oz chicken livers and toss them about a bit. Thread the seasoned livers on to skewers and brush with olive oil. Cook under, or over, a preheated hot grill for 2 minutes; turn and cook the other side. Serve with a tomato and onion salad and soft white bread such as a bap or English muffin. For 2.

A Salad of Chicken Livers, Gorgonzola and Grapes

Cut 100g/4oz ripe Gorgonzola cheese into cubes. Wash 4 large handfuls of salad leaves and divide between two plates. Cook 225g/8oz chicken livers in a little butter for a couple of minutes till brown outside. Make a simple salad dressing with a little olive or walnut oil and lemon juice and black pepper. Scoop out the livers with a draining spoon and scatter them over the salad. Throw a handful of green grapes – seedless muscats would be delicious – into the pan, pour in the dressing (about a wineglass full), warm for 1 minute and then pour over the chicken livers and baby salad leaves. For 2.

CHAPTER 8

Grains, Beans and Lentils

My love of grains, lentils and the bean family grows by the day. I find their warmth, frugality and comforting qualities of far more interest than meat. They have a certain charm and offer something of a challenge to the cook. Until I took a closer look I had thought that this would be a short chapter, assuming a length of cooking time beyond our tight deadline. I couldn't have been more wrong, and this is now one of my favourite sections in the book.

Quick cooks will make the most of the tinned flageolets and haricots, the brown, blue and green lentils and the rice and couscous that cook within half an hour. It is only in their dried form that the larger beans are excluded. Most lentils will cook in 30 minutes.

This is one area of cookery that has become exciting of late. And it can only get better. First stop, though, is to rid these wonderful ingredients of their wholefood image – in my opinion a large millstone round their necks.

BULGUR, QUINOA AND COUSCOUS

Texture is almost as fascinating an attribute of food as flavour. This may in some way explain my love of grains; the crystalline texture of quick-cooking bulgur, the extraordinary round bobbles of Andean quinoa and the soothing charm of Middle Eastern couscous. Grains in their many forms are a constant source of delight to me, and several are suited to the restraints of this collection.

Summer isn't summer without a Cypriot salad of cracked wheat (bulgur) and lush, emerald green parsley. I add whatever is around, tomatoes, apricots (leaving their soft downy skin intact) or cucumber, to produce a bowl nourishing enough to eat as it stands rather than demote it to the role of accompaniment.

A recent trip to South America confirmed my interest in quinoa. Most health-food shops have it, and a few supermarkets. Once tasted, it is impossible to forget its fluffy round texture and faint bitterness. It can be used in place of rice in a pilaf, or as a soothing base for a salad of bright flavours.

Couscous is a wonderfully versatile grain, which I use both as a salad ingredient and in its traditional form as a starchy bedfellow for spicy North African stews. In high summer its grains make a substantial salad with ripe scarlet tomatoes and black olives. In winter I steam the grains, which are, in fact, invariably pre-cooked and take barely 20 minutes, and treat them as a bolster for a golden saffron-spiced vegetable stew.

Classic Tabbouleh

....

A fast, bright tasting salad from the Lebanon with a fluffy, grainy texture.

Soak the cracked wheat, bulgur, call it what you will, in just enough water to cover it for 15 minutes. Meanwhile, chop the herbs quite finely, and put them into a large bowl with the lemon juice, olive oil and spring onions, also chopped.

Wring out the bulgur wheat with your hands. You should be left with moist, rather than wet, grains. Throw them into the salad bowl with the cucumber and a fair seasoning of salt and pepper. Toss gently and leave for a few minutes before serving.

▶ D*on't stint on the mint or the parsley. Both must be in tiptop condition and used in generous amounts*

For 2, as an accompaniment
•
75g/3oz bulgur wheat
50g/2oz flat-leaf parsley
25g/1oz mint
2 tablespoons lemon juice
2 tablespoons olive oil
4 spring onions, chopped
½ cucumber, finely diced

Red Onion, Chilli and Lime Tabbouleh

....

Vivid flavours for a mild-mannered grain. Use spring onions if the red onions you have are not really mild and sweet.

Soak the wheat as above. Chop the onion and parsley finely. Mix with the remaining ingredients and salt and pepper. Squeeze out the wheat and toss with the dressing.

For 2, as a side dish
•
75g/3oz bulgur wheat
1 medium, sweet red onion
50g/2oz flat-leaf parsley
1 medium-hot red chilli pepper, seeded and finely chopped
juice of 3 limes
3 tablespoons olive oil

Red and Yellow Pepper Pilaf

....

For 2, as a light supper

•

25g/1oz butter

2 tablespoons olive oil

1 small onion or shallot, chopped

1 plump clove of garlic, crushed

1 medium-hot red chilli pepper, finely chopped and seeded if you wish

1 red and 1 yellow pepper, seeded and sliced into eighths lengthways

½ teaspoon paprika

225g/8oz bulgur wheat or 100g/4oz quinoa

300ml/½ pint boiling vegetable stock or water

a small handful of coriander leaves, chopped

Pilaf need not just mean rice cooked with onions and stock. Quinoa or bulgur respond well to being cooked in the same way. As long as the grain is small and willing to soak up the butter and stock then it is suitable for the pilaf treatment. When I have time, I often make a barley pilaf with mushrooms and thyme, though sadly it takes too long to include here.

Melt the butter in the olive oil in a medium-sized pan over a moderate heat. Add the onion or shallot and cook until it is translucent and starts to soften, and then add the garlic and the chilli. Cook for 2 minutes, add the peppers, sauté for a couple of minutes till they start to soften and then add the paprika, wheat or quinoa, salt and the boiling stock or water.

Simmer gently for 15–20 minutes till the peppers are tender and the grain has soaked up most of the liquid (if it becomes dry, add a little more stock). Stir in the chopped coriander with a fork and eat warm.

....

▶ I *have served this bright pilaf with grilled goat's cheese and salad leaves as a light lunch, and it seemed to go down rather well*

Couscous

············

Half a pound of couscous is more than enough for two people. Officially that is a rather awkward 225g, but you know that. I usually steam it in a colander that I have lined with a new J-cloth to stop the grains falling through. The colander is placed over a pan of simmering water for about 20 minutes until it is hot right through to the centre.

Couscous Niçoise

············

Cook the beans in boiling salted water till they are bright green and tender, about 6 minutes. They are there to add crunch to the soft grain, so cook them slightly less than you would for a vegetable accompaniment. Drain and run cold water through them to stop them cooking.

Meanwhile, soak the couscous with a little water, about 150ml/¼ pint will be enough although it will not appear so at first. Leave for about 10 minutes and then crumble the lumps that form between your fingers. When the grain has swelled a little, stir in the cooked beans, the tomatoes cut into small dice, and the olives, anchovies and herbs.

Make the dressing by whisking together the ingredients and seasoning generously with salt and freshly ground black pepper. Toss the salad with the dressing, set aside for 10 minutes, or longer if you have it, and then serve with lemon wedges.

For 2

•

100g/4oz French beans, cut in half lengthways

225g/8oz couscous

4 tomatoes, ripe but firm

10 black olives, stoned and halved

4 anchovy fillets, rinsed

a large handful of flat-leaf parsley, chopped

2 tablespoons chopped coriander leaves

lemon wedges, to serve

For the dressing:

•

1 plump young clove of garlic, crushed to a paste

3 tablespoons extra virgin olive oil

1 teaspoon lemon juice

Peach and Almond Couscous

....

For 2

•

100g/4oz couscous

50g/2oz (a good handful) flat-leaf parsley

25g/1oz mint

juice of 2 lemons

2 tablespoons olive oil

4 small spring onions, chopped

3 medium, ripe, juicy peaches

2 tablespoons flaked almonds, toasted

A sublime accompaniment – but only if the peaches are ripe – to fish, poultry or meat. A lovely summer lunch with Parma ham and summer pudding to follow. There is a recipe for a cheat's version in *Real Fast Puddings*.

Sprinkle the couscous with 100ml/4fl oz water, leave for 10 minutes, then break up the lumps that form with your fingers. Chop the parsley and mint, but not too finely, and mix with the lemon juice and olive oil in a salad bowl. Add the spring onions to the dressing.

Halve and stone the peaches and cut the flesh into large dice, saving as much of the juice as you can. Doing this over the dressing bowl is one way. Add the peach flesh to the dressing along with the couscous. Throw in the toasted almonds and toss gently.

Cinnamon-scented Couscous

....

For 2, as an accompaniment

•

225g/8oz couscous

50g/2oz butter

½ teaspoon ground cinnamon

3 tablespoons pine nuts

50g/2oz sultanas

A sweetly spiced hot accompaniment to stews, grills and pan-fries.

Sprinkle 150ml/¼ pint water on to the couscous, leave for 10 minutes, then break up the lumps that form with your fingers. Melt the butter in a sauté pan and fry the couscous with the remaining ingredients for 3–4 minutes till warm and fragrant.

RICE

In the last twenty years rice has become an accepted part of our midweek cooking. Before that it was regarded as a rather weird alternative. Unless it was baked in milk until it softened and formed a golden skin, and was eaten with jam for pudding.

In much of the world a meal without rice is unthinkable. In China, Thailand and India it could be said that life revolves around this extraordinary white grain. I enjoy the aromatic, spiced pilafs of India, the garlicky fried rice of China and the sticky risottos of Italy, though I wouldn't want to eat rice every day. In my kitchen at least, rice is the most useful of storecupboard ingredients next to pasta and rarely does a week go by without it forming the basis of a quick weekday supper.

There are a myriad of different rices, only a handful of which are to hand in the shops here. I have not yet taken a shine to the glutinous sticky rices (the sushi rice) so beloved of the Japanese, but I have developed a deep affection for the creamy result you get when Italian Arborio rice is slowly simmered with stock for a risotto. If you have never thought to buy basmati rice for pilaf, then I urge you to do so, if only for the wonderful smell as it cooks.

To gloss over the technicalities I refer to rice in this book only as long grain, by which I mean Indian basmati (though strictly speaking the term also covers Sunlong, Thai Fragrant and Texmati rice), and Arborio, which is the medium grain used for risotto. A simplification perhaps, but it suits the purposes of the book. Though if you see Carnaroli next to the Arborio, buy it. It is even better.

The Risotto

············

I have known the Arborio rice traditionally used in a risotto to be cooked in 20 minutes. But this is an exception, and I am the first to admit that this classic Italian dish, a soothing blend of rice, butter, onions and stock, only just makes it into this 30-minute collection of recipes.

Even if it took 40 I would beg your tolerance so that I could include some risotto recipes. There are few suppers so simple, so satisfying and so appealing to the hungry. Risotto demands a little respect; it is easy enough to cook but several rules must apply if the results are to be truly velvety.

• The rice must be Arborio, the small, round grain whose outer coat of soft starch dissolves to give the customary velvety texture to the risotto
• The stock must be a decent one, the more gelatinous the better. Chilled fresh stock will do the job well enough, or use just water rather than a stock cube. It must be added hot, so keep a pan at a very gentle simmer by the side
• The timing is fairly crucial. The rice is cooked when it is tender and pleasant to eat but still has a bite to it. It shouldn't really be chalky (if I have to get it wrong I would rather my portion be over- than undercooked), but should have a silky, creamy texture. But it must have a bit of bite, otherwise you might as well eat porridge

▶ *I use any old pan for making risotto, but I speak as someone whose pans all have solid bottoms. (Any pan with a thin base was burned black and thrown out long ago.) The most suitable pan is one of enamelled cast iron or heavy stainless steel. Purists suggest that risotto should be spread out on a plate and allowed to cool a little before eating – apparently it tastes better. Sorry, but I like mine hot, straight from the pot*

Pancetta and Parmesan Risotto

Pancetta is Italian bacon. But what bacon! Moist and mildly spiced, it has a generous amount of sweetly scented fat that melts into the butter to give a fine cooking medium for the onions. Pancetta deserves a wider distribution but you should be able to find it in the nearest Italian delicatessen. Buy it in the piece, which won't come cheap, rather than the silly wafer-thin slices the supermarkets offer.

In a heavy-based pan cook the onion and pancetta in the butter until the onion is soft. About 5 minutes. Add the rice and stir for a minute while it fries lightly in the butter. Pour in a ladleful of stock.

Let the rice simmer gently, adding another ladle or two of stock as it is absorbed by the rice. Stir almost, but not quite, continuously, till the rice has taken up all the stock. If you intend to have salad too, make it near the cooker so that you can keep an eye on the rice.

Stir in the butter and grated cheese, taste, and add salt if necessary. Eat immediately.

For 2
•
I small onion, finely chopped
75g/3oz pancetta, diced
50g/2oz butter
275g/10oz Arborio rice
I litre/1¾ pints hot chicken stock
a large knob of butter
50g/2oz grated Parmesan cheese

Leek, Tarragon and Mushroom Risotto

············

For 2
•

3 small tender leeks

50g/2oz butter

225g/8oz assorted small mushrooms, wild or cultivated, wiped

2 tablespoons chopped tarragon

275g/10oz Arborio rice

1 litre/1¾ pints hot chicken or vegetable stock

a large knob of butter

2 tablespoons coarsely chopped parsley

A very different animal indeed to the one above, this fresh mushroom risotto can be made with any funghi. Use apricot-coloured chanterelles or black musty trompettes de mort if that is what you have (though I would eat them simply sautéed myself), but tiny juicy champignons de Paris or even little white button mushrooms are good cooked in this way.

Cut the leeks, discarding the very dark green bits, into small rings about 1cm/½ inch thick. Wash them thoroughly in a colander under running water to remove any grit or sand trapped between the layers. Cook them in the butter over a moderate heat for about 7–8 minutes, until they soften and become translucent. They should not colour.

Cut the mushrooms into bite-sized pieces. Chunks are more succulent than thin slices. Add them to the leeks and stir to coat them in butter. Cook for 2 minutes. Add the tarragon and the rice. Stir to coat the rice with the butter and then pour on a ladleful of hot stock.

Cook until the rice has absorbed the stock and then add more hot stock, stirring from time to time. If you run out of stock and the rice is still not tender, carry on with water. When the rice has taken up all the stock and is, as they say, al dente, stir in the large knob of butter and season with salt and the parsley. Eat hot.

The Pilaf

············

The *pullao* of India, or *polow* of Persia, is a soothing and substantial blend of rice and spice. Made with basmati rice, even using the quick method opposite, this is a frugal and relatively authentic accompaniment to any of the Indian-style dishes in the book.

A simple rice pilaf has a mildly spicy and utterly comforting smell, especially if made with basmati rice. I can think of few things more appropriate after an illness than a bowl of delicately spiced rice. At the other extreme, jewelled with dried fruits, nuts and saffron, it is befitting of the most glamorous of celebratory meals.

But the pilaf only just sneaks into this collection. A traditional recipe will normally include a soaking of over 30 minutes. I have got round this by giving the rice an initial boiling before it meets the butter and spices. Unorthodox, but a practical answer for those like me, who are not the sort to soak the rice before they go to work of a morning.

Fragrant Rice

....

True to its name, though less so if you use ready-ground cardamom and cannot locate any lime leaves. A lovely rice, warming and golden, much of its magic relies on these two ingredients. Crush the green cardamom pods lightly to expose the oval black seeds, or take the seeds out first if you prefer. The cooked pods can be left on the side of the plate, or fished out before you serve the rice.

Wash the rice in a colander under running water. Warm the oil in a heavy-based, deep pan and fry the shallot till golden, for about 2 minutes. Add the cinnamon, turmeric and crushed cardamom pods, and fry for 2 minutes until their fragrance rises and the cardamom pods have puffed up. Add the lime leaves, rice and stock.

Bring to the boil and then turn down to a moderate heat and simmer for 15 minutes, covered with a lid. Do not stir, peep or fiddle. After 15 minutes lift the lid and check; if the grains are tender and there is virtually no liquid left at the bottom, stir it gently with a fork to fluff up and serve.

For 2, as a side dish
•
225g/8oz long-grain rice
2 tablespoons groundnut oil
I shallot, finely chopped
I stick of cinnamon
I teaspoon ground turmeric
I teaspoon green cardamom pods, crushed
2 kaffir lime leaves
350ml/12fl oz chicken or vegetable stock

Coconut Rice

....

For 2, as a side dish

•

225g/8oz long-grain rice
a large knob of butter
300ml/10fl oz coconut milk
a bay leaf
1 teaspoon finely grated lemon zest
a few coriander leaves, chopped

I first encountered coconut rice in a plane. I won't say it was the best introduction to the genre and I ate it more out of boredom than anything else. You know how you do? Since then I have become very fond of this gentle, fragrant accompaniment.

Rinse the rice in a sieve under running water. Melt the butter in a deep saucepan and add the rice, cooking it over a moderate heat for a minute or two, stirring all the time.

Pour in the coconut milk and add the bay leaf and half a teaspoon of salt. Bring to the boil, and simmer for 20 minutes until the rice has absorbed the milk. You would do well to check every now and then that it is not burning. When there is little or no liquid left, cover with a lid or cloth and leave to steam, off the heat, for 5–10 minutes. It will fluff up a little. Stir in slightly more butter, the grated lemon zest and the coriander and fish out the bay leaf.

A Few Good Things to Add to Fragrant Rice

....

The three fragrant rice dishes above, coconut rice and the simple basmati pilafs are interesting enough as an accompaniment to richer dishes, but can be embellished to provide a simple lunch or supper dish in themselves.

Soak a good pinch of saffron, about 20 threads, in 4 teaspoons warm water. Soften 50g/2oz butter in a small pan. It should be warm and almost liquid. Mix the two together to give a glowing golden liquor with fine scarlet strands of saffron. Stir into the rice as you fluff the grains with a fork just before eating.

Saffron-buttered Pilaf

Add a handful each of shelled pistachios and toasted almond flakes and a tablespoon grated orange zest to the buttered saffron rice above and you have something approaching the splendid, extravagant 'jewelled rice' served at Persian wedding feasts. Tradition decrees grated carrots, crystallized sugar and dried fruit, too, but this should be grand enough for a weekday supper.

Pistachio and Almond Pilaf

Halve and stone two medium, ripe peaches. Cut the flesh into dice, losing as little juice as possible. Fold the chopped fruit into 100ml/4fl oz thick yoghurt. Follow the fragrant rice recipe above. When the rice is cooked, remove the lid and fold in the yoghurt mixture, before replacing the lid and allowing to stand for 10 minutes.

Peach and Yoghurt Pilaf

....

▶ A *few other thoughts, added at the end of cooking before 'standing': ½ cucumber shredded and stirred into yoghurt, a handful of chopped blanched spinach leaves, sesame seeds, or chopped tinned tomatoes and coriander leaves*

A Few Things to do with Cooked Rice

....

I always cook too much rice. Apparently this is not an uncommon phenomenon. These next few recipes are for those who have a similar habit.

Anyway, finding a bowl of cooked rice in the fridge can be a joy. Especially if you don't particularly feel like cooking. It doesn't matter if it is lightly seasoned already, left over from its principal dish, in fact it will probably help. It should be fresh, though. No more than a day or two old.

If it is stuck together in an unappetizing lump, and it probably is, then you must separate the grains. Crumbling them in your fingers is a good enough method, though I have seen Thai cooks chop the lump with a large knife, which I think is a little excessive. Dumping the lot in a large sieve and running cold water through it works too, but take care not to waterlog the rice.

If I remember, I stir a drop of olive oil into the cooked rice before I refrigerate it. If I remember. The following ideas are far from 'twenty original ways with leftover rice', most are classic dishes that call for cooked rice rather than freshly cooked.

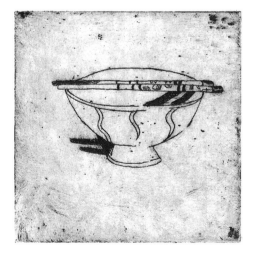

Chicken Biryani

Biryani is not traditional Indian fast food. It is a layered Moghul casserole, the meat being slowly braised and mixed with cooked spiced rice, then cooked again before being garnished with fried onions, toasted nuts and silver foil. I have foodwriter Sri Owen to thank for freeing me from such tyranny. In her beautiful and definitive work, *The Rice Book*, she includes this quick version and is the first to admit its unauthenticity. I would agree, but add that Ms Owen's recipe successfully keeps both the original dish's spicing and its supreme comforting quality. The long ingredients list is actually less frightening when you take a closer look.

Wash the rice and drain. Boil 1.7 litres/3 pints water in a large saucepan. When it boils, put in ½ teaspoon salt and the rice, a little at a time so that the water stays on the boil. Stir once and keep at a rolling boil for 8 minutes. Drain the rice in a colander and set aside.

In another large saucepan heat the oil, and fry the shallots, the garlic and ginger for 2 minutes, stirring all the time. Lift out 1 tablespoon of the shallots and set aside. Put in the chicken slices. Increase the heat and stir-fry the chicken for 3 minutes. Now add all the ground ingredients, stir again for a few seconds only, add the yoghurt, and continue stirring for 1 minute. Add the sugar and raisins and adjust the seasoning. Then pile the rice on top of the chicken and sauce.

Cover the saucepan with foil or a tea towel and put the lid on tightly. Lower the heat and leave it to cook undisturbed for 10 minutes. Remove from the heat and let it rest, undisturbed and with the cover still tightly on, for 5 more minutes. Then uncover and sprinkle the remaining shallots and the almonds over the dish.

For 4

•

225g/8oz long-grain rice

2 tablespoons olive oil

2 shallots, chopped, plus 1 tablespoon chopped shallots to garnish

2 cloves of garlic, chopped

1 teaspoon finely chopped fresh root ginger

4 boneless chicken breasts, sliced diagonally into thin slices

½ teaspoon chilli powder

½ teaspoon ground cumin

1 teaspoon ground coriander

a pinch of freshly grated nutmeg

¼ teaspoon ground cinnamon

¼ teaspoon ground turmeric

175ml/6fl oz yoghurt

1 teaspoon sugar

3 tablespoons raisins or sultanas, if you like

2 tablespoons ground almonds, to garnish

▶ *I recently made a vegetarian version of this by replacing the chicken with quartered chestnut mushrooms. I should like to try it with aubergine slices too, though no doubt it would take a little while longer*

Basil-scented Vegetable Rice

············

For 2, as a light supper dish

•

3 tablespoons groundnut oil

2 cloves of garlic, sliced

2 small hot red chilli peppers, seeded and finely chopped

2 shallots, chopped

100g/4oz tiny button mushrooms

100g/4oz broccoli, snapped into small florets

a handful of green beans, stalks removed and sliced into 5cm/2 inch lengths

225g/8oz cooked long-grain rice

1 teaspoon sugar

2 tablespoons light soy sauce

12 large basil leaves

This is a purely vegetable version of Khao Phat, the Thai fried rice that normally contains both pork and shellfish. Thai friends who make this for me now know to put fewer chillies in it than they do for themselves. I thought I was going to explode the first time they made it. I give here 'my' soft version, but the quantity of chillies is up to you. My friends use four small, very hot chillies, the little ones that blow your head off.

Heat the oil in a hot wok till a little smoke rises, add the garlic and chillies, and fry till the garlic is dark golden. Add the shallots, fry for 1 minute, and then add the mushrooms and broccoli. Fry for 2 minutes until the greens are bright and starting to soften.

Add the beans, fry for 1 minute, and then stir in the cooked rice, sugar and soy. Toss gently and stir while the rice heats and the vegetables cook, about 3–4 minutes. Tear the basil leaves into shreds and scatter them over the rice. Eat hot.

▶ *Thai basil differs slightly from the sweet peppery leaf we know here. It is still fragile, but its leaves are tinged with mauve and it has a more aniseed flavour. For most purposes, Italian basil is a perfectly reasonable substitute. See the ingredients chapter for more detail*

Spicy Fridge Rice

....

Some intelligence called for here. If you have some cooked rice in the fridge you may well have other good things in there too. What follows is a basic spicy rice that will act as a base to which you can add leftovers to produce a quick, not to say frugal supper. Leftovers is a difficult word, rather like offal. But the alternatives are even worse, as in 'variety meats'. Whatever you call them they must be in good condition; crisp cooked greens, diced chicken or perhaps a casserole or curry.

Fry the garlic and ginger in the oil in a wok or frying-pan. Add the mustard seeds, and when they start to pop add the turmeric, chilli and rice. Stir. Cook for 2 minutes or until the rice is thoroughly hot, then stir in any of the following:

• diced cooked chicken, stir-fried for 2 minutes in a little oil
• cooked greens (spinach is best), chopped roughly, added with the spices and before the rice
• mushrooms, again added before the rice and cooked for 2 minutes
• leftover ratatouille, or meat or chicken casserole, or even curry – warm it slowly, and then bring to the boil; as it starts to boil stir in the spiced rice, and eat hot
• Sunday's roast, the meat stripped from the bones and torn into bite-sized pieces. Stir-fry till hot and then add any gravy or pan juices – they will work well with the spices in the rice

For 2

•

1 plump clove of garlic, chopped
small knob of fresh root ginger, peeled and shredded
2 tablespoons groundnut oil
1 teaspoon mustard seeds
½ teaspoon ground turmeric
1 teaspoon hot chilli powder
225g/8oz cooked long-grain rice

BEANS AND LENTILS

Taking an hour or two to soak and almost as long to cook, the bean family hardly fits into this book. But the ones available in cans are not so bad as you might expect. Chick-peas can superbly. Butter beans and flageolet are little worse for their time in a tin while fluffier-textured cannellini are only slightly less successful. Though it depends on the brand. Lentils, on the other hand, are distinctly less of a success, losing all their bite. Then again, you can cook a lentil from dry in 20 minutes.

I would hate to be without a tin or two of beans. As emergency fare, they have got me out of trouble more times than I can remember. Sweet green flageolets stirred through with garlicky pesto for an accompaniment to lamb when I have neither veg nor spud, pretty white cannellini beans cooked with cream and tarragon for an instant supper for an overlooked vegetarian, and chick-peas whizzed to a nutty dip when the cupboard was truly bare.

Almost every nation's cooking has its traditional bean and lentil dishes; the warming French cassoulet, the more-ish Egyptian falafel, and that gloriously spicy, fragrant Indian sludge we know as dal. This is some of the finest eating there is. And yet there are those who only ever eat them in a sweet, bland tomato sauce.

This is an indulgent and somewhat whimsical collection of bean and lentil recipes. I have included my favourites, green flageolets, white cannellini, firm nutty chick-peas and earthy lentils. Cast aside are red kidney beans, which I find coarse, black beans, which turn too easily to grey sludge, and mung beans, which I prefer in their sprouted form, when they taste like little fresh green peas. But I do include the charming borlotti with its pink and mauve marbling, though like all of them, it needs a thorough rinse in cold running water to rid it of its viscous canning liquor.

Canned beans need no cooking, having already been cooked in the can. Warm them gently, just covered with water, and you may catch them while they still have some bite, some nuttiness and some sweetness. Many is the time I have come home tired, cold and in need of a drink, to find that a tin of beans, made hot and stirred through with nothing more than a few slices of spicy sausage and a grating of Parmesan, restores me within half an hour.

Butter Beans

....

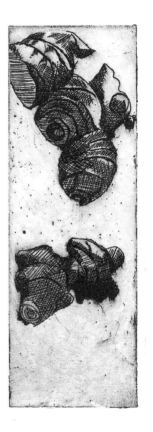

The bean world's answer to the beefsteak. The butter bean is a true whopper with a soft mealy texture, delightfully fluffy inside yet firm enough not to break up in the tin. Mild-flavoured and nutty, the butter bean soaks up cooking juices like a sponge, making it also one of the most delicious beans.

Traditionally used in large, slow-cooked casseroles, this king of beans is just as well suited to a quick supper. Baked with bacon, mustard and cheese it makes a wonderfully savoury supper. Best of all, I like it whizzed into a purée and drizzled with olive oil, eaten with lightly cooked spring greens or purple sprouting broccoli.

The butter bean's floury texture has an affinity with cream, cheese, sausage and ham. Mustard brings out the best in a butter bean. You can do a great deal worse than dress a tin of rinsed butter beans with a warm vinaigrette into which you have stirred a goodly amount of grainy mustard and chives.

Butter Beans with Bacon and Mustard

....

For 2

•

1 × 400g/14oz tin butter beans

4 rashers smoked streaky bacon

1 tablespoon groundnut oil

1 shallot or small onion, finely chopped

100ml/4fl oz dry white wine

100ml/4fl oz double cream

1 tablespoon grainy mustard

1 teaspoon smooth Dijon mustard

50g/2oz grated Cheddar cheese

2 rounds of hot toast

Fat creamy beans in a savoury sauce which makes a change from the ubiquitous tomatoey glop. The result will be hardly the worse if you prefer to leave out the bacon. Or substitute any other beans you may have in the cupboard.

Tip the beans into a colander and rinse them under the cold tap. Cut the bacon into thin strips and fry them in the oil till the bacon fat is golden. Add the shallot or onion and cook till soft and translucent.

Pour off any surplus fat and tip in the beans. Add the wine and bring to the boil. Turn down the heat and simmer till the liquid has reduced by half. Add the cream, stir in both mustards and bring gently back to the boil. Simmer for a couple of minutes and then stir in the cheese. Taste and add salt and pepper if it needs it. Tip over the rounds of hot toast, buttered if you wish.

▶ *F*at, mealy, nutty butter beans somehow suffer less from incarceration in a tin than other pulses, emerging sweet and tender

Opposite Baked Bananas with Passion Fruit (page 246)
Over, left Hot Salad of Tropical Fruits (page 245); *right* Filo Pastry with Mascarpone, Chocolate and Almonds (page 244)

Warm Butter-bean Purée with Spring Greens

....

A very favourite dish of mine combining a rich butter-bean cream with hot, fresh greens. The contrast between the earthy beans and the fresh, unseasoned leaves is something I particularly enjoy. Bread, of the white crusty sort, is essential.

Rinse the beans in a sieve under running water. Tip them into a blender or food processor. Add the garlic and purée to a smooth paste. Blend in 3 tablespoons of the oil, lemon juice to taste, and salt and pepper. Scoop into a heavy-based small pan set over a low heat. Warm gently with a tablespoon of oil, stirring often. It should not get too hot. Just warm is fine.

Rinse the greens, but do not shake them dry. You can cut them into smaller pieces if you like. I tend to leave them in whole, separated leaves. Put them into a pan over a medium heat with 2 tablespoons of water, cover with a lid, and cook in their own water till they wilt, about 3–4 minutes. Shake the pan from time to time.

Scoop the purée on to a large warm plate. Sprinkle over a little paprika. Drain the greens and place half on each plate, on top of the beans. Drizzle the last spoonful of olive oil over the lot and eat with crusty white bread.

For I as a light supper or lunch
•
I × 400g/14oz tin butter beans
3 cloves of new garlic, peeled
7 tablespoons extra virgin olive oil
lemon juice
I large handful spring greens or sprouting broccoli
paprika

Baked Pears with Honey and Juniper (page 249)

Cannellini Beans

....

The Tuscans are devoted to this bean. In Florence, in shop after shop, these smooth white beans spill out of striped sacks. A white kidney bean, it appears in hearty soups and in salads with spinach or tuna. The real joy of the cannellini bean is its texture. Cooked for 30 minutes, its fluffy inside whips up to a wonderfully light purée.

More than any other bean, cannellini vary from brand to brand. Choose Italian packed cans with small beans if you have a choice. They will take little more than 3–4 minutes' warming through in water or soup, after which time they start to cook. For which read overcook.

If you are unlucky and these fragile beans are mashed a little in the tin there is not much point in trying to save them – mash them with black pepper and garlic butter and heat gently with some chopped parsley. Serve them as a purée, to accompany grilled fish or chicken.

Cannellini Bean Croquettes

....

For 2

•

1 × 400g/14oz tin cannellini or butter beans

1 clove of garlic, peeled

1 shallot, chopped

1 egg

5 tablespoons finely grated Parmesan cheese

1 tablespoon chopped tarragon

1 tablespoon plain flour

beaten egg and fine breadcrumbs for coating

groundnut oil for frying

I have a charming, rather tatty little book, printed in 1899, of Italian vegetable recipes. *Leaves from our Tuscan Kitchen* by Janet Ross has been an enormous source of inspiration to me over the years, it being an ideas book rather than a collection of detailed recipes. These little bean cakes started life as 'Beans (Haricots), Croquettes of', from her book. I have replaced the author's balm mint with tarragon, and removed her vinegar altogether. Needless to say, her instructions to soak the beans all night long, 'boil over a slow fire for about an hour. Drain and dry them again and put them into boiling water for another hour', has been superseded by my 'rinse the beans and whizz them in the food processor'. Miss Ross's beautiful poetry lost in search of a quick supper.

Drain the beans and rinse them. Whizz them in a food processor or blender with the garlic, shallot, egg, cheese, tarragon (or parsley if there is none) and place in the fridge for 15 minutes. Shape the mixture into 8 little croquettes or patties. Patties are quicker. The mixture is quite soft. You will need floured hands.

Dip carefully into beaten egg using a fork, and then into breadcrumbs, patting down firmly to make sure they stick. Fry till golden in shallow oil. Drain on kitchen paper. Serve hot with tomato sauce or, dare I say it, ketchup.

Two Beans with Chilli and Coriander

A side dish rather than a main course, this is a simple mixture of two types of bean cooked briefly with olive oil and chillies. It makes a clean-tasting accompaniment to grilled fish or chicken.

Rinse the beans in a sieve under running water to get rid of their packing liquid. Put them into a pan, just cover with water, and bring slowly to the boil. Turn down the heat, add half the olive oil and the chilli. Simmer for 7 minutes till heated through. Drain thoroughly, taking care not to crush the beans. Place them in a bowl, pour over the second tablespoon of oil and grind over a little pepper. You can crush a pinch or two of sea salt over them too if you like. Toss gently with coriander.

For 2, as an accompaniment
•
1 × 400g/14oz tin cannellini beans
1 × 400g/14oz tin borlotti beans
2 tablespoons extra virgin olive oil (your best)
1 small, hot red chilli pepper, seeded and finely chopped
1 tablespoon chopped coriander leaves

▶ *Borlotti beans are a beautiful dull pink and maroon marbled bean. They must be quite something when freshly picked, though I have never eaten them that way. Available in tins in Italian grocers, they make the best of salads when tossed in a lemony dressing with finely chopped shallots, tiny spinach leaves and freshly ground black pepper*

Flageolets

....

A jewel of a bean. Tiny, oval and delicate, this pale green kidney bean is my favourite. Even in a tin, it keeps some of its fresh green flavour and delicacy. Probably the most expensive member of the bean family, it is good enough to eat on its own, although a little olive oil and some lemon will lift its spirits even higher.

When warm, this is a fragile bean and should be heated gently so as not to overcook. It is at its happiest in lamb dishes, either together in a casserole or as a grill with the beans served alongside. Sometimes, when my body craves for a meal that is fat-, meat- and sugar-free, I mix warm flageolets with lightly steamed spinach drizzled with olive oil and lemon juice. A clean, green supper.

In high summer, the flageolet makes a fine salad. At its simplest with a handful of chopped parsley and shreds of cucumber, or tossed gently with line-caught tuna and chopped tomatoes, it will form the backbone of a summer lunch. It will produce the prettiest salad of all when mixed gently with cold, flaked, poached salmon. Especially if you make the flakes of salmon bite-sized.

As always, rinse thoroughly of its canning liquid, then warm gently either in simmering water for 4 minutes or with a little olive oil.

Flageolets with Young Garlic
....

Late summer and early autumn sees the arrival of the first of the season's dried beans and the last of the young summer garlic. Sadly, even the youngest beans need soaking and boiling for a good half hour. But tinned are more than passable, particularly if you rinse them thoroughly and scent them with freshly chopped flat-leaf parsley and a very good olive oil. I have been known to eat a plate of these with hunks torn from a crusty loaf, though I suppose most people will prefer them as an accompaniment.

Drain the flageolets and rinse them thoroughly in cold running water. Putting them in a sieve will save you fishing them out of the plug hole. Put them into a pan and just cover with cold water. Add 1 tablespoon of the olive oil and a little salt, and bring them slowly to the boil.

Let them simmer for 5 minutes till thoroughly hot. Meanwhile, slice the garlic, which as I have said must be young, and place it in a deep plate or bowl. Drain the beans and toss them gently (so as not to break them up) with the olive oil, sliced garlic and chopped parsley. Eat warm, while the fragrance of the olive oil and garlic is still in the air.

For 2, as a side dish
•
1 × 400g/14oz tin flageolet beans
2 tablespoons extra virgin olive oil (your best)
4 plump cloves of young garlic
1 tablespoon roughly chopped parsley

Flageolets with Prosciutto
....

The most delightful of combinations, even when the beans are from a tin.

Follow the recipe above. When the beans are tossed with the olive oil, garlic and parsley, shred 4 slices of Parma ham into long strips (the easiest way to do this is to roll them up together and then cut them crossways with a large sharp knife), and stir them into the beans. Eat while warm, perhaps with a salad of new potatoes.

Flageolets and Cannellini Beans with Pesto

············

For 2

•

2 medium potatoes, peeled, or 6 large new potatoes, wiped

1 × 400g/14oz tin flageolet beans

1 × 400g/14oz tin cannellini beans

4 tablespoons ready-made pesto

1 tablespoon olive oil

The prettiest of beans stirred through with the fragrant Italian basil and garlic purée, pesto.

Cut the potatoes into large bite-sized pieces. Cook them till tender in boiling salted water, about 15 minutes.

Meanwhile, drain the beans and rinse. After about 10 minutes add them to the potatoes. Bring back to the boil and continue to cook over a moderate heat for 5 minutes or until the potatoes are tender and the beans are hot. Do not overcook the beans – they won't take much cooking before becoming too soft.

Drain the potatoes and beans. Put them back into the pan, turn off the heat and gently – no, very gently – stir in the pesto. The potatoes will absorb some of it quite quickly. Add a little oil if it appears dry. Or even more pesto, if there is some in the jar. Eat while warm.

CHICK-PEAS

The most resilient of the pulses, standing up to hours of soaking, boiling, canning and cooking. The only way to ruin a chick-pea is to let it boil dry during the long cooking needed to render it tender.

Chick-peas can be of use to the short of time, but only if you buy them in tins. I have cooked them from dry (after a 48-hour soak) and there seemed to be no advantage over opening a tin. Hazelnut-shaped and nutty to taste, they have a knobbly feel in the mouth that is both unique and pleasing. Their nutty flavour is what makes the Middle Eastern hummus so more-ish, and what makes them so delicious when mashed and deep-fried as Israel's crunchy falafel.

They are known as garbanzos in America and Spain. A name that amuses me for some reason. Especially when it is said with an American accent.

Roasted, Spiced Chick-peas

A side dish for simply cooked fish or perhaps for grilled chicken. On the other hand, you could serve them with drinks.

Drain, rinse and dry the chick-peas. Lay them in a single layer on a baking sheet, stir the oil with the garlic and drizzle over the peas. Roast them in a preheated hot oven, 230°C/450°F (gas mark 8), for 15 minutes. Remove from the oven, dry on paper towels and then toss them while still hot in the cumin, chilli and salt and freshly ground pepper.

For 2
•
1 × 400g/14oz tin chick-peas
2 tablespoons olive oil
2 large cloves of garlic, finely crushed
½ teaspoon ground cumin
a pinch, a large one, of chilli powder

Chick-peas with Aubergine and Spinach

For 2

•

1 × 400g/14oz tin chick-peas

2 medium aubergines, cut into 2.5cm/1 inch cubes

8 tablespoons olive oil

2.5cm/1 inch knob of fresh root ginger, peeled and grated

4 cloves of garlic, sliced

1 hot green chilli pepper, seeded and chopped

1 teaspoon ground coriander

1 teaspoon ground cumin

1 × 400g/14oz tin chopped tomatoes

225g/8oz spinach, chopped roughly

An Indian mixture, its spiciness depending on how many chillies you put in, which plays the crisp bite of the chick-peas off against the soft aubergine. A delightfully sloppy mixture, best scooped up with an Indian flatbread such as soft, warm chapatti or lighter puffy poori.

Rinse the chick-peas to get rid of the canning liquor. Fry the aubergine cubes in the oil till golden on the outside and tender within, about 10 minutes. Remove with a draining spoon.

If there is no oil left in the pan, then add a little more. When it is hot, add the ginger, garlic and chilli, and fry for 1 minute, stirring constantly so that it does not burn. Add the coriander and cumin and cook for 30 seconds, taking care not to burn the spices – lower the heat if you have to. Add the tomatoes and their juice, chick-peas and about 225ml/8fl oz water. Bring to the boil and turn down to a simmer.

Cook for 15 minutes, add the spinach and bring to the boil, cook for a further minute or two till the spinach is tender. Season with salt and pepper, and serve hot.

Chick-peas and Potatoes

....

This extraordinarily frugal mixture of spiced starches is known in both India and the Middle East. Scooped up with warm pitta or naan bread, it makes one of the most warming, comforting suppers imaginable. Though hardly the prettiest, for all its autumn colours.

Drain, rinse and dry the chick-peas, heat the oil in a frying-pan and cook the cumin seeds till they start to turn golden brown and smell both sweet and spicy. Cut the potatoes into large bite-sized pieces. Add the onion and cook till golden brown at the edges.

Add the curry powder to the onion, cook for a minute or two, then add the tomatoes and their juice, chick-peas, potatoes, 225ml/8fl oz water and the lemon juice. Season generously with salt and pepper. Simmer for 15 minutes and serve.

For 2

•

1 × 400g/14oz tin chick-peas

4 tablespoons olive oil

1 teaspoon cumin seeds

4 medium potatoes, boiled (yesterday's leftovers are fine)

1 medium onion, chopped

1 tablespoon curry powder

450g/1lb or 1 × 400g/14oz tin tomatoes, chopped

1 tablespoon lemon juice

Falafel

....

For 2

•

2 × 400g/14oz tins chick-peas
6 plump cloves of garlic, crushed
2 teaspoons ground coriander
2 teaspoons ground cumin
1 medium onion, chopped
2 tablespoons plain flour
1 tablespoon chopped parsley
groundnut oil for deep-frying

Crisp outside, soft inside and spiced with garlic, cumin and coriander, these fluffy chick-pea fritters from Israel are, to my mind, the finest street food of all. They are easy enough to make at home, either in the traditional manner, as deep-fried, slightly flattened balls, or as little flat patties cooked in shallow fat. Eat them as you wish, though stuffed into pitta bread with salad and a drizzle of tahini is pretty hard to beat.

Drain, rinse and dry the chick-peas. Blend in a food processor with the garlic, spices and onion till smooth. Scoop into a bowl and stir in the flour and the parsley. Season with salt and pepper.

Stir the mixture thoroughly – it should be thick enough to roll into balls. With floured hands, roll the chick-pea mixture into balls about the size of golf balls, maybe a little smaller. Deep-fry the balls in 10cm/4 inches hot fat. Alternatively, flatten them into patties and shallow-fry them for 2 minutes on each side, till crisp.

▶ *Serve them hot, stuffed into warm pitta bread. Traditionally, a cucumber and tomato salad would be stuffed in there too*

▶ *Although the nutty, bitter and slightly slimy tahini is one of the traditional lubricants for these crisp fritters, I much prefer yoghurt. Particularly when it has had a little cayenne pepper and some chopped mint stirred into it and is spooned over the falafel as you eat*

▶ *Falafel are found all over the Middle East. They are the local answer to America's hamburger and the great British sandwich. Some cooks use yeast or baking powder to lighten them, though I prefer a slightly firmer falafel myself. With a raising agent they are more likely to break up as they fry (I once had a panful dissolve before my eyes). They are also good flattened into burger shapes and cooked in shallow oil, spiced with a whole chilli*

LENTILS

Once the butt of vegetarian jokes, the humble lentil is now enjoying its five minutes of fame. The lentil is now trendy. Quite why it was ever banished to the further reaches of vegetarian cooking remains a mystery. I love the texture, the earthy, spicy flavour and the warm homely smell as it cooks. It rarely needs soaking, and taking less than 25 minutes to cook, the lentil family fits happily into the 30-minute cook's repertoire.

In India I have seen more varieties of lentil than I thought was possible, bursting from their sacks in dark, dusty shops. In Britain we rely on three or four major varieties. Tiny orange or yellow ones, and small brown or slate green Le Puy are the most usual. Indian and French cooks understand the lentil. In India it may well come as a yellow or brown spiced mush, fragrant with onions and butter, while in France you are more likely to be served diminutive green-grey Le Puy lentils with ham or lamb.

To the quick cook it is invaluable. Use it as a base for a mushroom and onion-rich soup, as a bed on which to serve slices of duck or as the main ingredient in a curry to scoop up with warm naan. I love it too as a side dish, lightly cooked till nutty, and then stirred through with fresh fruits, redcurrants, blueberries or sliced ripe scarlet peaches.

Dal

....

Serves 2, with rice

•

225g/8oz yellow lentils (toovar dal)

½ teaspoon ground turmeric

75g/3oz ghee, butter or oil

½ teaspoon cumin seeds

1 medium onion, sliced

2 cloves of garlic, sliced

1 small chilli pepper, red or green, chopped

1 tablespoon finely chopped coriander leaves

Dal is, along with mashed potatoes, real custard and crisp-crusted bread, one of my favourite foods. It is a general Indian term for lentils and dried beans, though to most people, me included, dal means the silky, sloppy, spicy mush made from yellow split peas and red or yellow lentils. As this is supposed to be a collection of quick recipes, and split peas need soaking and take a good 45 minutes to cook, I have used lentils throughout.

Rinse the lentils in a sieve under running water and check carefully for little stones. Put the lentils into a pan with the turmeric, a good teaspoon of salt and enough water to cover, about 725ml/1¼ pints. Bring to the boil, stirring. Turn down the heat and simmer for 25 minutes, stirring occasionally, by which time they should be easy to squash. If not, cook for a further 5 minutes.

Meanwhile, make the spiced butter. Heat the ghee, butter or oil in a shallow pan, add the cumin seeds and cook for a few seconds till they turn dark brown. Add the onion and the garlic, and cook until both turn a deep nutty golden brown. About 20 minutes. They should be darker than you would cook them for a European dish. Stir them so they do not burn. Add the chilli and cook for a further 3 minutes.

When the lentils have absorbed all the water beat them with a wooden spoon for a minute or two to a soft, wet purée. Scoop into a warm dish. Pour the spiced butter over the top and scatter over the coriander leaves. Serve warm, with rice.

▶ **B**aghar *or tadka is the Indian name for the spiced butter used with dishes such as dal. The point is to flavour and perfume the dish. Ghee, the clarified Indian butter, is generally preferred, though vegetable oil is often used. I prefer a mixture of butter and oil (the butter tastes better – the oil stops it burning). It is then perfumed with onions and chilli, and sometimes garlic and spices*

Lentils and A Few Good Things To Stir into Them

....

I often cook myself a bowl of lentils. The blue-green-grey Le Puy variety have a pleasingly earthy, nutty flavour if not cooked for too long. With a glass of fruit juice and some sweet grapes afterwards, they make a solitary lunch that is both comforting and clean-tasting, frugal and light. Somewhat monastic perhaps, but such a dish is a pleasant enough change from richer, more complicated things.

About 75–100g/3–4oz best quality French or Italian lentils will be firm and nutty after 15 minutes' cooking, a further 5 will render them pleasantly floury inside. But you don't have to eat them as is.

• ripe Gorgonzola cheese, warmed in a non-stick saucepan till it starts to melt, stirred into the lentils with a little black pepper

• a blob or two of garlic butter

• grated – or shaved if you are feeling trendy – Parmesan cheese, stirred in with a little extra virgin olive oil

• pancetta, the fat Italian cured bacon, diced and fried

• gloriously ripe tomatoes and a handful of basil leaves

• snippets of cold cuts (cold roast duck is wonderful) or shreds of ham or prosciutto, with a dressing made with olive oil and mellow balsamic or sherry vinegar

▶ *Some lentils are of more interest to the 30-minute cook than others. Diminutive red (actually it's more salmon pink) ones cook quickly, though their flavour needs bolstering with spices. Little yellow ones seem sturdier and possibly have a better flavour. They fluff up impressively when beaten with a wooden spoon for a thick spicy dal dish. Posh Le Puy have a nuttiness to them that makes them the best flavoured. They cook in 20 minutes (even less if new season's) and are quite a bit more expensive. But we are only talking pence per pound. Earthy-tasting brown lentils, provided they are the tiny ones, will be tender but firm after 20 minutes or so*

Red Lentils with Turmeric and Mustard Seeds

....

Photograph between pages 64 and 65

For 2
•

I large onion, finely chopped

I tablespoon groundnut oil

2 cloves of garlic, sliced

I bay leaf

I tablespoon ground turmeric

I tablespoon mild or hot curry powder

I small red chilli pepper, seeded and chopped

I tablespoon mustard seeds

I teaspoon cumin seeds

450g/ I lb small red lentils

850ml/I ½ pints vegetable stock or water

coriander leaves

Fry the chopped onion in the groundnut oil till it is soft and translucent, add the sliced garlic cloves and bay leaf and stir in. Continue cooking for 2 minutes over a medium heat and then stir in the turmeric, curry powder, chopped chilli, mustard and cumin seeds. Fry the spices with the onion and garlic till fragrant and then pour in the red lentils with the stock or water.

Stir the mixture, season with salt, and leave to simmer for 12–15 minutes, until the lentils are tender but before they turn to sludge. If the water has not almost all been absorbed, then simmer until it has. Check the seasoning – you may want to add pepper – and then serve in bowls with warm naan.

▶ *Traditionally, a piece of warm, flat naan is torn off and used to scoop up a mouthful of the spiced lentils. It is a lovely way to eat, feeling the warm food in your hand. But it is only one way. Use a spoon or fork if eating from the hand is not your thing, or pile the lentils on to the naan, then cut through both with a knife and fork, just as if you were eating beans on toast. Which, in a way, you are*

CHAPTER 9

Snacks, Cheese and Puddings

I could write an entire book on snacks, the fast food you throw together to appease a rumbling stomach. Unfortunately, I am running out of space and time and must limit my suggestions to a healthy handful of my favourites. Toasted croissants oozing with melted cheese, a crisp and flaky parcel of warm Camembert and a plate of ripe fruits and piquant goat's cheese are some of my favourite things to eat.

I cannot be alone in finding a hot, crisp morsel of food, held in the hand and eaten standing up, as some of the most satisfying food of all. There is a frisson of spontaneity about such eating that sharpens the appetite like nothing else, apart from sea air. I often think I could live on snacks and short eats. In fact, sometimes I do.

SNACKS AND CHEESE

Baked Camembert

....

For 2

•

225g/8oz puff pastry, defrosted
I small Camembert cheese
a little beaten egg

A sexy combination of crisp puff pastry and melting cheese. Serve with a leafy salad, chicory and frisée perhaps, with a mustardy dressing.

Get the oven really hot, 220°C/425°F (gas mark 7). Cut the pastry in half and on a lightly floured surface roll out two circles, about 4cm/1½ inches larger than your Camembert, one circle slightly bigger than the other. Lay the smaller circle on a baking sheet, take the cheese out of its box and peel off the paper, then lay the cheese on top of the pastry.

With a pastry brush or your fingers, wet the edge of the pastry thoroughly with the beaten egg. Place the larger disc of pastry on top of the cheese. Press the overhanging pastry on to the base pastry and then trim both to give a 2cm/¾ inch border. Seal the pastry to stop the cheese leaking – this is best done with the prongs of a fork. Push hard to seal, but not so hard that you slice through to the baking sheet.

Brush all over with beaten egg and cut two small slits in the top to let out the steam. Bake in the preheated oven for 15–20 minutes until the pastry is golden brown and puffed up. If you can bear to leave it to cool for 10 minutes before cutting into it, then the cheese will ooze voluptuously rather than pouring out.

▶ *This is the best use I have found yet for one of those wretched cheeses that just won't ripen properly. A firm cheese is easier to handle than one ripe enough to burst its seams, and it is less likely to leak through the pastry. A wedge of Brie can be used instead but is more of a hassle to wrap*

Pitta Sandwich with Hummus, Feta, and Caramelized Onions

....

Wonderful scents, evocative of the Middle East, fill the kitchen every time I make this sandwich, even though the ingredients smack of a desperate trip to the corner shop. Even the lowliest food shop seems to carry little tubs of chick-pea dip, plastic-wrapped planks of salty white Feta, and bags of oval pitta breads. And there is always an onion knocking around somewhere.

Peel the onion and slice it into thin rings. Cook it with a little olive oil in a shallow pan till the rings soften and turn crusty brown at the edges. This is when the natural sugars in the onion have caramelized, lifting the whole snack on to a higher plane than if you made it with a raw onion. The onion is really the whole point of this. Stir in a few thyme leaves if you have some. Dried are fine in this instance.

Meanwhile, cut the Feta into bite-sized lumps or smaller. Any larger and they tend to roll out. Toast the pittas till puffed and golden. Split each pitta round the edge to make a large pocket, fill with hummus, onions and Feta in no particular order, and eat immediately. The filling may need a good grind from the pepper mill, but no salt.

For 2
•
1 medium onion
1 tablespoon olive oil
a few thyme leaves
225g/8oz Feta cheese
6 tablespoons hummus
2 pitta breads

Ciabatta with Black Olive Paste, Prosciutto and Warm Mozzarella

....

This sandwich, like many of my better ideas, was the result of a midnight fridge raid. It smells as good as the inside of a cool Italian deli on a hot day. Enough for two sandwiches.

Slice a small ciabatta (or a third of a big one) horizontally to give two flat airy bases. Toast lightly; they should go no more than pale gold in colour and still have their characteristic chewiness. Spread each with black olive paste. Be generous, it's not *that* expensive. Lay one slice of prosciutto on top of each. There are two ways of doing this: you can either leave each slice whole, in which case you risk dragging the whole slice out of the sandwich, leaving you looking like a spaniel with its tongue hanging out, or you can take the elegant route and cut them into thin strips. The latter is the method to use if there is the possibility anyone might see you eating.

Thinly slice a ball of Mozzarella cheese and cover each prosciutto sandwich with it. Season both with a drizzle of olive oil, salt and quite a lot of pepper. Cook under a hot grill till the cheese softens. Stop before the cheese colours more than a little, when it will toughen. Eat immediately.

Toasted Croissants with Mushrooms, Onions and Melted Cheese

....

Photograph between pages 96 and 97

One of my favourite sandwiches, and a most successful way to bring a slightly tired croissant to life.

Fry a small onion, peeled and sliced into rings, in a little oil till soft. It will take about 10 minutes to turn soft and golden. After 5 minutes or so, add a few mushrooms, thinly sliced. Meanwhile, split two large croissants, toast the cut sides till golden. Spread generously with mustard, a French grainy one for preference.

When the onion and mushrooms are golden and tender, scoop them out of the pan with a draining spoon and place on top of the mustardy bottom halves of the croissants. Place thick shavings of cheese – Cheddar or Gruyère is fine – over the mushrooms and place under a hot grill till the cheese melts. Replace the top halves and eat hot. Substitute slices of prosciutto for the mushrooms if you wish.

Purple Figs with Ricotta and Prosciutto
....

Photograph between pages 96 and 97

Velvety purple figs are with us from early autumn to late spring. Their tenderness makes them tricky to carry home, but their flavour is worth the extra care needed. A light lunch or supper dish this, or a starter for a more formal meal.

Cut a cross in each fig – you had better wipe them first – from stalk to flower end. Gently squeeze the figs so that they open out like water lilies. Put them on a plate.

Season the Ricotta with black pepper and some of the marjoram or oregano leaves. Slice the prosciutto into ribbons. Spoon the seasoned Ricotta into the figs and scatter over the remaining herbs. A few slices of ciabatta might be welcome, if only to add a little substantiality.

For each person
•
3 fat figs, ripe but not squashy

3 tablespoons Ricotta cheese, fresh and moist

marjoram or oregano leaves

1 slice of prosciutto

ciabatta, to serve

....

▶ *Nectarines and peaches can be used instead, when they are in season*

PUDDINGS

Although I have already written an entire book of puddings that can be made in 30 minutes (called *Real Fast Puddings*, incidentally, and packed to the gills with ideas for quick puds), I want to include a few here as well.

British cooking is one of the few that takes puddings seriously. The French have wonderful pastries and the Italians have the best ices in the world, but they are invariably bought rather than made at home. Indian cooking has some wonderful sweetmeats but they are not easy to prepare. Chinese puddings, or what passes for them, are something of an acquired taste. To put it mildly. The rest of the world seems to finish their meal with fruit.

I see nothing wrong with this, except I think they are missing something very special. So, even though this book is mostly concerned with food from countries that are unaware of how good a proper pudding can be, I have included a few gooey, sticky, fruity things just for fun.

Filo Pastry with Mascarpone, Chocolate and Almonds

....

Photograph between pages 224 and 225

For 8

•

450g/1lb Mascarpone cheese

100g/4oz ground almonds

50g/2oz plain chocolate chips

grated zest of an orange

50g/2oz sultanas

100g/4oz raisins

1 × 400g/14oz pack of filo pastry, defrosted

50g/2oz butter, melted

2 tablespoons shelled pistachios

A slightly updated (that is, less sweet) version of the traditional pastries of the Middle East; the wonderful contrast between the crackling pastry and the soft interior is really the reason for its inclusion. It serves eight, but will keep in a cool place for a day. The Mascarpone cheese filling is not as unorthodox as it may sound – many such pastries are filled with sweetened Ricotta cheese. I have taken something of a liberty with the 30-minute rule.

Set the oven at 200°C/400°F (gas mark 6). Scoop the Mascarpone into a bowl and stir in the almonds, chocolate, orange zest and dried fruit. Mix thoroughly. Brush a baking tin 30 × 20cm/12 × 8 inches and at least 2.5cm/1 inch high lightly with butter.

Cover the base of the baking tin with two pieces of filo pastry, brush them with some of the melted butter and lay another two sheets on top. Lay the remaining sheets of pastry, one by one, in the baking tin, each piece half covering the base of the tin and half hanging over the sides. Brush with butter and repeat so that each piece is now at least two sheets thick. Brush again with butter.

Add the Mascarpone and smooth level with the back of a spoon. Now lift each double piece of pastry hanging over the sides and fold it into the middle, twisting it into a large curl as you do so. The top of the pie should be pretty much covered with pastry. Brush with any remaining butter and top with the pistachios. Bake in the preheated oven till golden brown, about 20 minutes. If you can, leave for a little while before serving.

Hot Salad of Tropical Fruits

....

Photograph between pages 224 and 225

Hot tropical fruits in a sticky lime syrup. Serve with balls of vanilla ice cream.

Put the sugar in a thick-bottomed pan with 225ml/8fl oz water. Bring to the boil over a moderate heat until the sugar has dissolved. Add the tamarillos, turn down the heat and simmer gently for 10 minutes, or until the fruit is tender. Remove from the heat and pour into a heatproof serving bowl.

Meanwhile, peel and slice the grapefruit, papaya, mango, kiwi fruit, guava, peach and banana. Cut the passion fruit in half and squeeze the seeds over the sliced fruits. Remove the tamarillos from the syrup and slice them, about as thick as pound coins. It would be nice to peel them, though not essential. Add them to the fruits. Stir the lime juice into the syrup, pour over the fruits and serve warm with lime quarters.

For 2–4

•

100g/4oz caster sugar

2 tamarillos

1 pink grapefruit

1 ripe papaya

1 ripe mango

1 kiwi fruit

1 ripe guava

1 ripe peach

1 banana

2 passion fruit

juice of 2 limes

quartered lime, to serve

Photograph opposite page 224

For 4

•

4 ripe bananas, peeled
2 tablespoons runny honey
a little lemon juice
juice of ½ orange
6 passion fruits

Baked Bananas with Passion Fruit

....

Hot bananas have a seductive richness about them. Some might say too rich. The tart passion fruit serves the purpose of contrasting that richness and offering one of the most fragrant fast puddings imaginable.

Wrap up each banana in kitchen foil leaving the top open. The easy way to do this is to place the foil flat on a work surface. Place a banana on each one, then bring up the sides of the foil to make little packets for the fruit. Drizzle the honey over the bananas. Squeeze a little lemon juice in each packet and then drizzle over the orange juice. Cut the passion fruit in half and squeeze four of the halves over the banana parcels.

Scrunch together the foil at the top to seal. Bake in a preheated oven at 200°C/400°F (gas mark 6) for about 20 minutes. Test for doneness with a skewer. Put the parcels on to plates and hand round. Give everyone two halves of a passion fruit. Each diner should squeeze their passion fruit on to their bananas as they open the packet. The scent will be exquisite.

▶ A *passion fruit is ripe when it is severely wrinkled. But it should still weigh heavy in the hand. That is a sign that it is full of juice*

Blueberry Muffins with Crème Fraîche

....

Warm, fruity cakes best eaten with tart crème fraîche. You will almost get them done in 30 minutes. Buttermilk is available from a surprising number of supermarkets. You will find it among the cream.

Preheat the oven to 200°C/400°F (gas mark 6). Butter 12 deep bun tins.

Sift the flour with the baking powder into a large bowl, stir in the sugar and the salt. Break the egg into a second bowl, then beat in the buttermilk or milk. Stir in the melted butter, then pour the mixture into the flour. Stir for half-a-dozen strokes. Then stop. The mixture will be a bit lumpy. No matter.

Divide half the mixture between the bun tins. Drop a few blueberries into each tin, then add the remaining mixture. Bake in the centre of the oven for 20 minutes or until firm and golden. Cool slightly, then slide a knife round the outside of each muffin to loosen it from the tin and serve with crème fraîche and a fork.

Makes 12

•

250g/8oz plain flour

1 tablespoon baking powder

4 tablespoons caster sugar

½ teaspoon salt

1 size 3 egg

225ml/8fl oz buttermilk or milk

50g/2oz butter, melted

100g/4oz blueberries

crème fraîche, to serve

Grilled Plums and Blackberries with Hot Mascarpone and Sugar

....

A simple mélange of dark fruits, molten cream cheese and sugar. The plums must be ripe, otherwise the dish loses all its voluptuousness.

Cut the plums in half and remove the stones. Put them, snuggled up together, in an ovenproof dish. Scatter over the blackberries and trickle over the booze. Place a teaspoon of Mascarpone in each hollow and sprinkle over the sugar.

Place under a preheated hot grill till the sugar melts and the cream cheese runs: about 5–8 minutes. Eat warm from the grill.

For 2

•

4 ripe plums

a few blackberries

2 teaspoons brandy or kirsch

8 heaped teaspoons Mascarpone cheese

4 tablespoons caster sugar

Some 10-Minute Puddings

....

Strawberries and Grand Marnier

Cut the hulled strawberries in half if they are small; in quarters if they are a little on the large side. Sprinkle them with Grand Marnier, or Cointreau, whichever of the orange-based liqueurs you have, and set them aside a while before eating.

Raspberries and Rosewater

Sprinkle each serving of raspberries with a little rosewater. About 1 tablespoon per 100g/4oz berries. If the berries are ripe, and I hope they are, the scent will be quite heavenly.

Baked Red Fruits

For 2

•

25g/1oz butter

2 good double handfuls of red berries, raspberries, blackberries, red and blackcurrants

2 tablespoons red fruit conserve

2 tablespoons kirsch or framboise

double cream, to serve

Cooking fruit in parcels is not a twee affectation. The method has a point. The foil successfully seals in the fragrant steam, cooking the berries quickly and providing a cloud of scented steam when the foil is opened.

Place two pieces of kitchen foil on the table, about 25cm/10 inches square. Butter them and turn up the sides. Place a good double handful of berries, raspberries, blackberries, red and blackcurrants in the centre. Add the conserve, sprinkle with kirsch or framboise, and seal the parcels with a twist. Bake for 10 minutes in a preheated hot oven, 220°C/425°F (gas mark 7). When you open the parcels the smell will be quite intoxicating. Serve with cream.

Melon and Beaumes de Venise

Scoop out balls of melon with a baller or spoon. Drop them into wineglasses and pour over enough Beaumes de Venise, or other muscat, to come halfway up. Serve seriously chilled.

Orange and Angostura Salad

....

You haven't used the Angostura since Uncle Walter used to drink pink gin. It will probably still be all right, though.

Peel the oranges, taking care to remove the pith and save the escaping juice. Slice them in half and then into thin slices. Put them into a bowl, scatter with strawberries and add the Bitters. Toss very gently and then chill till you are ready to eat.

For 2
•
4 small oranges, heavily laden with juice

100g/4oz strawberries, hulled and halved

½ teaspoon Angostura Bitters

Tropical Fruit Salad with Honey

....

Dessert, yes – but even better for Sunday breakfast.

Peel the fruits, saving the juices as you go. Slice the peeled fruit into large chunks – nothing too small or they will turn mushy. Cut the passion fruit in half, squeeze the seeds out over the fruit and toss gently.

Drain off the juice into a small bowl. Stir in the honey and pour over the fruits. Chill and serve.

For 2
•
1 ripe papaya

1 ripe mango

1 banana, slightly underripe

2 passion fruit

2 tablespoons orange-blossom runny honey

Baked Pears with Honey and Juniper

....

Photograph opposite page 225

Tiny, ripe pears are best for this recipe. Unless you wish to extend the cooking time for a larger fruit. Use sliced pears if it suits you better.

Place the pears in an ovenproof dish. Slice them if they are large. Add the other ingredients and bake in a pre-heated oven, 200°C/400°F, gas mark 6, for 30 minutes till tender. Serve warm with crème fraîche.

For 4
•
8 small, ripe pears

4 tablespoons runny honey

2 tablespoons lemon juice

½ teaspoon coriander seeds, lightly crushed

8 juniper berries, lightly crushed

SELECT BIBLIOGRAPHY

Andrews, Colman, *Catalan Cuisine*, Headline, 1989

Bareham, Lindsey, *In Praise of the Potato*, Michael Joseph, 1989

Bareham, Lindsey, *A Celebration of Soup*, Michael Joseph, 1993

Bhumichitr, Vatcharin, *Thai Vegetarian Cooking*, Pavilion, 1991

Bissell, Frances, *Sainsbury's Book of Food*, 1989

Bissell, Frances, *Real Meat Cookbook*, Chatto and Windus, 1992

Boxer, Arabella, *A Visual Feast*, Century, 1992

Brown, Edward, *Tassajara Cooking*, Shamhala/Zen Centre, 1973

Brown, Lynda, *The Cook's Garden*, Century, 1990

Carrier, Robert, *Taste of Morocco*, Century, 1987

Christian, Glynn, *Glynn Christian's Delicatessen Handbook*, Macdonald, 1982

Costa, Margaret, *The Four Seasons Cookbook*, Nelson, 1970

David, Elizabeth, *A Book of Mediterranean Food*, John Lehman, 1950

David, Elizabeth, *French Provincial Cooking*, Michael Joseph, 1960

Del Conte, Anna, *Secrets from an Italian Kitchen*, Corgi, 1993

Floyd, Keith, *Far Flung Floyd*, Michael Joseph, 1993

Gavin, Paola, *Italian Vegetarian Cookery*, Optima, 1991

Graham, Peter, *Classic Cheese Cookery*, Penguin, 1988

Gary, Patience, *Honey from a Weed*, Prospect Books, 1986

Grigson, Jane, *Jane Grigson's Vegetable Book*, Michael Joseph, 1978

Grigson, Sophie, *Sophie Grigson's Ingredients Book*, Pyramid, 1991

Hambro, Natalie, *Particular Delights*, Jill Norman and Hobhouse, 1981

Hazan, Marcella, *Classic Italian Cookbook*, Macmillan, 1980

Holt, Geraldine, *Recipes from a French Herb Garden*, Conran Octopus, 1989

Jaffrey, Madhur, *Eastern Vegetarian Cooking*, Jonathan Cape, 1991

Lasalle, George, *East of Orphanides*, Kyle Cathie, 1991

Madison, Deborah, *Greens Cookbook*, Bantam, 1988

Maschler, Fay, *Eating In*, Bloomsbury, 1987

Nicholson, B. E., *Oxford Book of Food Plants*, Oxford University Press, 1969

Olney, Richard, *Simple French Food*, Jill Norman and Hobhouse, 1974

Owen, Sri, *Indonesian Food and Cookery*, Prospect Books, 1980

Owen, Sri, *The Rice Book*, Doubleday, 1994

Pomaine, Edouard de, *Cooking in Ten Minutes*, Cookery Book Club, 1989

Roden, Claudia, *A New Book of Middle Eastern Food*, Viking, 1985

Roden, Claudia, *Picnic*, Jill Norman and Hobhouse, 1981

Round, Jeremy, *The Independent Cook*, Barrie and Jenkins, 1985

Sahni, Julie, *Classic Indian Vegetarian Cooking*, Dorling Kindersley, 1987

Scott, David, *Demi-Veg Cookbook*, Bloomsbury, 1987

Scott, David, *Middle Eastern Vegetarian Cooking*, Rider, 1992

Slater, Nigel, *Real Fast Food*, Michael Joseph, 1992

Slater, Nigel, *Real Fast Puddings*, Michael Joseph, 1993

Slater, Nigel, *Marie Claire Cookbook*, Paul Hamlyn, 1992

Smith, Delia, *Delia Smith's Complete Cookery Course*, BBC Books, 1978

So, Yan Kit, *Classic Chinese Cookbook*, Dorling Kindersley, 1984

Solomon, Charmaine, *The Complete Asian Cookbook*, Grub Street, 1976

Speiler, Marlene, *Hot and Spicy*, Grafton, 1992

Stein, Richard, *English Seafood Cookery*, Penguin, 1988

Stobart, Tom, *Spices, Herbs and Flavourings*, Penguin, 1987

Waters, Alice, *Chez Panisse Menu Cookbook*, Chatto and Windus, 1982

INDEX